Tampa Review

Tampa Review is published twice each year by the University of Tampa Press. Founded in 1964 as *UT Poetry Review*, *Tampa Review* is the oldest continuously published literary journal in Florida. Subscriptions in the United States are $22 per year; basic subscription is the same outside the U.S., but write for mailing cost by surface mail. Payment should be made by money order or check payable in U.S. funds. International airmail rates are available and vary; write for specific information. Subscription copies not received will be replaced without charge only if notice of nonreceipt is given by subscribers within six months following publication.

Editorial and business correspondence should be addressed to *Tampa Review*, The University of Tampa, 401 West Kennedy Boulevard, Tampa, Florida 33606-1490. Manuscripts and queries must be accompanied by a stamped, self-addressed envelope. Manuscripts are read only during September, October, November, and December. See submission guidelines at http://tampareview.ut.edu

Tampa Review is indexed by *Index of American Periodical Verse* (Metuchen, N.J.: Scarecrow Press), *Annual Bibliography of English Language and Literature* (Cambridge, England: Modern Humanities Research Association), *POEMFINDER* (CD-ROM Poetry Index), *The American Humanities Index* (Albany, N.Y.: Whitston Publishing), and the *MLA International Bibliography*. Member of the Council of Literary Magazines and Presses (CLMP), Council of Editors of Learned Journals (CELJ), and the Florida Literary Arts Coalition (FLAC).

The editors gratefully acknowledge the assistance of Jim Lennon, Dorothy Cowden, and Kendra Frorup. Special thanks also to the entire University of Tampa Art Department.

Typography and design by Richard Mathews

Printed on acid free paper ∞

Manufactured in the United States of America

For additional information visit *Tampa Review* **at**
http://tampareview.ut.edu

Editor

Richard Mathews

Fiction Editors

Audrey Colombe
Gina Vivinetto
Richard Mathews

Nonfiction Editors

Daniel Dooghan
Elizabeth Winston

Poetry Editor

Erica Dawson

Editorial Assistants

Sean Donnelly
Joshua Steward

Staff Assistants

Jimmy Kelly

Contributing & Consulting Editor

J. M. Lennon

Published by the

University of Tampa Press

Tampa Review 47/48

Contents

ON THE COVER: Kendra Frorup. *McAllen.* 2013. Mixed media. 60 x 40 inches.

"McAllen" is the middle name of the artist's brother, Keith; Kendra Frorup created the work as a tribute following his death in a traffic accident last March. Absence is felt in the empty straw bag in the top half of the image, and in the empty arch that suggests departure in the bottom half. Tapping into digital technology, Frorup also employs "augmented reality" within the arch, and readers with the Aurasma app on an iPhone, iPad, or smart device can view the emptiness within that arch as a threshhold to moving images from their family home in the Turks and Caicos Islands. This leap into Augmented Reality is a first for *Tampa Review*, and a beautifully complex statement about the ways art leads us to express and understand multiple layers of reality. Much of Frorup's work involves perceiving and constructing meaning from emptiness. She approaches the work "with the mindset of a collector and an affection for disdained items, urban refuse, and industrial materials." A sense of place and history also pervades her work, As she has written, "The objects used within the artwork maintain their integrity to reflect where they have been, and the artwork I create is reflective of who I am."

Tampa Review 47/48

Contents (continued)

Corey George. *Bellatrix*. 2013. Archival ink jet print. 16 x 20 inches.

Kendra Frorup. *Iron Market*. 2013. Mixed media. 104 x 36 x 36 inches. Photo by J. M. Lennon.

A Family of Interest

When the shrapnel in my father's knees set off the metal detector, we had to sit and wait for someone from Homeland Security to show up. With everybody else boarded, half the flight crew seemed to wander back down the jet bridge pretending to be doing something official. The real reason, of course, was to check out the family of interest that was preventing the plane from taking off.

"Barbarians at the gate," Cora said, picking her celebrity crossword back up.

My antsy sister wasn't the only who couldn't sit still. Even my father was getting restless. Because he was on deployment, he had to wear his uniform, something he hates to do when he's off post. My mother looked like she was waiting on the governor's reprieve.

Later, as soon as the guy with so-called clearance authority stepped from the moving walkway, he started apologizing for having to inconvenience an American warrior. But then who could appreciate safety protocol better than a member of our own armed services? My father didn't take this as a question and silently marched off with him like a prisoner of war. He wasn't used to someone else giving the orders.

That's when Cora asked me if it wouldn't be just like Al-Qaeda to impersonate a bird colonel and the woman sitting in the next row glared over her shoulder at her again. Earlier, she'd helped her elderly mother board, and now, because of us, she was stuck here until they gave the go-ahead.

"Five letters across," Cora said, drumming her pencil on her movie magazine. "'Streep in *Prada*.' Starts with a 'b.'"

I covered my mouth so the woman couldn't hear me.

"Bitch," I whispered.

"B-i-t-c-h," my sister spelled the word out. "And staring me right in the face the whole time."

My mother suddenly reached over and patted Cora on the knee. "That's enough," she said and then nodded at me. "The two of you."

Because it was a hardship tour, we wouldn't see my father again until Christmas. And I tried not to think about this when I saw him emerge from the pilots' lounge. I didn't want his last memory of me to be blubbering when I said goodbye.

As he came back over to us, we all stood up.

"Who says waterboarding works," Cora said and I noticed the security guy give her a lopsided smirk.

"Speaking of water works," my father said. "I don't want to see any."

I knew that this was meant more for me than for Cora who's never cried at an airport in her life.

"You know why it's called the Green Zone, right?" she said to my father.

I was jealous of my sister's stiff upper lip. Mine was already starting to quiver.

"Because it's the ultimate gated community," she said.

My father steered me a safe distance away from her and my mother.

"Just remember to let your sister go in one ear and out the other," he said, keeping his back turned to them. "Kapish?"

Predictably, he didn't offer me a hug or even a pat on the shoulder. My father wasn't the touchy-feely sort.

As he turned around, my mother was dabbing at her eyes with a wad of Kleenex. And I thought how last week, she made us all go to church together, something she ordinarily required only on Holy Days of Obligation.

My father exhaled wearily and I got a whiff of the cigar he'd been smoking this morning. His staff gave him a box of Cuban coronas as a going-away present.

"Good," he said. "We're all copacetic."

Then, embracing my mother, he said something that made her smile bravely. The hard part came as we watched him pass through the detector without triggering World War III. Typically, he didn't turn to wave as the relieved security guy gave the rest of us a thumbs up.

Afterwards, my mother made Cora and me wait until the plane's departure time registered on the flight screen. But when she tried to say something, her voice caught and a kind of choked hiccup came out instead. An attendant at the check-in counter wheeled about as if a shot had been fired.

"Everything all right?" she said, thrusting the hinged panel up.

My mother only looked away. Cora, however, assumed her new role as family spokesperson.

"Everything's copacetic," she said and already I knew that I'd have to start letting things go in one ear and out the other.

For the last thirteen months my father had been acting post commander of Ft. Irwin which, after 9/11, became a training center for counter-insurgency. Although it's in the middle of the Mojave Desert, it's still the closest Army facility to Los Angeles. So instead of staying on in Dependent Housing, my mother put everything in storage and rented a furnished bungalow in Santa Monica. Because she didn't want my sister in public school her senior year (Cora skipped a grade), she handed her over to the nuns. And the only reason her daughter didn't go ballistic was because The Sisters of Charity School for Catholic Girls is situated high in the Hollywood Hills. Hills which my celebrity-obsessed sister fantasized would be alive with the sound of movie stars.

It didn't matter where I went. "Teddy adapts," my mother likes to say. This meant that I wound up having to catch the bus at six in the morning to PS-112, a multi-ethnic middle school halfway across town.

After my first week, Cora asked me how classes were going in "Bosnia/Herzegovina."

"I have mixed feelings," I said.

She looked at me a moment before acknowledging her baby brother's budding wit.

"It just goes to show," she said. "Even dull pencils can be sharpened."

My sister is stingy with praise and so I felt a little shiver of pride at her compliment even if it was backhanded.

At school, sitting in the last row, I tuned out any current event report that had to do with the war. Usually, it was about the latest explosive device

to go off in a crowded public square. More than once already I'd had the dream about the staff car pulling up in the driveway. The one where I open the front door to some glum-faced military chaplain who says, "The Secretary of the Army regrets to inform you . . ."

Cora didn't board on weekends so we picked her up right after her last class on Friday. My mother was afraid to drive back after dark on the tortuous mountain road which my sister called the Grace Kelly Parkway. As our celebrity tour guide, Cora took the wheel and pointed out which movie star lived behind which ivy-covered wall we passed on our roller coaster descent. With her non-stop running commentary ("Clooney sold that one to some producer who unloaded it on Oliver Stone") and the brakes being pumped around every curve, I got home just in time to spring from the back seat and puke in the Ligustrum.

Except for my sister's ridiculous movie magazines, my mother permitted no subscriptions of any kind, including the newspaper, to be delivered to the house. Nor did she have a land-line or cable installed. A media blackout was in effect at six and nine in the evening because the major news channels' coverage was considered too risky. "I don't need to hear about the generals' latest strategies," she proclaimed. "I've known most of those goombas since they came out of West Point with your father. And I wouldn't put one of them in charge of a commissary, never mind a war."

Within a month, Cora tried to start a political action committee at school which the nuns nixed. So she spent all her time at home working on ways to get Hollywood more involved in the anti-war effort. One Saturday, she left her door wide open which, of course, I wasn't to misinterpret as some kind of social invitation. I was simply being allowed to admire, at a distance, her floor-to-ceiling collage-in-progress.

She was pasting up the famous picture of Sean Penn that shows him hunched over after having just taken a swing at a paparazzo. Both his fists are clenched and there's a really crazy look on his face. "The sword," Cora said, flashing her scissors as I loitered in the hall, "is mightier than the pen."

She planned to mail a copy of the collage to "all the usual suspects." Civilians (non celebrities) could send a check to NOW! (Nuns Opposing

War) which had a post office box number in Santa Monica. It sounded pretty hair-brained and I asked her if it was legal.

My sister made her favorite clicking sound with her tongue. For extra effect, she didn't bother to answer until she'd completed the cropping of some starlet from a photograph of Woody Harrelson.

"You mean like Iraq?"

The following week, I came home from school to find my mother still in her bathrobe at the kitchen table.

"There's a card from your father on the counter," she said, her chin resting on her hands.

Her arms were exposed and appeared skinnier to me than usual.

"I'm having a peanut butter and jelly," I said. "You want one?"

She acted as if she hadn't heard me. "Read your father's note, honey. Tell me what you think."

It was one of his comic postcards, the only kind he really sent. He must have bought them before he left because they had nothing to do with where he was. This one showed a woman standing in the surf and holding two large coconuts that covered her naked breasts. "Hope to get to the beach this weekend," he'd written across the back.

"Your father thinks he's being funny," my mother said.

But I knew that he was just trying to keep us from worrying.

Thursday night, Cora called to tell us not to pick her up tomorrow. She was babysitting. My mother held her cell phone out to me.

"Your sister says we each get one guess who the parents are."

Cora's school had a bulletin board for posting babysitting notices which Mother Superior carefully vetted (e.g., same sex couples, foreign directors, any of the Baldwin brothers). Unlike my sister, most of her classmates were locals themselves and had been around people in the movie industry all their lives. So they were pretty blasé about celebrities.

My excited sister allowed me a second chance when I guessed Susan and Tim because everyone knew they'd split.

"Okay," I said. "Then Angelina and Brad."

"Give the phone back to Mom," Cora said irritably.

She finally revealed to my mother the name of the executive producer ("He works with Spielberg mostly") and his young third wife who would send a driver over to pick her up.

"I don't want you getting into any strange cars," my mother warned her.

Without my father around, she'd gotten kind of paranoid lately. For instance, as soon as it was dark out she double checked all the window locks. Not to mention replacing the back porch light with a bulb bright enough to perform surgery under.

Although it was a school night, I sat through another colorized Turner Classic with her. And afterwards, to keep me up a little longer, my mother asked the one question she knew worked better than caffeine: Why do I have a chip on my shoulder about my sister being such a chip off the old man's block?

"You don't like being your mother's son?" she teased me.

Despite its being true I still resented that Cora was always the one who reminded everybody of my father.

"You and I are two peas in a pod," she declared, pouring a "smidgen" more bourbon in her coke. "Just like your sister's your daddy's daughter."

She wasn't, of course, trying to hurt my feelings, something she didn't have to worry about with Cora. Unlike her son, her daughter had a thick hide, a trait, it went without saying, she inherited from the Colonel.

By the time I got to bed, I barely closed my eyes and I was dreaming about my father again. This time he was in our backyard in the desert, practice shooting with his M9 pistol. "That one," he said, aiming in the dark at the silhouette of a cactus. "It's the same prickly pear you see over in the Gulf." Then he blew the top off with a single shot and I opened my eyes.

The house was quiet except for the faint drone of the TV coming from my mother's bedroom. I tiptoed to the end of the hall and found her asleep with all the lights on. I quietly tried to ease the remote from her hand.

"What?" she said, her eyelids fluttering.

I could smell the liquor on her breath.

"You left the TV on."

"Leave it," she said sharply, but in another moment was snoring again.

Back in my own room, I sat up in bed with my hand on my chest. My heart was ricocheting around like it was trying to come up with an exit strategy. There had been a real edge to my mother's voice. It was the same way she started sounding with my father before he left. At night, even with their bedroom door shut, I could hear her arguing. He was deluding himself if he thought for a second that going over to that hell hole would win him his star. He'd been passed over twice. Did he really think the third time would be the charm? Who was he kidding? Because it wasn't his wife. Even his kids knew better. My mother turned to ask me if it wasn't true.

But my alarm suddenly went off and I woke up with my heart still racing.

Monday, for Current Events, Mannie who had a buzz cut and a chain necklace got to use the projection TV from Audio-Visual. He showed a clip from YouTube of a tank coming down the middle of a wide boulevard in Baghdad.

"That's the biggest tank in the world," he said.

Actually, the Abrams M1A2 was slightly larger but, like Cora says, nobody likes a pedant.

Mannie described how the insurgents would plant a bomb in the street, and how later when the tank passed over the spot, a sniper would shoot and explode it. Mannie froze the frame with the remote and pointed at the rooftop of one of the nearby buildings.

"Watch there," he said and pressed the slow motion button.

A second later a little white cloud blossomed exactly where he was pointing.

"Okay," Mannie said. "Here comes the good part."

And you could tell he'd practiced with the remote because right on cue there was an explosion and smoke puffed out from under the tank which stopped in its tracks.

"Ladies," Miss Hardy said when we didn't settle down quickly enough. "Gentlemen."

Mannie finished by telling us that the bomb wasn't strong enough to blow up the tank but that the crew probably didn't hear as good as they used to. Everybody laughed and even Miss Hardy had a hard time not smiling.

Usually I just doodled in my notebook when someone's current event was on the war. But my father's branch wasn't Artillery so I wasn't really worried about him riding around in a tank. What I did kind of worry about, though, was how whenever he's overseas he'll always

explore the outdoor markets. He especially liked to find the local haggler's row of dealers. Last Saturday, UPS delivered his first "Bundle from Baghdad," a small wooden crate that included a hand-carved teak jewelry box for my mother and a jade Buddha bedside lamp (with the light switch as the navel) for my sister. My own present came wrapped in a back issue of the *Army Times*. At first, I thought it was a scorched coconut but Cora recognized what it was immediately.

"Another gift of the magus," she said.

I separated the black strands of hair to reveal the shrunken head's two empty eye sockets. Its mouth was stitched shut.

"I didn't think Daddy could top the petrified bat," my sister said.

Miss Hardy waited until Mannie got back to his seat.

"Teddy," she said, peering in my direction. "I believe you're up."

It surprised me a little that I wasn't jittery when I got to the front of the classroom and unzipped my backpack. As I pulled out the shrunken head everyone seemed to lean forward in their seats and squint. But they didn't shriek or laugh or get unruly the way they did when the bomb exploded in Mannie's report. Instead, they all seemed to turn to stare at Miss Hardy as if for an explanation.

"Teddy," Miss Hardy said finally. "I'm afraid we have a problem."

She had a kind of pained look on her face so I didn't get to tell the class all the stuff I found out about shrunken heads on-line. For instance, how importing them to the States had been banned since the 1940s and how eighty percent of the ones on the black market were fake.

Miss Hardy thought I probably needed to take my current event down to Mr. Sanson's office. Which sort of made me feel sorry for her because Miss Hardy wasn't the kind of teacher who liked to send a student to see the vice principal. That was why I didn't try to make any excuses and instead just scooped up my backpack and left.

Halfway down the hall I could see that the door to the teacher's lounge was open. And as I came up to it, I glanced in and saw Mr. Sanson sitting by himself on the couch. He was watching CNN with the sound turned down.

"My man Theodore," he said when he saw me standing outside.

I wasn't sure what I was supposed to do. So I just told him that Miss Hardy had sent me to his office.

"Think of the vice principal's as sort of being like the county seat," he said, gazing back at the TV. "It's wherever the vice principal is sitting."

Mr. Sanson was kind of famous for being eccentric. Everybody said it was because he had a steel plate in his skull from Vietnam. But Cora said it was more likely from beating his head against the wall because of all the ignoramuses he had to deal with at PS-211.

After the reporter finished pointing out several buildings that were still smoldering in the distance, Mr. Sanson finally turned back to me.

"So, Theodore . . . the problem du jour?"

I unzipped my backpack.

As soon as Mr. Sanson saw the shrunken head, he clapped his hands together as if in prayer.

"My god, son. What have you done to our home room teacher?"

But he glanced back at the TV when several rifle shots went off. The reporter was squatting down with his hand on his helmet.

"Miss Hardy tells me your father's over there," the vice principal said, patting the couch. "Have a seat."

I wasn't sure what to do with the shrunken head so when I sat down I just arranged it on the empty cushion between us.

"Yes, sir."

As the reporter continued to describe what was going on behind him, Mr. Sanson threw his hands up.

"What the hell do they want from us?" he said.

When I didn't say anything, he nodded.

"Your family probably wonders the same thing," he said.

After a while, you could see an arm waving a white towel from one of the vacant windows of the charred building.

"I'd use it to sight on the son of a bitch," the vice principal said bitterly.

Then he slapped his knees and pulled a note pad out of his jacket pocket.

"You brought him into the classroom?" he said, resting his palm on top of the shrunken head.

"For Current Events."

"And I'm guessing Miss Hardy felt it was inappropriate."

"No, sir. I mean, yes, sir."

"What do you think, Theodore? She have a point?"

I nodded.

"All right," he said and jotted something down on the pad. "Here's what we do. We say a couple Hail Marys and make a perfect act of contrition. Sound fair?"

When I shrugged my shoulders, he folded the paper over and passed it to me.

"Give this to Miss Hardy." And he pointed his pen at the shrunken head. "You can leave homunculus with me."

Friday when we picked Cora up at school she was so hyper that she practically bounced into the car. Apparently, Sister Amelia who taught her modern film class had a brother who turned out to be some kind of hotshot at Disney. Anyway, every year the Academy Awards hires about twenty-five out-of-work actors. They're used to fill any seats that are temporarily vacated during the live telecast. Because the camera's always panning the audience, their job is to play musical chairs whenever someone's late getting back from the bathroom. Or, more likely Cora claimed, from snorting a line in one of the stalls. So Sister Amelia's brother had arranged to let her star pupil be one of the "fillers" at the Kodak Theater on Oscar Night.

Saturday morning, Cora had twenty-five copies of her collage printed at Kinkos. To save on postage, she used her *House Map to the Stars* to locate the most likely targets of opportunity in the Platinum Triangle. We were headed back down Sunset after stuffing half a dozen mailboxes in Bel Air when I decided to tell her about Mom's problem. My sister had burned a disc of the Best Original Song nominees, and I had to reach over and lower the volume to be heard.

"Falling slowly," Cora said, turning the sound back up on the CD. I didn't know if she was identifying the song ("Falling Slowly") or if she meant she'd talk to Mom about her drinking. Either way it was clear she was more interested in her karaoke than in discussing an intervention. And so I didn't say anything more about it.

It was nearly dark when we finished up with Holmby Hills but Cora had one last address she wanted to hit on the way back to the house.

At what looked like the Brandenburg Gate, she parked across the street from a mansion in Westwood.

"No pun intended," she said. "This guy virtually invented reality TV."

But she was suddenly looking past me. A woman in a white uniform had stepped through the gate's wrought iron entry way.

"Bingo!" Cora said and leaped from the car like it was on fire.

I watched her rush across the street, waving the envelope like she was delivering the grand prize from the Publisher's Clearing House Sweepstake. Unfortunately, the rich producer's housekeeper didn't seem to understand English. All she saw was another deranged wannabee actress storming the gates of her employer's home.

It was too late for Cora to halt her forward momentum and she skidded, arms flailing, directly into the blinding cloud of pepper spray. But she's her father's daughter all right and just like him a stoic. Clamping her palms over her eyes, she bent at the waist and then dropped to her knees on the concrete without ever making a sound.

There was a jug of water in the trunk (a holdover from the radiator tending to overheat in the desert) which I lugged across the street to empty over my sister's head.

Meanwhile, from the safety of the other side of the fence, the housekeeper had placed the can of repellent back in her uniform pocket and was casually lighting a cigarette as if waiting for the camera crew to set up the next take.

The following morning, Cora woke up with a rash on her face and was in and out of the bathroom experimenting with different applications of makeup.

"Tell the truth," she said to me after trying to camouflage the reddening with a rust-colored shade. "I look like Pippi Longstocking, don't I?"

In fact, it reminded me of the episode where Pippi comes down with the measles.

"What's the difference," I told her. "Everybody's going to be looking at Julia Roberts."

My frustrated sister wasn't sure how to take this but slammed the bathroom door after her anyway.

It wasn't really her blotchy skin that had her anxious about tomorrow night. Cora had come to the conclusion that her collage wasn't going to bring the troops home. So she spent the afternoon brainstorming about a more effective battle plan.

By the end of the day, she'd come to the realization that the most effective weapon for getting the truth into the American living room is television. And what better occasion than Oscar Night when half the world would be watching. More importantly they'd be watching her!

As usual, mine was a supporting role. I was to act surprised and ask the leading lady how this was possible.

"When the Best Picture's announced," my sister said slowly, as if coming up with her strategy off the cuff, "instead of filling one of the empty seats, I'll just follow the winner and his entourage down the aisle and up onto the stage."

There she'd unfurl her Get-out-of-Iraq banner in the primest of prime time. She would use a swatch from an old reserve parachute my father had given her. The silk was so fine she could fold it into the palm of her hand.

"All you have to do is look like you belong," she said. " Everyone out here's blinded by their self-absorption."

Sometimes with my sister, I didn't know for sure if she was just pulling my leg or really believed what she was saying. That's when she got a certain look. Like the one she had right now. And there's no point in trying to change her mind. So I didn't even try.

Later, after dinner, Cora headed back to her room with a pair of scissors and a black, felt tip marker borrowed from my school supplies.

There was supposed to be a partial lunar eclipse and Mr. Thompson said he'd give extra-credit for any crater timings we made. It was overcast but since my grade had become a big issue, I sprayed myself with insect repellent and put on a long-sleeve shirt.

After an hour of listening to my iPod, the clouds still hadn't opened long enough to get a clear view of the moon for more than thirty seconds. I decided to call it a night. But halfway back to the porch I stopped. My sister's voice was coming from the kitchen and it almost sounded as if she was trying not to cry. It's not something you hear every day, and so I set the telescope down and silently crossed the brick patio to the pair of french doors.

"I'll call Daddy if you don't," Cora was saying.

"Honey—"

"You're scaring Teddy and now you're starting to scare me."

"Sweetheart—"

"Honest to god, Mom. I'll pick up the phone--"

"All right. Fine."

It was quiet for a moment and the next time my sister said something she'd calmed down enough that she sounded more angry than upset. I tilted my head slightly, pressing my ear to the crack between the twin doors.

". . . how many stars have died that way?" Cora said. "Because it's a long list, Mom."

"Okay, honey. You've made your point."

"I flushed them down the toilet. There's no more left."

"That wasn't necessary."

"And if Teddy tells me he sees you taking anything, I'll call Daddy."

"Now you're turning your brother into a spy?"

When my heart started pounding so hard that all I could hear was a thumping in my ears, I set the telescope back up. But the clouds were still too low and it was useless to try to focus the lens piece. Everything was only going to look like it was underwater anyway.

Sunday afternoon, Cora had to report early to the George Eastman Room for her final run-through at the Kodak Theater. My mother and I stood in the driveway waving goodbye to her as she backed the van out into the street.

"Your sister's gone Hollywood on us," my mother said. "She's wearing more makeup than an opera singer."

Cora didn't tell her about the trigger-happy housekeeper. Instead, she blamed the rash on something she ate.

"I'm having a before-dinner cordial," my mother said.

"I thought they were for after dinner," I said.

She winked conspiratorially at me. "I like how you think, honey."

My mother retrieved a new bottle of bourbon. She'd hidden it from her watchdog daughter among the cleaning supplies under the kitchen sink.

"We have something to toast," she said, tearing the plastic seal off the top. "Your sister's television debut."

My double-take had my mother staring curiously at me.

"What?" she said. "You don't think we'll see her?"

I shrugged my shoulders, understanding that she merely meant that the camera might catch her filling someone's seat.

"Cora said it can be a fine line between a fan and a fanatic," I said.

She laughed, raising her glass. "Your sister crosses the line all right."

There was a definite pattern to my mother's drinking. She only began to get edgy after her second bourbon. Then she would start in on how my father didn't really think about his family the way a "loving father" should. How else to account for the silly postcards he sent and the even sillier things he wrote on the back of them. I stopped sticking any more up on the refrigerator after she took a Magic Marker to the grass mini-skirt one of the island women was wearing.

Before the evening news came on, my mother changed the channel to a cooking show. After a while, she finished her drink and stretched out on the couch. Already I could tell that her mood was starting to change so I didn't say anything when she asked me if I was hungry.

"I'll fix us something in a minute," she said, closing her eyes.

I waited until she was snoring before I turned the overhead light off and muted the sound on the TV. My mother wasn't really that interested in watching the Awards ceremony anyway. She didn't care who won any more than I did.

It was pretty close to the end of the show when I went out to the backyard. But I wasn't thinking about my grade which was probably a lost cause anyway. Instead, I pointed the telescope at my neighbor's house and adjusted the lens. The shade wasn't drawn on the recreation room and I could see their large flat screen TV tuned to the Oscars. Harrison Ford was opening the envelope so it had to be for Best Picture. Already my heart was doing back flips as I tilted the scope slightly so that the television picture blurred and the whole family came into focus in its place: mom, dad, siblings, all sitting together on the sectional leather couch and no one knowing what was going to happen next.

❖   ❖   ❖

Judith Werner

A Sense of Time Passing

Still not rescued, I watch
wild birds disdain my privet's
berries, black like buttons
of a too-early prince caught
in Sleeping Beauty's briar.

Its spindle-shaped flowers
are spilling a fragrance
like soporific wine,
as if dandelions
and violets might escape

the lawn through branches knit
with leaves that fold on midribs
like tiny yawns guarding
the sleep of a hundred
suburban Novembers.

David Starkey

On the Ninth Anniversary of the Death of Derrida

The day begins in fog, mist clinging
to hilltops, birds erratic

in their song. Above the ocean,
air and its attendant wrongs.

Along the coasts of the world,
books have been left out overnight

on wooden tables and in the seats
of plastic chairs, their pages curling

at the corners, letters etched with salt.
On a dew-wet beach in Indonesia,

Rilke's eszetts have lost their sibilance
and Trakl's umlauts—damp, smeared,

illegible—no longer have the power
to round the vowels they rest upon.

A Sliver of Heat

From the tar bubbles comes the Cyclops sun.
Come grasshoppers, sleeveless girls, yellows
Imbued with the cries of childhood.

from the white birch trees' inset eyes
Comes the burn-wound
Of remembered infant-song.

There grasshoppers, strewn like paper clips,
Flew up when footfalls disturbed dead calm.
Wings so light it seemed they were made of paper

Appeared to glide in childhood.
At night the earth collided with comet hair
And you wanted to tip the Milky Way

Into your parched throat, drain the cream
As well as all that curdled in argument
Grown full with midday.

From the burn-wound of childhood
Where cicadas, second-hand cars, oil siphoned
Into engines where, a storm came

And dropped its thunder-rain.
There the rainbow would swim grudgingly
In a little pool of grease.

Winter Tree

There are no words at the end of the day,
there is only this bare branched tree in a field of fog
and the birds that come and go as they please.

By now the sun is finding its way to other side of the continent,
leaving us in the dark.

It's true that the poor will always be poor
and that the few carry on the tradition,
like a dam that hordes the perpetual flow of the river
as the land dries up
from that which belongs to us all.

Winter tree in a field of fog
with its colors drained at the branches,
how patient you are, how foreboding,
lifting the wind quietly tonight—

in the cold hush of snow.

Santiago Echeverry. *Flex*. 2012. Digital photo. Archival ink on photographic paper. 30 x 24 inches.

Hunger Season

I borrowed three hundred dollars from my father to buy my mother's Honda Civic out of the Minneapolis impound lot, and I'll be damned if I ever pay him back. Just before the money changed hands, on the drive from the Hennepin County Jail to his house in White Bear Lake, he informed me that because of the DUI, I couldn't get into Canada, where he'd told me on a fishing trip years before that he was divorcing my mother. I told him Canada meant more to him than to me, at least in the way he was talking about it. I felt cheated like a goldfish falling into a toilet bowl feels cheated. My stomach was a cauldron and acid gnawed at its lining. Despite my numbing hangover, I felt the anger of a jilted son. I was twenty-three and living in my mother's townhome in Minnetonka. I was ashamed to call her because she needed the car for a date that night. She always drove, to show she didn't need anything.

My father—this was in his living room—wouldn't even hand me the money. "I've done enough for you, haven't I?" he said when I asked him to drive me to the impound lot. "Do you think I don't have anything to do today?" He set the money on the glass-topped coffee table while I called for a cab, and then we waited, alone in his house. He wouldn't let me out of his sight. A framed photograph of his son from his second wife hung next to the clock. Kyle, a teenager, who my father hid from me like a secret. "I should have never answered," he said about my early morning call. "I should have let that damn phone ring." He was like a relapsing addict paying to forget his shame. I wanted to scream at him, "It's the addiction!" But I didn't. He'd seen enough of Kyle to feel safe writing me off. He'd take his name back if he could.

All I did was watch that stack of twenties on the table. I swear those twenties seemed alive. They seemed like a dying gasp. Like they'd been crawling toward me for hours.

❖ ❖ ❖

Outside, the gray morning sky spit dry flakes of snow. "Where to?" the driver said when I slid into the backseat of the cab. Red blood vessels webbed his eyes like directionless rivers. I was good with accents and could tell he came from Africa. East Africa, probably.

"Impound lot," I said. "Minneapolis."

What can be said about those barstool nights? Some take from those nights what they offer, and some give up everything they have, without ever being asked. I just wished I knew which one I was. I thought about Wyatt volunteering his couch while we drank in Uptown the night before. His apartment building stood just around the corner from the bar. But I'd nodded at the girl on the other side of him, and after another beer he left because he worked the morning shift at the Perkins diner, and I stayed late buying vodka tonics for the girl, who disappeared as soon as I stepped into the bathroom.

From the cab, White Bear Lake seemed to have a flatness that extended beyond its terrain. And I longed for variation in my hapless life. Everything I'd seen of the world until then was a failure of the imagination. Everyplace I went was everyplace I'd been. But I'd never been anywhere. I leaned forward and rested my elbows on the back of the front seat. "Where from?" I said to the driver.

"Eritrea," he said, checking me in the rearview mirror. "You know?"

I knew enough. I followed world events like a hawk. I scoured all kinds of newspapers, hunting for ideas. I knew the time when the food ran out, before the next harvest came in, and that where he came from they called it hunger season. I knew borders shifted for reasons having little to do with the territory changing hands. I knew the nations of this world: how they came together, why they fell apart. "The war?" I said.

"Pardon?" he said.

"You left because of the war?"

"What war, man?"

"You know," I said. "The war."

"Nah, man," he said. "I left to go to school."

"School?"

"Yeah, man, school," he said. "You go to school, right? College?"

"No," I said. "I don't go to school."

"No school?" he said. "You look like a student. Like you go to school."

I leaned back and kept an eye on the meter. We passed a sign for the impound lot. The driver smiled, revealing straight and yellow teeth. "Towed?" he said.

I said, "Towed."

❖   ❖   ❖

I paid the fine, and back outside the shuttle van driver, an elderly, overweight man wearing aviator sunglasses despite the overcast sky, studied my paperwork, then the clipboard on the dash. He looked like a war veteran who still talked about the war. "DUI," he said as he slung his seatbelt over his shoulder, "you had the Civic." The van crept along a muddy path running between parallel rows of cars. The artificial pinecone smell of the heat vent air freshener permeated my clothes. The snow was falling harder.

"There it is," I said, pointing up ahead. "It's maroon." Past my mother's car, past the rows upon rows of impounded vehicles, past the chain link fence, the elevated freeway punctured the city center. "Can I ask you something?" I said. "My father says I can't go to Canada, now. Do you know anything about that? I never know whether to trust him."

"They've got a law," the driver said. "What you did is a felony up there."

"I was driving five miles under the limit."

"We get jokers like you in here all the time," he said. He shifted into park in front of my mother's car. "Your dad's right, though," he said. "Forget Canada."

Up on the freeway, the traffic murmured. Cars zipped to and fro. These people that surrounded me! Why did they insist on keeping their options open? They weren't going anywhere.

Back in my mother's car, I pumped the gas pedal as the engine wheezed. The radio worked, and I listened to a talk show. I opened the hood, but the engine looked normal. I trudged toward the office, which seemed like a mirage through the falling snow. The wind bit into my face, and I shivered and folded my arms against my body. I

wore no jacket and clothes from the night before. The van crawled back down the path toward me, its headlights dim. When it reached me it slowed to a stop and the driver rolled down his window.

"You can't be walking out here," he said. "We got a policy."

"The car won't start."

A beautiful young woman rode in the passenger seat, and she regarded me with what I interpreted as great pity. I have a theory, see, that people like myself tip the scale in favor of others. I suffered out there in the cold so this woman could live a predictable life. She wore a scarf that I knew would be soft to the touch, cashmere, probably, or baby alpaca, but I would never feel that scarf, and she seemed impossible in that place, a mirage herself. I felt sure her car had been towed unjustly.

"Spark plugs," the driver was saying. "You can bank on it."

The wreckage of a mashed car in the row of cars behind me reflected from the lenses of his sunglasses. I thought, You have the answers, my friend. Share with me your knowledge of the world. I'm ready for it. I maintained my calm, though, for the woman's sake, and took him at his word, because there was no better choice. "I'll just walk up to the office, then," I said, "if that's all right."

In the office, I plugged quarters into the pay phone and dialed my father's number, which I'd always had memorized. Kyle answered. I pretended I didn't recognize his voice. "Hello," I said. "Is David there?"

"I'm not supposed to talk to you."

"Well," I said, "here we are."

"I think it's dumb," Kyle said. "I've always thought so. I tried calling you last week."

"Life can be dumb," I said. "Why did you call?"

"Dad says you hang out with a drug dealer. He said you're on the fast track to nowhere."

"Is this an intervention?" I said.

"I need some pot for a party."

"I don't know anything about that."

"Come on," he said. "I already told some girls."

He reminded me of myself at that age, on the edge of something. Like if I could just see it, I'd know what it was. "Can you pick me up?" I said. The last time I'd smoked pot, when I worked at Perkins with Wyatt, I had vomited. I read later that you could be allergic. Wyatt told me stick to alcohol, which I'd done. But pipes and filters and little plastic bags still littered Wyatt's apartment. "Bring some money," I said to Kyle.

"How much?" he said.

"All of it." While I waited I imagined our father, his incredulous smile, mixing his worlds like I mixed my drinks. I wanted to tell him, none of this was by choice. But I'd never told him anything.

❖ ❖ ❖

At Perkins, I asked for a booth and ordered coffee for us both. Kyle wore a Twins baseball cap and had wispy sideburns. When the waitress brought our coffee, I asked for Wyatt. Kyle studied his coffee as if he'd find his future somewhere in its murky depths. "Cream?" I said. I peeled open one of the small containers for myself. "Sugar?"

"No," he said. "No, thanks."

He fiddled with the handle of his mug and then finally slurped some coffee, which he then spit out. Across from him, I imagined myself, briefly, as his savior.

"Who's Wyatt?" he said, wiping the table with his shirtsleeve. "Is he the guy?"

"A friend," I said. "He knows engines."

The waitress whispered on her way by that she'd found Wyatt out back by the dumpsters. "Wait here," I told Kyle, and pushed through the swinging doors into the kitchen. On my way to the back entrance I nodded to the Mexican in front of the big stainless steel sink. I'd known him before I'd been fired, or stopped showing up, whichever had happened first. He seemed exactly as I remembered him: satisfied, for some reason, in his greasy apron and ratty jeans and a sweat-stained t-shirt, as if he held some secret that was useless for him to share.

I found Wyatt leaning against the brick facade of the building, smoking a cigarette. He wore a dirty apron and a hair net. "Bum me a smoke?" I said. Wyatt flipped me his pack and I shook out a cigarette and lit up. We studied the row of dark green dumpsters. "You hung over?" Wyatt said, finally. "We were three sheets to the wind. I'm hanging like a motherfucker. I can't hardly stand."

"They got me good," I said. "Right after you left." I told him about the girl who'd stranded me at the bar, about the car, about the spark plugs. "You've got to help me fix it," I said.

"Bullshit," Wyatt said. "I offered you my couch."

I flicked my cigarette away. It bounced against a dumpster and sparked to the ground. "Jesus Christ," I said. "What the shit. My mom needs the car."

Wyatt itched his blond beard, then his neck. "This place is so goddamned dry," he said. "It's the driest place I've ever been. And I've been to the desert."

"The arctic is a desert," I said. "It's a cold desert."

"I been to the desert," he said. "You don't have to tell me it's dry."

I told him about my brother.

"He ain't really your brother," he said. "That's not what you call him."

"He's pretty much my brother."

"That's misleading."

"Well," I said, "that's what it feels like."

"I'm off in an hour," he said. "Can you wait that long? Or are your panties too far up your ass?"

"I'm glad I quit here," I said, after I knew he'd help me. "I hate this goddamn place."

❖ ❖ ❖

At the auto supply store, Wyatt stopped partway down aisle four, in front of the spark plugs. I turned to Kyle. "Do you have the money?"

"How much?"

"A hundred," I guessed.

"Make it one-fifty," Wyatt said. One by one he plucked spark plugs from the shelf and tucked them into a deep pocket of his parka. "Eyes on me," he said, when I glanced at the cashier. He smelled like pancakes and artificial maple syrup. He zipped shut the pocket and continued toward the checkout lane, carrying a socket wrench. I waited by the oil section while Kyle dug into his pocket and counted out the bills. I studied the label on a quart of synthetic oil, which I'd read was better than regular oil.

"Is Wyatt getting the pot?" Kyle said.

"He's paying for the wrench."

My stomach felt much better, as I had known it would. Pain was part of my routine. It passed, like everything else. I drank Perkins coffee from a Styrofoam cup. I stuffed Kyle's money into my pocket. "Don't worry," I said. "I'm keeping this separate from my other money."

Back in the car, with Wyatt directing in the front passenger seat, we merged onto the freeway. Wyatt held a spark plug in midair, examining it as if he were turning a diamond in the light, as if by stealing the spark plug he had created it and was now admiring his craftsmanship. "I have to tell my father something," Kyle was saying. "He thinks the money is for basketball shoes."

"Not a bad excuse," I said, watching the passing office buildings. "Not bad at all." The buildings were gray in the fading light like they were gray during the day. I thought of my father and me as this: countries that bordered each other, ancestral rivals, struggling endlessly, connected forever, advancing and retreating over the same pathetic patch of ground. I just wanted to give Kyle something my father couldn't, and all I could give him was what he shouldn't have.

"Get off at this exit," Wyatt said. "See the Subway sign?" Kyle pulled off the freeway and into the parking lot. Wyatt opened his door. "Wait here," he said. "You want anything?"

He was gone before we could answer. Kyle fingered a spark plug. "Did Wyatt really steal these?" he said. I didn't reply. He scratched his matted hair with the bill of his baseball cap. I could tell he wanted to say more, but he didn't, until Wyatt sloshed back toward us through the slush. Then he said, "Dave, I have to tell Dad something. Does Wyatt have it? Is that why he went in there? I didn't know it would take this long."

What did he want from me? I could only do so much. He was going to have to learn how to operate on his own, with his lines of support severed. He needed to figure out, like everyone else needed to figure out, that this world is a lonely world. "Don't worry," I said. "It'll be fine." Kyle, oh, Kyle! At the end of your road, he will be there waiting. My head exploded with knowledge I had no idea how to convey. I squeezed shut my eyes, and focused on the tangible, on what was in front of me. I opened my eyes. Wyatt crossed my vision and I knew, once in the car, he would turn toward me with a grin.

❖ ❖ ❖

Wyatt lit a joint on the drive to the impound lot. "The smell," Kyle said when he held it out to him. "This is my mom's car."

"Too late," Wyatt said. "It's already lit."

Kyle didn't know to do anything except for what we said, or what we did. He dragged and passed the joint back to me. Wyatt rolled his window down an inch. "See?" he said. "Fresh air. Feel it on your face." Without smoking, I passed the joint to Wyatt. After a few rounds of this, Wyatt snubbed it out, and said, "That's all for now." Wyatt went silent, and Kyle giggled intermittently, and in the back seat I felt the loneliness of the sober man in a drunken crowd.

When we parked in front of the impound lot office, Kyle said, "I'm parched. My throat is dry." I sent him inside to drink from the water fountain. Wyatt followed me down to my mother's car. "You should have stayed with him," he said. "He's going to need some help."

"I'm afraid of what he might be doing," I said. "I think he's calling our father."

"Is this the father that took you fishing, then divorced your mom?"

"That's the father," I said. "I was five years old."

We came to the car. "Pop the hood," Wyatt said. I pulled the latch and dangled my legs out the open door and waited while Wyatt worked. "All done," I heard him yell. "Try it now." The engine sputtered, then caught, and as it idled Kyle walked down the path toward us. The snow had turned wet and heavy, coating the vehicles and the ground and making everything seem clean and intact. As Kyle approached he scooped a handful from the top of a car and held it to his forehead. Wyatt slammed shut the hood. "He's not going to make it," he said. "I should have cut him off."

"It must be his first time."

"We should have asked him."

I opened the back door. Kyle didn't even break his stride. In a fluid motion he fell into the back seat. Wyatt said, "No basketball shoes tonight."

"What should we do?" I said.

"He's your brother. You tell me."

"We can't stay here," I said. To stay would feel like admitting to something we couldn't take back. "I can't take him home like this."

"You could leave him out in front of your dad's place, in the car."

"It seems like he should have a choice."

Wyatt looked around. "We shouldn't leave anything," he said. "We don't want to come back here."

❖ ❖ ❖

I found my father's car parked at an angle in my mother's driveway, its headlights shining on the garage door. "Kyle," I said, not expecting a reply. "What gives?"

"I called him," he said. He was sitting up. "I don't know if I can stand."

Wyatt walked up the driveway from where he'd parked on the street. "This must be the father," he said. "This I've got to see." We helped Kyle out of the back seat and up the walk.

Balls! When I swung open that door! My mother was planted in front of the gas fireplace, which burned a low, blue and orange flame. Dressed to the hilt, ready for her date, venom dripping from her eyes. I could smell her perfume. My father launched his volleys from the walkway behind the couch, the only obstacle preventing them from finally tearing each other to pieces. The taunts. The mockeries. The insinuations. They hurtled across the room like arrows. There was barely room for me to stand!

"Here's the little bastard now," my father was saying. He smirked at me. He was in his groove, I could tell right away. This was what he worked to be better at. "Did you have a good day at the office?"

"You leave him out of this!" shrieked my mother.

Something washed out of me right then, a long unwanted allegiance to this place I'd been born into, to these people who failed to see the world was so vast it hid them from what they did to each other. I liked to think I could see. I liked to think I knew exactly what I did. I stepped aside and let Wyatt drag Kyle into the house. My father started toward Kyle, with his pale face and his blank eyes, and Kyle struggled to find his feet. "What the fuck?" my father said, shifting his attention to me. "What did you do to him?"

❖ ❖ ❖

I knelt to untie my shoes, which were soaked and speckled with mud. I felt like I was years in the future, reliving a memory. Wyatt helped Kyle over to the recliner, tracking dirty snow across the carpet, and then settled down onto the couch. He

seemed eager to know what would happen next. I wasn't surprised that Kyle had compromised us, but I'd hoped he'd be stronger. Still, I couldn't hold his mistakes against him. In his formative years, he didn't yet know the rules. In that way, I envied him. He wasn't used to interrogation. He didn't know to never give it up. Ever.

Like any memory I knew how it would end, and I left them all there and shuffled into the kitchen. My socks slid across the linoleum. I poked around in the refrigerator and snagged a container of blueberry yogurt. Eating healthy was part of my plan to grow ancient and withered with a furrowed face, reflecting back on my accomplishments. There would be wisdom there, I was sure. In the living room, the yelling acquired a rhythmic quality, lulling me back to my roots, to my early childhood. I peeled the foil cover off the yogurt container and licked the bottom of the cover clean.

Through the window above the sink, I watched the snow blanketing the earth as I ladled yogurt into my mouth and thought about the cab driver who had driven me to the impound lot that morning. I'd added twenty dollars when I paid him the fare. I felt sure his family back in Eritrea needed his help, though in truth I hadn't the slightest idea. The cab driver tucked the money into his shirt pocket and said, "Thank you, friend," as I clambered out of the cab and jogged away to rescue my mother's car.

❖ ❖ ❖

I know different people might say different things. Some might say I hadn't earned the money so it was easier to waste, and that in a nutshell is the problem with this country. Some might say it would be criminal to not repay the three hundred dollars, plus interest.

But it's my shred of truth and I'll do with it what I want. I say think about what you've taken yourself, from those who would help you. I say remember from where you came. I say remember looking straight up at the world as the swirling water pulled you down, before you tell someone else what they are allowed to do to survive.

❖ ❖ ❖

Sarah Crossland

In the Breath of Ten Thousand Metals

Almadén, Spain—1583

We have all committed crimes. Whether or not
they are the ones we were accused of—lifting
a loaf of bread from its carrier with spell-weighted
fingers, a lost blue horse, the wife we forsook
for cold islands of macabeo in the night—guilt
forms in our hands each day like a pound
of cinnabar. Pander metal, the always hunted
or latticed. Lustering as the deep-knowing
sky that watches us. It's that we want the guilt,
we want the heaven, we want the red lead.
And we are told to find it. Or soon our bodies
will fall into the long, entropic tomb rimmed
with its unavoidable scatflowers. In our two
shirts, the breeches and stockings, the single
hood we wear to bring darkness close to us
as it will come—the apothecary, the cup
of water as large as a child's hand, the sun
that imprisons us more than the men who say
they have imprisoned us—all of the provisions
we are given for each day to pass are not
enough. With buckets, we bail the rain out
after the dog-hungry storms. There is nowhere
for it but over our shoulders, back behind us
in the place we just have walked. Some men
write to their mothers and ask for coming
back. Back beneath their melancholic skirts,
calico and ugly as the face of someone who has
spent the evening with her own yeasty tears.
To where the wind won't fiss, where
the mercury in its fat pails won't find a way
to talk to us. There are sounds and there are
soundings. In the hymnals, it is not the same.
The chaplain, who is one of us, asks silver
coins for when we will not give over our
hour to God. And where is he down among
the mines, hero of the picaresque whose name
does not have surrender in it? It is taking
our hands—the poison—it is a beautiful thief
to talk to us. To tell us the rivets. The spangles
which could be horses in the night. Instead
of dreams, the whitening shape. Into a cup of wine.

An ear crinkles in the fire, a sole or a pot
of shoes right before the oven's door. Not a crown
to our heads but something blooming. Listen, our
teeth have found a way out. The hell is with us
inside and forever now, it is our own unending
skeleton. Every bell, every bell that has turned
will turn and turn to gold. There will be no
justice for any man. Only our toxic bodies,
which after all are innocent.

Discernment

a furious hunger for simplicity

−Tomas Tranströmer

The hawk-cluttered sky tangles with
clouds tossed in wind's tomfoolery;
stealthy, amnesiac light loiters,
poulticing blights of seasons past
(though spirit stores hard-copy, gusts
etch data in memory). Will chill not
numb our faults' persistent aches?

There's refreshment in searing wind—
what it doesn't savage it may salve:
January's regimen acts astringent to the
wayward, bewildered spirit, shearing
layers of deceit from rimed thought,
cleansing mind (almost) for another
attempt at snagging the apple's savor.

•　　　•　　　•

At the verge of green depths, clarity;
yet veiled within (always) the tentative—
deer stock-still scenting the wind
birds converging on the hour of migration
leaves tuned to life-sap's orchestration
to spew fireworks against the sky.

In clefts deep in mountains hues spill
for no eye: keener, more vivid perhaps,
tonalities of birdsong, clapperless bells
quickening pulse through brilliant sky,
attuned to a discerning ear that might
sate our furious hunger for simplicity.

Visible Breath

These dead leaves are hypnotized by snow.
She watches from the window, sees
numb fires of clouds becoming black stains,
oracles of birds. She imagines *before*
and *after*, as though they are as tactile
as the greenhouse where, by day, light
sweats and short-sighted winter loses
itself in fevered loam. She was *with him*
then *alone*. The varicose veins of days
meander beneath the skin, this sermon
of stars when she is sleeping, this breath
she holds in abeyance in her lungs,
all the earth a sustenance of dead
grass and drifts against the fence,
sleeping the way a pickup on the highway
spins its pirouette on ice before coming
to a graceful stop beside a bar ditch. *He touched*
her arm then walked away. In dreams there is
a vortex of weeds at the yard's edge,
and snow falls from an invisible mask,
as far away as a small confessional
of geese, the retreating V bound
to the earth and yet escaping it.
Once he seemed as familiar as a red
sun in a gray lake. Now he is stone
and smoke and hemorrhaging clouds.

Ina Kaur. *Liberating Restrains*. 2010. Color etching, relief, and blind embossment. 24 x 18 inches.

Discovering Terra Incognita

Polar exploration is at once the cleanest and most isolated way of having a bad time that has been devised.

–Apsley Cherry-Garrard
Worst Journey in the World

Before I came to Antarctica, I still believed it was the last place on earth left to explore. I grew up with Scott's journals; I traced routes from Palmer Station to Queen Maude Land on a map, and stared for hours at photographs of calved glaciers in the St. Paul Science Museum. I would spread a map across my bedroom floor and trace my finger along the coast. I memorized the names—the Gamburtzev Mountains, Vostok, the Pole of Inaccessibility, Dry Valleys, the Queen Maude Mountains, the Mertz Glacier, Casey Station, Vinson Massif— and always, before I folded it along worn edges, I traced the longitudes to their intersection. South Pole, it read, labeled in bold.

So when Raytheon Polar Services hired me as a General Construction Assistant, even though I knew I was a glorified snow shoveler, even though I understood that the job would be thankless, I still imagined I had joined ranks with those explorers who came south in search of glory and greatness and some inner sense of worth that continued to elude me. I expected to feel lost in an untried landscape. I expected the wind and cold and the glare of never-ending sun. I expected that the people I worked with would be the sort who fell naturally to the fringes of the map. But I never guessed that the bottom of the world would be quite so—weird.

In the final days of October, I flew to Denver for training—tedious corporate lectures held in warm classrooms imbued with the promise of the earth's southern terminus. After four days of deployment paperwork and company protocols, Raytheon put me on a plane from Denver to Los Angeles, then Honolulu to Sydney to Christchurch, New Zealand. I sat in a hotel room for three days waiting for the weather to clear over the Southern Ocean. At last I reached the Ice: McMurdo Station, the last layover before my flight to the South Pole. Here then, was my first view of Terra Incognita—the Unknown Land, Antarctica.

❖ ❖ ❖

As far as the eye could see, there was nothing but an icy shroud, white ruins, tabula rasa.
He hadn't a minute to lose.
He was going to populate this wilderness.

–Blaise Cendrars, *Dan Yack*

Ice began hundreds of miles ahead of the continent, great chunks floating closer and closer together until I peered through the portholes of a C-17 cargo transport plane onto a white so white it made my eyes ache. I fought to discern the contours of landfall and, slowly, the clouds tinged grey on their edges. I noticed striations far below— crevasses and ascents of the Trans-Antarctic Mountains—and when we began our descent to the sea ice off Ross Island's coast, I glimpsed long fractures, snow-packed ridges, and pockmarked blue ice blown barren by the polar wind.

We landed in late afternoon. Fifty of us, dressed in red parkas, bunny boots, and ski goggles, stepped onto the Ross Ice Shelf at 77.51 degrees south latitude. Snow feathered its way to crystalline horizons; sea and land merged with sky, dancing together in bloodless miasma.

The thermometer read eighteen degrees below zero; cold sunlight circled the southern sky. A mile away, station buildings sprawled—tan and green, stark and industrial—up the smoking side of Mt. Erebus. Along the distant shore, where the Victoria Range jutted out of McMurdo Sound, the only color came from black volcanic rock and the atmosphere's pallid blue arc.

A century earlier, Sir Robert Falcon Scott set off on his doomed expedition from this same spit of land. His hut, still standing and pristine, was visible a mile away on Cape Evans. Colored flags checkered the ice, marking the roadways and runways across the pack. The ageless shack, the red of our parkas, the growling of machinery, and the station, with its two taverns, coffee-shop, visitor center, and decommissioned nuclear power plant, felt pathetically impermanent, like a surreal painting where the sense of scale has been created through an overwhelming white space.

Standing on Antarctic ice for the first time, I felt like an intruder. It was if I had departed from earth. To simply survive here was to live a post-apocalyptic existence. To feel and smell the reality of 12.4 million square miles of frozen expanse, to place upon a scale the fathomless weight of that much ice pressed upon the earth, left me winded. The land—and my mind—felt as if they had been flipped upside down.

Ice crystals bit into my eyes, a pressure ridge thrust blue ice onto the edge of the runway. I caught a whiff of jet fuel from the plane, watched as it lifted into sky and headed back north to Christchurch. We climbed into a transport vehicle—the name "Ivan the Terrabus" imprinted on its side—and bounced toward the station amid a rumble of machinery, voices, and crackling sea ice. The pleasure was maddening.

❖ ❖ ❖

I have felt all the time that the diet of dog does not agree with me.

–Dr. Xavier Mertz, Mawson Expedition, 1911

The Antarctic Plateau doesn't warm enough to land a plane on it until the end of October. So though I'd been hired to work at South Pole Station, I spent two weeks at McMurdo, scooping snow off diesel pipelines and reorganizing drums of oil in an old freight canister out near the abandoned power plant. For two weeks, I shuffled between buildings to see nightly science lectures. I visited the library and taverns, sent postcards to my parents, and played cribbage over glasses of red wine in Quonset huts.

One afternoon I hiked out to Cape Evans and visited Scott's hut. Rows of books still sat as they had for a century. The shelves were still lined with canned meat, fish, vegetables, and a few hunks of preserved seal. A pipe rack for his several smoking pieces still rested in the corner. The hut felt like a museum display, the supplies like

impossible attempts to stave off homesickness. The scene struck me as ridiculous. Pork rind and a chessboard couldn't make Antarctica feel like the green pastures of England. That much, at least, was obvious. I zipped my parka against a stiffening wind and walked the mile back to the base.

That evening, at the coffee shop and tavern, a pair of workers sat in a corner, playing a guitar and a stand-up bass borrowed from the station's music room. In the next building over, people exercised on treadmills and Stairmasters after their workday. In the dining hall, they had served Pad Thai and Massaman curry for supper. And at last it occurred to me: these incongruous possessions serve to remind us that our efforts to tame Antarctica are themselves absurd. In a landscape where nothing is familiar, superfluity is essential. We can't cope without it.

I lived in limbo while I waited for my flight to my real job at the Pole. Really though, it was worse than limbo, because I stayed in Man Camp. When they distributed keys to all new arrivals on the first day, I was left standing with two other guys in the hallway.

"We, uh, didn't get keys," I said to the woman in charge of orientation. She looked at my paperwork and giggled.

"Your room doesn't have a key. That's Man Camp."

"Man Camp?" I said.

"You'll see," she said, and called to a welder in the doorway, "Hey, you wanna show these guys Man Camp." The welder just laughed.

Man Camp was designed as a one-night layover for workers passing through to other stations on the continent, and as such could hold nearly fifty people, who, as per policy, all happened to be men. The thermostat blasted heat twenty-four hours a day, keeping the room at a consistent ninety degrees, but when I opened a window to cool off, I woke up in the morning with frost on my eyebrows. I spent the nights feverish, my nose numbed by cold, my feet damp with sweat. A climatologist bound for the pole managed to get on the season's first flight, but I was on the manifest for flight nine or ten.

One night a group of Australians passed through on their way to Casey Station, drank their last hard booze for the season, and passed out on whichever bed they happened to trip over. I returned that night to a naked and snoring Aussie in my bunk. For the last week, I slept in the hallway.

The roads of McMurdo are made from wind-pummeled volcanic rock, and after a few days in McMurdo, we transients waiting for the weather to break over the interior began to take on the same grey appearance as the land around us. Soot covered the sides of buildings. Rows of steel pipe, transporting diesel, water, electricity, and excrement surrounded the station like a fence and made the promise of the unblemished, wild outside that much more alluring. We sought the warmth of taverns to escape the diesel smell that saturated the air around town.

To nurse our hangovers one day, my friend Emily and I skied out onto the Erebus Glacier. We stopped at the fire station, checked out a radio for emergencies, and glided across the ice. Every ten feet, red and blue flags jutted up from the Styrofoam snow, and zigzags of black ribbon denoted hidden crevasses. Halfway up, a bulbous hut, stocked with food, sleeping bags, and stoves, served as a survival shelter.

The view in Antarctica relies on a skewed perception. Moisture on breath turns instantly into ice crystals, but it is not simply that you can see the steam. Exhalations seem to suspend in the rarified air, and on sunny days, the atmosphere shimmers with a million microscopic flashes, a hoarfrost with nothing to cling to but exposed skin and hair. Occasionally, the crystals linger long enough to glimpse a flash of rainbow. Once, deep in the tunnels under South Pole, I controlled my breathing while holding a cupped hand under my chin. In the beam of my headlamp, I watched the vapor hover in the still air for a moment, then fall in visible shards onto my glove.

On the glacier, Emily looked out at the Ross Sea along the distorted horizon and said, "My favorite color is white. Once you've seen ice like this, white never seems plain . . . there are so many different kinds of white it blows my mind."

I attended sea ice training. Five people, decked out in Extreme Cold Weather gear, climbed into a tracked vehicle and lumbered out toward Razorback Island several miles up the coast. The wind was light—we could see four or five flags in front of our vehicle. The miles zipped by across bare ice; snow whipped sideways toward the distant Dry Valleys. As we paused to take a depth sampling, a lone Adelie penguin waddled and slid into view. In a month, three hundred thousand more would arrive at Ross Island, but on this frigid spring morning, open water was fifty miles distant, and the tiny bird moved inland at a steady pace. It appeared as a grey speck, a comma on blank paper.

In October, Air Force transport jets land on the sea ice, but by January, McMurdo Sound becomes open water peppered with icebergs, and excursions such as ours become impossible. The sea dissolves into a jigsaw puzzle of jumbled floes, and migrating whales, seals, and birds flock to Ross Island in a cacophony of sound. After less than two months, the super-saline currents that surround the continent push polar air back down; the ketabatic winds blow down the glaciers. By February, life flees north and darkness returns.

On our way back to the station, our vehicle, called a piston bully, stopped by Razorback Island to visit the breeding grounds of Weddell Seals. A hundred blubbery blobs bleated and wallowed in their own afterbirth along a rift in the sea ice. Not far away, a glacier extended out from the land, floating on McMurdo Sound, and we climbed into a crevasse that had burst open a few hundred yards from shore. Above me, two hundred feet of ice churned its way out from shore—in the silence I imagined I felt a bobbing of the tides. Impulsively, I licked a tendril of ice; it froze to my tongue, and for a moment I was gripped by a fear that the glacier might calve.

The last dregs of the long winter clung desperately to the coast, making flights to the pole irregular and dangerous. Workers and scientists filtered through Man Camp, a summer populace spreading across the continent. My desire to escape McMurdo grew strong. Because I didn't have regular work, Raytheon had made me a lackey. I filled out time sheets, set up army tents, organized lumber, and helped build a mini-golf course for a carpentry shop costume party. I went as Ziggy Stardust. Three bands played on a rough-cut stage; other party-goers dressed up as pirates, penguins, scissors, krill, and the Blue Man Group.

McMurdo, despite the thousand inhabitants, the bars, the yoga classes, the seals and penguins, made me masochistic. I wanted more cold and fewer people. I wanted endless white space and a spinning compass. I came to regard the station as a tiny stain, like an abandoned cabin in a wilderness or rover tracks on the moon. McMurdo acted as the last outpost on the edge of the map, but I hadn't yet fallen off the bottom. Besides, after a week sleeping in a hallway, colder, windier, and more bizarre didn't sound too bad.

At last I left for South Pole Station. On the last day, I met a New Zealander while I climbed to the cross on Ob Hill above the station. We talked about our jobs, about the sacrifices and philosophies that had filtered south. I told him I was headed to the Pole to shovel snow.

"Not too many people can say they've shoveled snow in Antarctica, mate," he said.

Across the sound, Mount Discovery shimmered in the month-long sunset. A handful of seals, looking like spackled black dots, lay strewn along a distant pressure ridge. I checked my watch, buttoned my parka, and turned back down the hill to catch my flight.

❖ ❖ ❖

And so you will travel nearly alone, but those with whom you sledge will not be shopkeepers: that is worth a good deal.

-Apsley Cherry Garrard

In 1911, the only extraneous item Roald Amundsen carried on his quest to the South Pole was his journal. The Norwegian had by then spent three winters held fast in Arctic ice. He had walked five hundred miles from the Beaufort Sea to Eagle, Alaska—and back—to telegraph news of his successful traverse of the Northwest Passage. He had survived in barren country and had found a colonial sensibility to be ineffective for polar travel. Amundsen meticulously planned his bid, considered every step from Norway to the Pole. A plaque on the wall in South Pole Station notes that his sled dogs gained weight on the journey.

The Amundsen Expedition arrived at ninety degrees south latitude on December 14, a tired outline set against a backdrop of unceasing white ice, where sky cannot be discerned from solid ground.

"So we arrived and were able to plant our flag at the geographical South Pole," he wrote, claiming the world's southern axis for himself and his country.

A month later, Sir Robert Falcon Scott turned up, wasting away from malnutrition. He had brought ponies to carry him to the pole, but the first horse died on deck two nights after setting sail from New Zealand, and none had survived the voyage. Scott would not make it back from the Antarctic Plateau alive. Eleven miles from his supply depot, a rescue crew found him frozen. "The Pole," he had written. "Yes, but under very different circumstances from those expected."

Triumph and tragedy.

We trickle south in search of a perception unachievable elsewhere. A recruitment ad for Ernest Shackleton's Endurance Expedition in 1912 advertised a "hazardous journey, small wages, bitter cold, long months of complete darkness, constant danger, and small chance of success." More than five thousand people applied, and Shackleton spent months selecting his crew from the pool.

Perhaps for some—the intrepid and legendary explorers and today's possessed polar workers—the inexplicable pull of the pole is the sufferance of a magnetic drive. I still wonder today: what happens when a life's meaning is found atop of 9,301 feet of ice?

Those who live and work at the South Pole, whether dishwasher or astrophysicist, approach the ice with a sense of awe that borders on religious conviction. I met architects who had quit high-paying jobs to load cargo, scuba instructors hired to clean toilets, and a poet who drove a forklift. One woman, who had grown up as a bear hunting guide on the Alaskan Peninsula dated a lobster fisherman from New England. They both put up siding on the station.

My job was simple. Every winter, blowing snow consumes any place left open to the elements—every hole, every ventilation duct, every place where even a screw works loose. Mountains develop between the massive sub-ice fuel storage tanks. Drifts obliterate entire buildings. Each summer season, a mile of storage materials, organized in rows called "the berms," must be uncovered. Raytheon hires a small army of workers to uncover the buried station and help with odd jobs.

For four months, I dug out boxes of station garbage, uncovered four-meter tall stacks of random metal pipe, shoveled off sheeting and L-brackets, bales of wire, old tires, lumber, t-shirts, and frozen lobsters. I spent a week tucked under the floor of the station's storage arch, bolting shelving to the floor by hand. Temperatures in the crawlspace where I worked never fluctuated—they remained a constant forty degrees below zero. We dug deep channels into the icecap and ran hundreds of meters worth of cable, we used chainsaws to cut blocks of ice that had encased the station's pillar supports. I shoveled out telescopes, wind generators, latrines, and forgotten military rations, all—as we reminded ourselves again and again—in the name of science.

Scientific research at the South Pole is, for the most part, pretty esoteric. Telescopes measure ions in the upper atmosphere; meteorologists study weather behaviors in order to predict global climate changes. Those who support these projects, "Polies," as we are called, are meant to believe that this research places us on the brink of scientific discovery. The entire station becomes, in many ways, imbued with the sense that some larger thing is at work here.

We cannot perfectly describe the experience of a world where earth and sky are indistinguishable, but we may be able to measure it. The largest scientific project in Antarctica, ICECUBE, attempts to quantify and trace an unfathomably small subatomic particle—the neutrino. A grant from the National Science Foundation has built a kilometer-square telescope buried a mile and a half into the ice. Five thousand basketball-sized sensors measure the rare reactions of these particles and trace them to their origins in galactic nebulae.

What little we know of neutrinos makes their potential all the more powerful. They are among the most abundant particles in the universe. A German scientist explained to me that "every second, a billion neutrinos pass through the nail on my pinkie finger, but across an entire lifetime, they may only react once in the space of a living room." One day at dinner this German researcher admitted to me his hopes for the project—that with ICECUBE, we might pinpoint the Big Bang's location in the universe. And a visiting physicist, after a talk one evening, said, "The statistical improbability of the Big Bang having actually occurred on any sort of universe-forming level of explosive photonic reactions, is so remote that nothing but divine influence could explain its existence."

These opinions, that by use of a scientific method we might discover the divine, and that the ICECUBE project places us on the cusp of this discovery, seems a uniquely Antarctic sentiment. Here the lines between theory and reality become blurred, perhaps because we do not yet understand this polar landscape. We have experienced the physicality of the Antarctic for less than a century, and it remains difficult for us to believe that an entire landscape exists where the only perceivable entities are imprecise—there must be more than simply ice and light.

I assisted in installing the wires for the ICECUBE telescope. For a week, we used an ancient snowmachine to drag nearly thirty million dollars worth of cable from the cavernous holes they had been lowered into, each hole drilled with pressurized water, consuming seventy-five hundred gallons of jet fuel to dig deep enough, to the two-story computer room that would monitor the reactions.

I spent two days in the fetal position while the cables, a thousand feet long and as big around as my arm, were positioned. As snow blew around in unctuous gusts, ten people heaved these cables through a drainpipe to the second-story balcony of the computer building. Once, a tug rope broke, sent a dozen people tumbling backwards into the pooling drifts of snow. We almost destroyed the entire computer system.

❖   ❖   ❖

One comes to measure a place, too, not just for the beauty it may give, the balminess of its breezes, the insouciance and relaxation it encourages, the sublime pleasures it offers, but for what it teaches. …It is not so much that you want to return to indifferent or difficult places, but that you want not to forget.

–Barry Lopez

Around Christmas, workers gather to watch the arrival of the annual fuel traverse. Fuel use at the South Pole in the summertime exceeds twenty thousand gallons per week, and requires an expensive type of jet fuel. AN-8, used only in Antarctica, is purchased and transported either via cargo plane or by Caterpillars that drive eleven hundred miles from McMurdo, towing giant gut sacks of fuel on custom sledges.

Occasionally, skuas, Antarctica's aggressive scavenger gulls, will follow the traverse all the way to the pole, where they circle for days, disoriented, desperate, and unable to escape, before succumbing to exhaustion. Along with Amundsen's flag, they are buried by the snow, entombed by ice for the next hundred thousand years. Life here can only be buried.

A strange mythology has worked its way into the South Pole Station's culture. Each season workers uncover dozens of objects that reinforce an odd respect for the brief history of the station. For example, one day we found a stash of bacon bars left over from when the Navy had managed the station in the 1970s. After much debate, we tore open the packages and ate them in homage to the station's history. They were salty, basically bacon bits pressed into the shape of granola bars. A pipe insulator and weightlifter named John, who had worked at South Pole for more than seventeen seasons, remembered when boxes of these bacon bars had filled whole shelves in the old station.

One day a dozer operator broke through the upper crust of snow and fell, machine and all, twenty-five feet into the dining room of the original station. The structure had been abandoned and buried since 1959, and had migrated fifty yards from its original location in those decades. After the operator, Josiah, had been rescued, he told his story over curried chicken dinner.

"It was crazy. There were still plates of half-eaten food on the tables and coats on the benches. If we heated the steaks back up, they'd be edible," he said. Two days later, they retrieved the bulldozer and filled the hole, entombing those stories in the old dining room forever.

A former winter-over worker shared a story about the psychological effect of the South Pole without sunlight. After two months, one employee began compulsorily turning off every light in the station. When he started shutting off the dining hall lights, a group placed flashbulbs in front of his bedroom door. In response, he took his meals in his room, refusing to speak to anyone until the sunlight returned. Nobody could quite figure out why, when the world's only illumination came from the Aurora Australis, he spurned even the glow of a light bulb.

During a flight that tested the ability to airdrop supplies in the event of a winter emergency, a box of bread flour failed to deploy its parachute and exploded over the snow. After work, I went out to search for the location. I glimpsed a speck near the horizon I thought might be the shattered crate. A friend and I trudged across the flat landscape toward this lone blemish. After two kilometers, we arrived to find only a sastrugi ridge, pockmarked wind deformations in the icy crust. The box had been covered, the flour sifted into the atmosphere and dispersed across the continent.

Our stories mimic the heroics of the early explorers here. Like Scott, we are at best unprepared, overzealous amateurs, but it does not matter. We want to believe that our myths are true, that an Australian actually did die after drinking glycol filtered through a sock (supposedly, he'd heard the Russians at Vostok Station made vodka that way), or that someone did spend two months walking around the station turning off lights in order to keep the sun from returning. We want to believe these stories are truth, and they may be. Certainly, strange things do occur here, but it is the provable moments that come to feel most important.

The axis of our world shifts several meters each year, a slight defect at the pivot point of the planet. And so, every New Year's Day the words of Amundsen and Scott, inscribed as epitaphs at the geographic South Pole, are ceremonially moved to the newly measured, precise bottom of the earth. The station manager and perhaps a visiting explorer recite the triumphs of humans over landscape and embed a marker, newly commissioned each year, on the new site. It is a reorientation of the indiscernible.

The South Pole smoker's lounge is famous for wild parties and thirty years of un-dissipated cigarette haze. The lounge comes complete with a stocked bar, a handful of regulars, and a stripper pole for when parties get wild. At one such party, a naked electrician used a plumber as a snowboard and rode him down a pile of excavated snow outside the doorway.

We drank beer which had sat in cans for half a decade. Our chefs gave up jobs at world renowned restaurants to deep-fry tasteless vegetables stored for a decade. On clear days, halos and sun dogs encircled the ever-present sun. A tourist from China flew in for a one-day visit and developed heart palpitations upon his arrival. A group of us who held mostly expired First Responder and EMT certifications monitored his vitals in shifts for twenty-four hours before airlifting him out. He had departed from Puntarenas, Chile. When he awoke, his plane was bound for New Zealand.

The lack of bacterial life sucks odor from the air, and after four months of sweating in bunny boots, the only smell they emanate comes from spilled jet fuel. To get drinking water, a steam drill melts ice fifty feet below the surface.

This same water, reprocessed as waste, is dumped into hewn ice caverns. Giant stalactites of gray-water stab up from the cavern floor, the crystallized shit of an entire station, buried into the icecap.

The mean annual temperature is minus fifty-seven degrees Fahrenheit. The mean annual temperature at the North Pole is just minus eighteen degrees Fahrenheit. The coldest ever temperature at the South Pole was recorded June 23, 1982: it dropped to one hundred and seventeen degrees below zero, and even in summer, the temperature never rises above zero degrees. In the wintertime, a sort of impromptu club forms. To gain entrance, one must turn the station's sauna temperature to two hundred degrees Fahrenheit and endure the searing heat for several minutes; then, on a particularly cold day, pull on shoes, dash for the pole, touch it, and return to the sauna. The sprint is clothing-optional, and those who succeed enter the "300 Club," for having endured this temperature fluctuation.

❖ ❖ ❖

Who are the chairbound to belittle men of hardihood, however driven, foolish, incompetent and even without scruple some may be? What is this awful need we have to pull the brave ones down into the mob by exposing their human frailties and mistakes? Are we so incapable of peace within ourselves that we find the eminence of bolder men unbearable?"

– Peter Matthiesson, *End of the Earth*

The Terra Incognita of our minds has not disappeared; it is merely, like blowing whorls of snow, perpetually altering itself to fit the progressively shifting frontiers of human awareness. We must be reminded that there is as much value in what Antarctica promises to teach as there is in what we have come to learn of the place. These paltry striated spaces, the organized human outposts of Antarctica, are defined by latitude and longitude, by meteorology and scientific measurements. Today, the continent is understood not through the glorious mythos of explorers, but through the quantifiable strictures of science. Yet Antarctica remains a perpetual frontier, and despite what we understand, the frigid beauty of that ice-shrouded world remains as mythical as ever.

My favorite painting is a work by the artist Xavier Cortada, on display at South Pole Station. It depicts the bust of Shackleton, wearing dirtied yellow suspenders, his face benevolent and tough, but blurred by the thickness of the paint on canvas. In the top right corner are the coordinates of the most southerly point the explorer reached. The materials for the work were gathered on the continent and include crystals from Mt. Erebus, seawater from McMurdo Sound, and soil from Ross Island and the Dry Valleys. How fitting to our conceptions that these natural materials depict a constructed and foreign object to the Antarctic landscape, that the image is displayed in the place that eluded its subject for a lifetime.

The South Pole offers a place for the imaginative to form theories on the origins of the cosmos, but the truth is that other places on the continent are far stranger—inaccessible, hidden by frost, they exist in the realm of story, and make up part of the folklore that defines humankind's brief presence on the continent.

The Dry Valleys of the Central Trans-Antarctic Mountains are noted for the scattering of mummified crabeater seals strewn across the ice free valleys. A few scientists fly by helicopter to the Valleys each year to measure the decomposition rates of the trapped and frozen remains. Decades of wind eventually curve their bodies and freeze-dry their skin and, like burned paper, the seals drift away across the years in chalky fragments.

The world's largest unfrozen lake rests below three miles of ice cap under Vostok Station. The Gamburtzev Mountain Range is over nine thousand feet above sea level, but can only be mapped using sonar, for the peaks are still under a mile of ice. I once talked to a pilot who had flown a Twin Otter flight over the Pole of Inaccessibility, the furthest point from the coast and the most remote spot on the planet. He claimed that an enormous stone statue of Lenin had been erected by the Soviets, and that his bust still stuck up from the snow.

Working each day in the cold and wind, I became accustomed to the lifelessness. Scientific presentations, musical concerts, and a visit from Sir David Attenborough and his documentary film crew, distracted me from the tedium of an imageless landscape. Only when I arrived back in New Zealand did I understand how the deficient nature of the polar world had affected me. To emerge from a place that belies understanding is to realize its importance. Antarctica, it would seem, contains that kinetic potential which can connect us to the imagined desires and landscapes of our souls.

For me, the unfamiliar and harsh desolation is a strange solace. I have sought it elsewhere, but never quite felt the pure release of spirit associated with the Ice.

Only the Southern Polar plateau offers an absolute nothing. If we seek a clearing of the mind, Antarctica's interior offers the sole opportunity for the known landscape to share in scouring clean our mind's excesses. I remember the night before I flew back to New Zealand, in the bright 3 a.m. sun, a moment when the bulldozers, snowmachines, and airplanes, the wind and snow even, fell silent. This glimpse of a complete serenity brought me to my knees; I realized the potential of ice, and it crushed me to a humbled speck.

Antarctica demands to be spoken of differently. I turn to the penguin pair huddled on the ice for advice on survival. I imagine the Dry Valley seals embracing the dry wind on their skin for eternity. We can learn to encounter desolation with a given joy.

One day, when most workers were asleep, I sat alone in the sauna until the heat had worked deep into my organs. Then with a whoop, I crashed through the storm doors into the everlasting daylight. In seconds, my skin was a sheen of frost, every hair grasping to retain the warm moisture, lest it escape to the dried plateau. My feet pounded the Styrofoam snow, needle points stabbing my heels, crystals froze my eyelids shut. A bulldozer had manipulated the surface into a gradual hill, and with a leap, I rolled downward. My sides and legs chafed against the ice, rubbed raw as if they'd seen sandpaper. Before I returned to the safety of the station, I scooped a handful of blown powder to my face and rubbed the ancient elements into my hair.

❖ ❖ ❖

F. Daniel Rzicznek

Of Hindrance

No faces yet for the dead—
no names, places, or certainties.

The little dog in the soul sits
cocking his head at the newscasters.

No faces yet for the wounded.
Little dog goes mad, howling now

for the million languages to answer:
which has a word for snow-

on-pines-and-the-wind-
banging-like-a-dull-axe-chopping?

An overwhelming majority of
headwounds. Glass bowl

of naval oranges—trees waltzing
outside the hospital window.

~

There is a narrow stretch where
the current slows over gravel and shale.

It is a popular place to cross.

A Deeper Telling

In a voice made almost
entirely of breath, she asks
me, *Tell me?* My tongue
touches folds at the tip
of my palate, *"o"* drags
air from my throat.

If she were in my mouth,
she could say, *Say a vowel*,
to feel the arrangements I
was making, spoken in order
from front to back—*bills,*
penalties, documents, drives,
cash, lockout, nothing in ink.

This seems somehow a deeper
telling, disguised in an assembly
of acoustics and sound, divined
from me in an alternate tongue.
No is tactile, forceful, bold in
a way that *yes* is anything else.

John Wall Barger

Lament of the Ex-Encyclopedia Salesman with a Pretty Thai Lady on His Arm

I woke & my fingernails were long. Where I moved
I drew blood. She, descendent of opium fields,
chose me. In this intermezzo of luck
I am ridiculous. Her digital photos reveal me:
pants tucked in high over my gut, staring out
at morning beach umbrellas past a big red nose,
eyes shocked as if readjusting to bad news.
While dancing I step on her foot & she laughs.
Her poised look asks, "Surprised I try to please,
farang?" My capacity to worship endures.
My capacity to endure is played out. I tell her
I don't like heels. Don't they make it hard to walk
on sand? She winks. She reveals little. Tipsy
on Jell-O spritzers, she let it slip that as a kid she
had a pet bunny that chased trucks. Why
did her bunny do that? So much is inconceivable,
sunstruck on our backs under a banyan tree
that eddies like a river but slower than time,
like Paganini violins. Tar coats my throat
& I stare at stars—no, between—at blackness
declared unmanifest, unthinkable, immutable.
The moth of night eats the linen sky. Time
siphons love. Her hand is small & brown in mine.

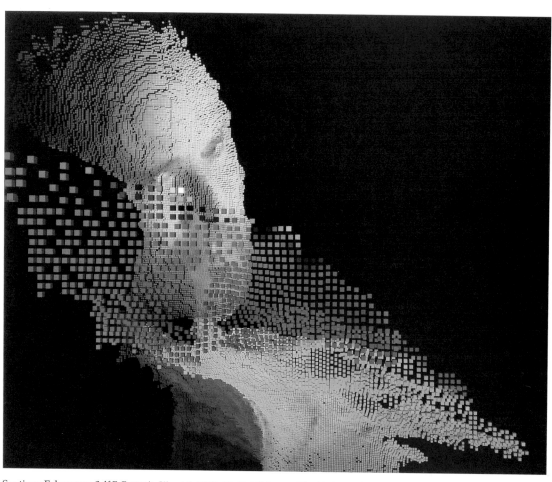

Santiago Echeverry. *Self E-Portrait, Kinect 1*. 2013. Digital Print, archival ink on photographic paper. 30 x 24 inches.

Home Waters

My brother Bill knows most of the natural springs in north Florida. He camps near the clear, rushing water of Blue Springs or, his favorite, the Econfina (ee-kin-fine-uh). For years, he led canoe trips for birdwatchers down the Choctawhatchee (chalk-tuh-hatch-ee) and other waterways throughout the Panhandle. But it wasn't hunting the ivory-billed woodpecker that taught him to move silently through the water.

❖ ❖ ❖

The water in Florida's natural springs is cold and clean. Filtered by limestone rock, the fresh water is as clear and perfect as blown glass. The source, or boil, is coated with colors of minerals deposited by the rushing waters—greens and blues, orange and pink. Hundreds of these portals pump millions of gallons a day from Florida's natural underground aquifer, the Floridan, the river that runs beneath the peninsula. Most of the springs aren't widely known; many are unmarked. Once they get "discovered," divers congregate at the boil many feet below, stirring up the silt with their fins, clouding the water. Even at the surface, though, the force of the flow is strong enough for me to swim as hard as I can and make no forward progress.

❖ ❖ ❖

Early on a steamy August morning a few years ago, Lowell Kelly, a local developer, came by my brother Bill's place on Blue Creek, in Ponce de Leon, Florida. He had hired Bill to do some day labor for him, so Kelly and his friend Kevin Hicks were to drive Bill to the worksite. Nearing sixty, Bill came prepared, with his water supply, lunch, and favorite hand tools. They told him to sit in the truck behind the shotgun seat and then drove past the small, remote Gator Pond, stopping near a dense, green wall of overgrowth that blocked access to the larger swamp. Kelly got out on the driver's side and ran around the back of the

truck, so that when Bill stepped out, Kelly was running at him with a baseball bat, screaming about his money. The first blow landed on Bill's head and spun him around. My brother is a big man and didn't hit the ground right away, but he was surprised —literally blindsided—by the assault and stunned by the actual blow to his head. Kelly had a moment to swing again, but this time, Bill instinctively pulled back, and the bat glanced hard off the left side of his head, inflicting more sharp pain. Blood began to pour from his torn left ear, and he stumbled back. That's when he noticed that Hicks was standing by the open truck door, his right hand hidden. Bill assumed he held a gun. When my brother slipped and hit the muddy ground, Kelly was over him quickly and beat him hard, in the gut, the chest, the legs, no longer with the advantage of surprise, but with the relish of a guy on top. Bill managed to scramble away from Kelly and stood, trying to shield his head from more blows, which allowed Kelly to bash Bill's elbows and belly.

❖ ❖ ❖

My brothers and I will jump into any body of water we find. Well, I may pick my way in, but the three of them (Bill, the oldest; Byron, just younger than I; and Bobby, the youngest) jump. They play games, mostly involving Frisbees, complicated rules, and fifty years of paybacks. Sometimes I swim around them in wide circles, paddling and bending to the right, then I turn around and circle to the left, like in a folk dance.

❖ ❖ ❖

Kelly wiped the slippery, bloody bat on his jeans before chasing Bill into a blind alley of land surrounded by swampy muck. When the dry land ran out, Bill turned and faced Kelly again, having a hard time seeing through the curtain of blood, thinking only *there is nowhere else to go.* Bill stumbled toward Kelly, who turned and ran back toward the truck, even though he still held the bat. So Bill, with no other options, stepped off solid ground into the muddy, lumpy swamp. He lay down, fast, on his belly. Taking a gulp of air, he went under the gray water. He slithered and slid, like his fellow animals in the water. Kelly and Hicks searched for him, yelling murderous threats. Kelly's voice could be heard for a long time, his ranting growing first louder, more insistent, and eventually more resigned, when they didn't find him. The thought of Hicks's gun kept my brother hidden. He stayed in the swamp, mostly underwater, for hours. He made no sound. He feared that lifting his head or making any noise would get him shot. He was sure that they had not intended for him to leave the swamp alive. Bill told me later that you have no fear of snakes or gators when men are hunting you with guns.

❖ ❖ ❖

Bill paddles the big kayak out from Pass-a-Grille into the Gulf of Mexico. I sit in the bow, feeling strange not to be paddling, too, but he assures me it's okay. He wants to do this for me, because my injured elbow keeps me from getting out on the water myself. I tell him about the last time I kayaked here, when we were surrounded by dolphins. A group of about fifteen, including juveniles, circled our boat for several minutes, jumping and playing, before heading up the beach on their morning rounds. He tells me about his search for good shelling places. He and his girlfriend Lynn want to sell shell-decorated frames and mirrors to tourists. We head south to the cut at the bottom of the barrier islands that make up Pinellas County beaches. The current is strong here and the water, very choppy. We turn into the channel, fighting the outgoing tide, as Tampa Bay waters relocate into the Gulf on their twice-daily journey. We jog right and left, slapped by the waves, our bow in the air. I move forward to weigh us down and now sit facing him, holding onto the sides. He gestures with his chin toward the north side of the channel. I look over my shoulder: the dropping tide reveals a spot of tucked-away, drifted sand and heaps of shells beyond two small docks. He steers us around the docks; we pull the boat half ashore and wade to the gorgeous pile of shells, big and tiny, rounded and pointy, white and pink and gray and orange, caught by the currents in this bend of shoreline. "We'll come back here from

the road later," Bill says. "I'll show you my new contraption. It's two milk crates hanging from a yoke on my shoulders, so I can tip the crates into the surf. It works real good."

On our way out of the channel, we ride the tide, and he uses the paddle only to steer. He has practiced, smooth motions. We don't talk about terrible things that can happen. We're wet from the splash and, as we turn north, we face a chilly February breeze. But the sun and his confident, quiet paddling make me think about taking a nap.

❖ ❖ ❖

From the swamp, Kelly drove to Bill's shop and roared into the driveway. He hollered at Lynn, Bill's girlfriend, that he had "hurt Bill, hurt him real bad." He threw Bill's belongings onto the dusty ground and said he would kill him if he made it home. Kelly ranted about Bill having stolen $30,000 from his truck on Friday when Bill had last worked for him.

Here's the thing about my big brother: He is scrupulous about things like honesty and thievery. He once found a full bank bag in a Winn-Dixie parking lot and turned the whole thing in. He and Lynn live very close to the bone, mostly growing many varieties of bamboo, running a small shop just off I-10 called "Flutes and Vegetables," and leading nature trips. That, and they host visiting music acts on their wooden stage among the old live oaks and younger, leaping bamboos. They don't lock their doors. They're smart and spiritual, but not God-fearing churchgoers, so they stand out in their tiny Southern town. She has bountiful wavy black hair, with streaks of gray; he wears his white hair in a ponytail and often has a beard. His name in local parts is "Bamboo Bill," and the Bill is pronounced "Bee-ull." After Kelly's visit, Lynn was scared, but she knew for certain that Bill hadn't taken Kelly's money.

❖ ❖ ❖

The November after my mom died, all her kids and our spouses and children (nineteen in all) camped at Blue Springs (the one near the town of High Springs, in north central Florida). The weather was a prominent guest, too: First, it was too cold even to sleep; then, as we warmed, the sleepy bees woke up, stinging two of the kids; and then it began to rain and didn't stop. My brother Byron, the tie-dye artist, had brought us each a t-shirt. We wore them on the last day, as we walked down the winding wooden boardwalk along the creek that leads from the boil to the Santa Fe River, strung out in ones and twos, lollipops of color against the gray downpour and the dark green scrub brush. Dyes dripped down our shorts and legs. At the final lookout, we leaned against the rough railing and watched the rain flowing into the river's flow, all that water headed to the Gulf. Bob, my youngest brother, carried the can of her ashes, and we passed it along, down the railing. Silent, each of us poured a little of her remains into the wet air. Down went the brief spray of gray ash. Down went the surprising chunks. Down went the rain. Down went the river to the Gulf, where she loved to swim.

❖ ❖ ❖

Bill managed to cross the swamp on his belly and emerged onto a short dirt road called Bunny Trail. As is often the case in rural areas, Bill happened to know Little Jimmy, who lived in the last of three small houses on that road; Bill limped to his door and banged. Then he called Lynn and the Sheriff. When Lynn finally found him, Bill was covered in mud and blood, and his left ear was hanging forward, barely attached to his head. He was alternately calm and euphoric, so happy to be alive and—for the moment—safe. Their journey through the medical system, without health insurance or cash, began at the wholly inadequate Doctors Memorial Hospital in Bonifay. As it turned out, the only medical care Bill's ear received was administered by Lynn and their friend, the other Jimmi, who had some colloidal silver in his possession.

At the Holmes County Sheriff's Department, Kelly was charged with Aggravated Battery. Hicks was not charged, which may have been because several close relatives of his work for the Corrections Department. Kelly's bail was set at $15,000.

❖ ❖ ❖

"Aunt Molly, you gotta talk to Pa. He's real messed up and won't talk to me." Lately, my teenaged nephew Harvey and I had been talking on the telephone about his conflicts with his father, my brother Bill. But now I couldn't understand what he was saying through his agitation and the remains of what we call a cracker accent,

even though he repeated it to me. What had happened to my brother? What?

Bobby, our youngest brother, called me back from the parking lot outside a biker bar. He'd just finished packing keyboards and amps into his van after a gig and was weeping quietly about Bill being beaten so badly. He kept talking about the baseball bat, about what a good ball player Bill had been. I remembered showing up in Parma, Ohio, one summer in my twenties, surprising Bill at a bright green baseball field. In my mind I could see him again, leaning on the green fence in the late afternoon summer light, the kind that lingers so you don't believe the day will ever end. I watched him play in the National Slow Pitch Softball Tournament, drank a lot of beer, and yelled myself hoarse. His team, Nelson Painting, became national champs; Bill hit eleven home runs.

❖ ❖ ❖

Bill's initial calm-giddiness soon gave way to alternating panic and weeping, trouble making even simple decisions, and constant worry. The other thing you ought to know about Bill is that he had always occupied a confident, quiet, masculine space. He was overwhelmed by the assault and doubly troubled by his emotional reaction to it. He told me he couldn't let his kids see him like this. Then, when word got around that Kelly had hired someone to "finish the job," Bill realized that they couldn't stay home, couldn't run their shop, couldn't take care of the extensive plant nursery. Turns out, Kelly has two prior convictions for Aggravated Battery and one for Solicitation, having paid someone to hurt a third party. A longtime lawyer in the Florida panhandle told a friend of Bill's, "That Lowell Kelly is crazier than a cockroach on bug spray."

Bill told me not to come. It's not safe here. Lynn told me I'm the only one he can talk to. Bill told me *don't let Byron* (our middle brother) *come up here, with a gun. They have a bigger army than we do, and more weapons.*

❖ ❖ ❖

I floated on my back, eyes closed, half listening to the kids challenge each other and to my brothers' ancient taunts. I felt light raindrops on my eyelids, my lips. The water from the sky rolled off my face into the spring pool. When the sprinkling stopped, I opened my eyes. The light gray clouds bleached to white, then gray again, propelled across the distant blue. I wondered what I could say about my mother, later, when we gathered in a circle to honor her.

Except when there's a drought, rain interspersed with sunlight is common in Florida. So, it follows that rainbows are common. I have resisted being impressed by them. But, on this day, between the showers, looking up from floating in the spring, I saw something I'd never seen before. It was a rainbow, but it was upside down; it arced in a U shape, rather than the conventional two-ends-near-the-ground orientation. Immediately, I lifted my head and turned fully around, so I could look from a different angle, thinking I had seen it wrong. From any angle, the clear spectrum of colors presented itself in this strange shape. "Hey, Bob," I called to my nearest brother, "did you see that?" I pointed at the sky.

He rolled his head around and, seeing it, chuckled, "Now, that's a rainbow. That's a Mom rainbow."

Byron saw it and hollered, in his huge voice, "It's smiling!"

I looked up again, checking: Still there. I thought, this is our Cheshire Cat, our mother haunting us, looking goofy and unlikely.

❖ ❖ ❖

My brother and Lynn went into hiding. They've moved from place to place ever since, sometimes resting with friends, but always for a short time and always hovering near enough that Lynn could visit her ailing mother every couple of weeks. They stayed in places without heat or power in the coldest winter anyone can remember. Lynn developed a cough that hung on too long. Bill's bruises began to fade and his ear began to heal, but his moodiness and jumpiness stayed. Amid ongoing periods of confusion and abdominal pain, he hatched and abandoned a hundred plans—for the next safe stop, to sell enough of their belongings to buy food and gas. They never put anything in their names, which meant that they couldn't really live anywhere or get jobs. After they discovered that one of Kelly's prior convictions involved pipe bombs in the mailboxes of people he believed had stolen marijuana from him, they couldn't have anyone pick up their mail for them, either.

❖ ❖ ❖

Along St. Pete Beach runs a shifting sandbar. At low tide, you can often walk out to it through darker green, chest-high water and be back in shallow water with a visible white sand bottom. You can carry young children through the dark moat, and they can stand, almost on the beach again, but no longer on the water's edge. When our kids were little, we would haul the whole passel of cousins out there to explore. Once, my son Matt and I found the sandbar covered with a coat of sand dollars. He bent down in that chubby toddler, wide-stance way and picked one up. He held out the gray, fuzzy disk to me, squinting up into the bright day. I turned it over to see the tiny, moving, living parts, swishing it in the water again, to keep the animal moist. "Put out your hand like this," I showed him my outstretched palm. Then I put the sand dollar on his hand, and we waited for him to feel the tiny tickles.

A man in the water nearby called over, "Did you see all these sand dollars?" He held up a mesh bag full of them. We nodded. "Do you want some to take home, young man? I'll give you some."

Matt looked at the sand dollar, still on his hand, and said, "But this *is* their home."

❖ ❖ ❖

In January 2010, five months after the beating, everyone was finally deposed, following which the State's Attorney charged Hicks, the second guy, with Principal to Aggravated Battery. Kelly's charge was maintained. Because Bill and Lynn's depositions were credible, their risk level seemed to increase: their testimony could hurt both Kelly and Hicks. So, they focused their lives around each court date, thinking each time that there would be some resolution; instead, each one led only to another continuance, and they went back into hiding. No one could tell for sure how realistic Bill's fear was, but the consensus remained that Kelly's dangerousness followed from his being foolish, vengeful, and unpredictable, and because he had enormous resources.

❖ ❖ ❖

Prior to living in Florida, we had been knocked about, the way the rough ocean throws around shells and driftwood. Children in a little boat, with no one at the helm, we were subject to the bad things that happen to unprotected children. We shipwrecked onto the quiet shore of the Gulf of Mexico. We learned to swim and sit in the sun. We learned to eat fruit from the trees and fish from the water. Suited to the rhythms of the place, we became "natives."

❖ ❖ ❖

In April, when Bill and Lynn had been on the road for eight months, the *Deepwater Horizon* well exploded in the Gulf of Mexico. In response to what has been called the largest environmental disaster in United States history, local disaster relief efforts, alongside British Petroleum-supported clean-up operations, began in May. Small companies rushed in to train "hazwoppers" (hazardous waste operations workers, as distinguished from the "hazmat" people, who handle the actual material), offering motel housing, a generous per diem, and good pay. When he heard about the training course, Bill had just set up their table at a large flea market in central Florida. Like gypsies with their cart, he and Lynn had become itinerant merchants, traveling with small craft items, knickknacks, and photographs. A series of rainy weekends had made the setting-up effort almost worthless, but—as they pointed out—they didn't have anything better to do. On this sunny Sunday, they talked for only a few minutes about the training course before re-packing their little car and driving seven hours to Panama City Beach. They slept a few hours in the car and showed up early for the class at the Emerald Coast Church of God, both of them itching to be part of something good. Like everyone else who loves the Gulf, they worried about damage to the entire ecosystem. Bill reckons they looked terrific compared to most people who could be available on short notice to relocate and work full-time.

They both completed the course and started working, ten hours a day, seven days a week, on the beaches at Pensacola. Physically grueling because of the heat and the Tyvek suits, walking the beaches was only preparatory; no oil had arrived. Although that job didn't last long, Bill is used to physical labor and moved to other sites along the coast; he also completed online hazwopper supervisor training in the tired evenings.

❖ ❖ ❖

When I am away from the Gulf of Mexico, I refer to it as "my gulf": my home waters, my truest habitat. And I have always felt the waters there to be female, to be holding and accepting like a great Earth Mother, to be connected to the Divine Feminine. I always go in, even when a storm leaves darkness in the water and I will find grit in my bathingsuit later. Even when it's too cold and I have to wear a wetsuit. Even when no one else in sight is near the water. Sometimes a ritual submerging is enough, going down, as deep as the salt water lets me, coming up with wet seal skin. Sometimes, walking along these waters, any time of day or night, is when I remember who I am. Sometimes, though, I need to swim, swim far and strong through the streaming, swelling water.

Matt, now grown, and I visit Pass-a-Grille, where no oil has been sighted yet—to be in the water while we still can.

❖ ❖ ❖

Bill calls me from a boat heading into the Gulf from Panama City early in the morning. "You would love this. The sun on the water, the sweet salt air." I can hear the boat's engines, or maybe the wind.

"Is there any oil?" I ask, sitting up in bed.

"Not yet. We can't see underneath, where the actual oil is, just the sheen. But when we find it, we radio in coordinates, so they'll know where it probably is."

"And then what?"

"Other boats will go out with booming material and surround it. The hazmatters."

I checked the clock: 8. "Hey, do we need to get off the phone? I can call you tonight."

"No, it's good. I have a lot of minutes now. And this phone isn't traceable."

I lean back onto my pillow, free to picture him on the water. "So, how long will you be out on the boat?"

"All day. There are hundreds of these VOO boats, making money since they can't fish."

"Vroom boats, like power boats, you mean?"

"No, 'Vessel of Opportunity' boats. That's the fleet we have. But I don't work the boat at all."

"Oh, so you just get to be on the water…on a boat…in the Gulf."

"Now you see why I said you would love it."

❖ ❖ ❖

On September 2, 2010, another oil drilling platform burns in the Gulf of Mexico, following an explosion. The radio reports a mile-long sheen on the water. "No casualties" must mean that no humans working on the well died, because there will be unavoidable casualties in marine life.

Now, on September 3, the radio reports that neither an explosion nor a leak has occurred. Not only is this well in more shallow water and this mishap less serious than the *Deepwater Horizon* spill in April, we are told that pumping was stopped prior to the fire. That this leak compares favorably to the worst environmental disaster *ever* does not reassure me. That the second day's reports sound like obvious spin strengthens the doubts that already plague me. Government scientists and others recently reported that the massive oil that gushed for months from the *Deepwater* well is mostly gone. Gone? Even if it's in smaller bits and at greater depths and harder for us to see, it's still there. If it's consumed by oil-eating microbes, it's still there in the food chain. Dispersed doesn't mean rendered non-existent. Haven't we been paying attention all these years to the discourse about ecological systems and interdependent webs of life?

Now, on September 4, I read in the *Boston Globe* that 133 fires or explosions occurred on rigs in the Gulf of Mexico last year. My reactions teeter between personal grief about harm to the Gulf and angry mistrust of an anonymous system that allows this harm and then misinforms us about it.

I live a long way from my Florida Gulf Coast upbringing, and I miss my home waters. Now I need to go to the Gulf again, as I did after the big *Deepwater* spill. As I often do.

❖ ❖ ❖

Bill calls from the boat going into Appalachicola Bay at the end of the day. We talk about his place on Blue Creek, where the house and shop are surrounded by bamboo.

"Is there any chance you'll go back there?"

"No. That's done. We'll sell it soon as we can. We can't go back."

"Even after the trial?"

"We can't live in that town. I always want to leave as soon as we get there."

"Yeah, I know. But I'm sad about you leaving all the bamboo."

"Well, I dug up a bunch when we left, put them where people would appreciate them. When we find another place, we'll probably go back and get some more. But they're mostly set now, any-

way. Most bamboos are impossible to kill, once they're set. I just wish we could get some of them to grow where you are."

❖ ❖ ❖

Organisms that live in the intratidal zones, the areas between the high tide and low tide lines on the shore, have to be able to survive both flood conditions and periods of drought.

❖ ❖ ❖

In August 2010, almost a year after the assault, Bill was back working out of Panama City Beach, with a barge that accepted oily waste—except that hardly any came. He went out on a VOO boat, one of only four still operating at his venue, and sat on a tugboat next to the barge, waiting. His assignments had become unpredictable, and he expected every day to be told the job was over. Bill had heard talk about most of the oil being "gone," but didn't find it credible. Whenever oil was actually found, small boats with tanks surrounded it and sprayed dispersant. He figured all the remaining oil was below the surface and that the overuse of dispersants would damage everything the oil didn't. When the trial and the cleanup job ended, he and Lynn planned to head to other waters—or other lands—because he believed the waters of the Gulf, my gulf, wouldn't be producing anything good for a long time.

Despite the judge's announcement that there would be no more continuances, the August trial, scheduled to coincide with the one-year anniversary of the assault, was continued, yet again. Bill's job ended, but his hopes about protecting the Gulf had ended weeks earlier. He and Lynn went back on the road.

❖ ❖ ❖

In October—fourteen months after his assault—Bill and Lynn drove west along Highway 10, to meet me in New Orleans. I'd gone down, as I do every year, to help re-build homes damaged in the 2005 hurricanes. This year the economic recovery of New Orleans, another favorite Gulf area, had been set back further by the BP oil spill, but we didn't detect greater need among the already disenfranchised people with whom we work. For a couple of days, Bill and I worked together clapboarding the front of a house. Then he and Lynn left us at work and drove east to Tallahassee for pre-trial meetings and, we all hoped, the trial itself.

❖ ❖ ❖

Bill called me the next day while I painted kitchen cabinets. My hands were paint-spattered a deep rose color and my face was sweaty wet, as I fished my phone out of my back pocket and tried to hear him.

"I have to make the decision. The State's Attorney says it's my call." Had I walked into the middle of the conversation?

"Hang on; let me go outside." I set down my brush and weaved my way out of the house between people sanding the front porch, ducking between ladders and keeping my head down to keep the (probably lead paint) dust out of my face. I walked away from the house, wiped my cheek on my t-shirt, and pushed the bandana away from my ear. "Okay, what happened? Aren't you doing witness preparation today?"

"Kelly's lawyer offered a plea deal. Kelly would plead no contest and be adjudicated guilty. He'd be sentenced to two years of house arrest and eight years probation."

"Oh my God."

"Yeah. And I don't know what to do. I can't stand the thought of him not serving any time behind bars. Being stuck in one of his mansions is way too easy time for what he did to me. And we've been focused on the trial for so long. All our preparation . . . and writing . . . and thinking have been for this trial."

"When do you have to decide?"

"As soon as possible. The witnesses are all here. Maybe an hour?"

We spent most of that hour on the phone, while I walked around the Freret neighborhood. I saw enough houses in need of our services that I knew we wouldn't run out of rehabbing work any year soon.

❖ ❖ ❖

At Ft. DeSoto Beach, we wander along the shady pine-needled path, out onto hot sand. We walk between the dunes and the sea, then in the surf itself. We spot crabs skittering around in the shallows. In the hard sand above the tide line, we see hundreds of their holes, alongside collections of the tiny sand balls they throw out to make temporary homes, homes only till the next storm blows the surf across them or the next moon draws a higher tide.

Birds are all around—herons, egrets, sandpipers, gulls. I spot a small green heron I remember seeing here before. Lynn photographs the birds. She tells me about cranes, white geese, and swallow-tailed kites they've seen on their travels around Florida this year.

Bill loads buckets of shells into the rental car trunk, and we make our way, salty and sun-tired, across the first causeway. As we're stopped at the light before turning toward the Gulf beaches, Lynn points out ibises in a little pond by the side of the road. She raises her camera and shoots. On both sides are long pools of shallow water, overfull ditches surrounded by scrub foliage. Our light changes green, and, without warning, I U-turn.

"You didn't need to go and do that, Molly. I got a picture already." Lynn thinks I drive recklessly, but she doesn't live in Boston.

"No, no, I know." I can't say it right; I'm too excited. I pull off the road, pointing out my window, to the other end of the little pond, at the big pink birds with the funny bills. "Look! Are those roseate spoonbills?"

"You're right, you're right! Can we get closer?" Lynn has her camera poised.

I pull back onto the road, cross onto the other side, and drive up a dirt road that does not appear to be maintained for this purpose. Dense shrubs and scrub pines separate us from the strange, pink waders. We stop and search where we guess they are, but we can't find them again.

❖ ❖ ❖

In the end, Bill accepted the plea, because the verdict would be definite, rather than uncertain, as in a jury trial, and secure, meaning it wouldn't be subject to appeal. Without explanation, Kelly's sentence was changed to six and a half months house arrest and seven years probation. The agreement wasn't a relief for Bill and Lynn: The loss of their organizing principle left them feeling even more adrift. As they await the possibility of a civil suit, none of the things they had planned to do after the trial seem right anymore. And, in the two years that they have now been without a safe harbor, they've grown accustomed to being rudderless, with their few pleasures and their familiar frustrations. I wonder what will become of them now, on what shore they will land, and where they will put down roots.

❖ ❖ ❖

Looking Down

This year the town blooms brackish
and buildings crack with salt. I think
I'd sink in an estuary I could swallow
now I know that home
is where the lizards frill
for their diamond ladies
and that trees can shed their snakes
when they get full. But won't an ordinary hull
get thin and rusty? Won't the sunlight bend
our backs and slit our eyes? We all live, I guess,
with our decisions. I came to the city
like a clamshell tired of closing.
I looked for you like a mangrove
claws below the tide.

Mark Smith

The Green Helmet

A runner jogs past the bottle bush
across the way, red blossoms
toned down by all this fog today,
sneakers slapping on the concrete
like stropped leather. Bare-chested
in chilly weather he wears
backwards on his curly Irish head
a fireman's helmet that even
in the grayness of this scene
is clearly green. Surely no green
not itself upon a mint or parrot
has any need or right to be
that green. Especially on
a fireman's helmet flaunted
as the logo of a loutish jogger
feet reversed and running backward.

Man of Feeling

This morning my heart goes out to pines
punctured and slung with hammocks
in leisure's name, to the redbird
with bandit mask, accused of every crime.
I feel bonded all at once to dogs
on chains, reciting prison
diaries as I pass; suddenly I open
to the possum, ugly as the trash it picks.
Soon I will return to selfish queries:
What trophies have I stowed in cabinets?
How many rivers forked at my birth?
But today I want to harry vapid
questions—as smaller, quicker birds
do hawks and crows—to be overcome
by clotheslines pinned with cast-off
selves, my mouth blowing ovals of awe.
For years I could not care less
that the turtle and armadillo carry
caskets on their backs the span
of their lives, that the spider quilts
in a solitude so consuming it devours
what guests drop by. Yet warmth has found
an entrance, or picked some shackle inside,
and I even feel for kudzu, choking all.
Earlier this summer, without a qualm,
I bagged and dragged to the curb
a goose found floating in the boat slip,
made crude by some Evinrude or Merc.
But now as the sun bobs up, I might be
an earl in the Age of Reason, so completely
have I fallen under sympathy's sway.
I hum in chorus with the mournful woodwinds
of rotted elms. And face with desperate
affection the stucco homes—guarded,
blank—like the man I was just yesterday,
who welcomes, least of any, my embrace.

45th High School Reunion

It doesn't matter who's gearing up to run
for office in Maine or who has three grandkids
and just retired from being a dentist a lawyer
a hospital bookkeeper or if Maureen still drinks;
what matters

is that Tippy McHenry's father, sitting alone
in the St. Claire Nursing Home day room
after lunch, has a clean blanket over his knees,
his mind's one window letting a draft in now,
and that the early November light

still makes it through the torn shade
to lay its frail and dutiful beam across
the ugly linoleum. It matters that Tippy made sure
the family Steinway went with him,
and that she's asked his favorite nurse

to let him stay there after the trays are cleared;
and that his hands, although these days
they shake a bit like stippled leaves whose time
has almost come, still know more or less
what to do.

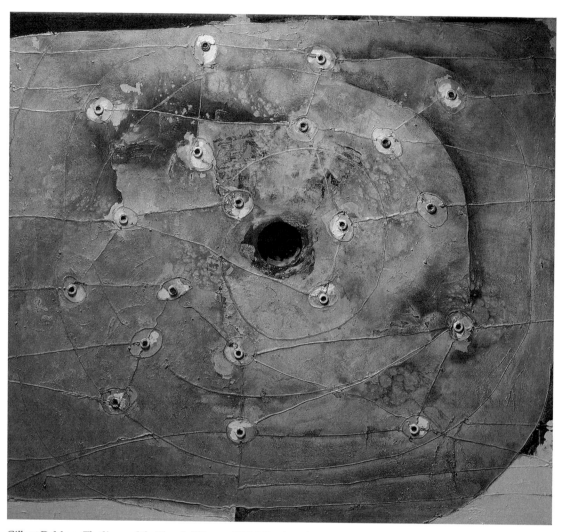

Gilbert DeMeza. *The Siren and the Wounded Sleeper*. 2013. Mixed media. 66 x 72 inches. Collection of Rebecca Skelton. Photo by J. M Lennon.

Exploring the Land of Cook

"Turn a rock," Temuti says, getting off the boat.

There are seven of us, but she's talking only to me.

"Turn a rock?"

English is not her first language so I assume I'm missing something. She bends over to show me that I should flip over a piece of coral rock. I flip a bleached-white slab of coral as the ocean laps baby waves over my bare feet.

"When you go on to new land you turn a rock for good luck," she explains. "It is to tell it that you are coming."

We are on Cook Islet, a slip of land that guards the horseshoe-shaped Christmas Island. I have been on this island and its collection of islets for two weeks now, renting a shack behind a church from a grumpy old priest. Temuti is the church cook, and she brings out tea each morning to chat. Yesterday she told me about the man she married when she was seventeen. He'd taken a knife to her more than once—fairly often from the scars running up and down her arms and legs. "But I loved him," she said. "My father and brothers told me they would kill him. They told me I should leave him. But I told them no." Then one day he went out fishing and never came back. His outrigger washed back on shore with marks from a shark attack. "I loved him then," she told me, "but that was the best thing that ever happened to me. The best thing. He might have killed me."

The trip to Cook was my idea, originally conceived as a solo trip to see some birds, but Temuti caught wind and changed the plan. Why go alone when you can bring a picnic? And family?

Cook Islet covers the mouth of Christmas as a separated chunk of the once circular coral atoll, so the boatride takes less than five minutes. Stepping inland, Temuti grabs the bags of food and heads with her cousin and cousin's daughter in the opposite direction from Bio, our guide, and Tiio, Temuti's nephew. Something I couldn't understand is said in I-Kiribati, the local Micronesian language.

"Are you not coming to see the birds?" I ask.

"No, it's too hot. We are going to the maneaba."

They had all been excited to come, but will now do what they might have done at home, head to the nearest maneaba—a thatched-roof, open-air hut—to sleep, talk, and eat. The heat is nearly unbearable out here though, and the air is still and humid, so I can hardly blame them.

The atoll Cook is part of is known to some for its fly-fishing and to others as the largest coral atoll in the world. Polynesians lived here on and off for centuries, but in the eighteenth century it was uninhabited when a Frenchman brought hundreds of Micronesians from two thousand miles away to plant half-a-million palm trees and harvest them for their meat. The five thousand people who live here now are their descendents, and the reason this atoll is part of the thirty-three-island Republic of Kiribati the British allowed independence in 1979. What it might be best known for though is the British and the U.S. nuclear testing that was done near and over civilian populations in the '50s and '60s.

But the atoll's recent history actually started here, on this tiny islet. The first noted visitor was Captain Cook, who landed on Cook Islet on Christmas Eve 1777. He named the islet after himself, and the entire atoll after the day he landed.

His visit was a short one, but he reported collecting three thousand pounds of turtle meat—a brutal irony considering the fact that this islet, his namesake, is now a bird and turtle reserve. In fact, the only animal besides sea turtle, bird, and crab allowed here now is the permit-paid human, and only with a guide from the Nature Conservation Unit. In this case, an enormous and amicable man named Bio.

"Tiio will go with you and Bio," Temuti says, walking away.

"Come," Bio says. He leads us over the coral rock berm and we can see that the small islet is blanketed in vine-like coastal scrub—greens and yellows pulled thin across sandy soil. It is more desolate of flora than I'd have thought, with trees and bushes only crowning the ocean fringe. Its highest point is perhaps two meters, and the land is largely covered in yellow ilima, stretching miniature hibiscus flowers and brown vine over the sandy soil.

A few hundred birds fly above, but as we step over the berm, masses of sooty terns rise up with a roar. There are suddenly thousands of them. I follow Bio into the ilima patches, and terns begin swooping at the backs of our heads. I can hardly blame them. Thousands, perhaps tens of thousands of eggs lie exposed on the ground between the ilima. We step carefully ahead, but it's not easy. There are birds and eggs scattered everywhere, and at least three times as many birds screaming above. It's like holding a baby while a mother shouts at you to be careful. The sound is deafening. It is the sound of a violent gale smothered by ten thousand angry squawks. It's impossible to talk to the person two feet from you without yelling, and Bio has just told me that he's had birds fly into his head. With so many birds, flying so closely, it's easy to see how they can veer to avoid each other and hit you.

According to the materials from the Nature Conservation Unit, there are an estimated six million sooty terns on Christmas Island. It is the largest sooty population in the world. And these oversized black and white terns are not the only inhabitants. This atoll is considered one of the most important breeding grounds in the Pacific. Hundreds of millions of birds pass through here each year.

Thousands of them now rise to our coming, bombing toward us until it's the next group's turn. I'm afraid that if we stop, the parents will see us as more of a threat and get more daring in their swipes at our heads. I'm ducking and dodging as I walk, afraid to pause, wondering if we should even be here.

Bio walks slowly, calmly. I watch a bird fly directly at his head and stop quickly, spreading wings as its feet fold the brim of his hat.

"Whoa," I say, flinching for him.

Bio hasn't even twitched. He looks at me, raising an eyebrow with a grin. He's laughing at me.

I look at Tiio, dodging with me, and we laugh at each other.

We pause to look at some sooty chicks. Though the name doesn't fit the stark black and white

adults, the chicks are soft and fuzzy gray, speckled light in black and white. We watch four stumble and waddle over a patch of creeping spiderling to the shade of a stunted beach heliotrope tree. Tiio looks over at me, and we share a childish smile. I'm still smiling when a sooty tern swipes at me, her wing grazing my ear as she pulls away. An image of a beak plunging into my skull passes through my head. I wince and let out a gasp.

"Whoa," Tiio says, laughing. "That was close."

I laugh too but am soon moving faster, ducking more, but beginning to relax enough to look around.

Alongside the sooties are fairy terns—curious, dove-like birds, angelic white with silent black eyes, who stand out as a deep breath on a crying island. And there is the Christmas Island warbler, a forgettably small, bland, gray-colored songbird—endemic to these islands and in danger of extinction, just like the green turtle Cook hunted so many years ago. Above all of these birds looms the majestic frigate, the Kiribati national bird, soaring above with a seven-foot wingspan that casts an intimidating shadow.

A hundred years ago, the whole atoll looked more like this small islet. It was a birds' paradise with nothing but crabs, scrub brush, and the occasional stay by passing Polynesians. Being the largest atoll in the world, sitting in the dead middle of the Pacific, it is a haven for migrating birds and traveling sailors. But the coconut plantations brought thousands of workers, hundreds of thousands of palms, and plantlife like breadfruit, taro, and pandanus. And they also brought rats, cats, and pigs who love to eat all of these exposed eggs.

This drastic shift created devastating problems for these birds. Most breed no more than once a year, one egg at a time, taking months or years to get a chick to its wings. Many of these birds are all the world has of the species, and eleven of the eighteen nesting species on Christmas are now limited to ocean-locked bits of lagoon flats and islets like the one I'm on today.

To stop the imported animals from killing too many birds, the government offers spading and neutering services and allows only male dogs on the atoll. The Nature Conservation Unit actively hunts feral cats.

You can imagine the outrage by some if this were to happen in the U.S. They hunt kittens?

And it is a controversy here, but not for the same reason. In 1999 a new species of rat, the ship rat, was accidentally introduced to the atoll. This rat, unlike the also-introduced Polynesian rat, climbs coconut trees, burrowing in to eat the coconut meat. Feral cats hunt these rats. So while some birdwatchers bring foreign cash, and conservation groups bring some investment, it cannot compete with the copra trade. And with so many wonderfully edible eggs around, it's hard to justify global-minded conservation policies to a people who live almost entirely off the land.

Bio's job, then, is to make sure we don't poach birds or eggs.

At six-feet-three and about two hundred and forty pounds, he would be an intimidating figure if he didn't walk with a soft bounce like a Tigger of men. He tells me that two years ago he was transferred from Tarawa, Kiribati's capital island two thousand miles to the west.

"Did you ask for the transfer?" I ask. We are at the crest of the first bay. The sea is a calm set of cerulean caps, the sky above soft blue in the hot haze.

"No, but I prefer it anyway. There are less people here."

"It is very crowded on Tarawa," Tiio agrees. Tiio and his wife moved here less than a year ago by choice. They are living with Temuti in her one-room home until they can build their own.

"It is easy to get food here," Bio adds. "You just step outside." Birds fly between us screaming. "This is much nicer than Tarawa."

Kiribati is one of the few countries left where most people are subsistence farmers. Less than ten percent of people work regularly within the cash economy here, but a shift is in the making. Western banks and nonprofits bring aid for food and medicine, and foreign media brings a promise of wealth. This money means that people no longer have to rely on infanticide and abortion, and they starve far less often, but the population has also boomed, making demands that the ecosystem cannot fill. This means they need more money than there are opportunities, and more debt than the economy can handle, so Kiribati is increasingly reliant on aid and imports, and the ecosystem is stretched to the point that there are major health concerns. Animal and human feces corrupt the water table, well water is overused and becomes saline, and the fishing waters are overfished and polluted.

"There is no need for money here," Tiio told me as we pulled coconuts a few days ago. "You have all you need around you."

It sounds like a dream, were it not on its way toward implosion.

Bio, Tiio, and I head away from the sooty terns to the less defensive boobies, noddies, shearwaters, and petrels. We are on the thinnest piece of the islet, at the crest of the second of two oceanside bays. The ocean shimmers clear, the sun picking up the bright reds and greens of the coral bottom. Natural coral channels run from the island—deep-cut chasms where fish hide in the irregularities of the coral walls. Bio points out a green turtle rolling at the ocean's surface fifty yards out. I can see nothing but the swirl and splash of the water.

"How often do you come out here?" I ask Bio.

"A few times a week."

"Do you come alone or with people?"

"Mostly we just come out to make sure there are no people or dead birds or anything."

"So do you count the birds or eggs?"

He gives a confused look.

"So that you know if there's a change?"

"No, we don't do anything like that."

Without any scientific data to track these birds, there seems no way to recognize a problem until it is so desperate that it becomes obvious to the casual observer.

Of course, Kiribati has other problems, ones that might turn a skeptic to say that Bio's job here is as much political posturing as practical solution. At an average altitude of two meters above sea level, Kiribati is in danger of an extinction of its own. The oceans are rising and expected to make most of Kiribati's islands uninhabitable in as little as forty years. They have already lost one island, in fact. So this small country's government carries the necessary burden of leading the charge to push larger nations to control greenhouse gases. It is the strongest of all environmental motivations, the one most often neglected because of a lack of foresight: the motivation of self-preservation.

The very existence of Cook Islet and the Nature Conservancy Unit seem like a way to say: "See? We're poor, and we still care for our environment. You're rich. Why don't you? Don't you realize you're slowly killing us?"

Bio's face begins wincing with each step. He stops to pull spurs from his feet. We've walked into a patch of scrub whose thorn-protected seeds dug into my bare feet a few times on Christmas.

"I forgot my shoes," he tells us after toughing it out for a while. Shoes are new to this society, a sign of wealth that is seen as unnecessary, though shoes seem plenty necessary in Bio's profession. "I'm going to walk back on the sand," he says, making his way to the beach.

Tiio and I continue down the vegetated areas where the birds are. There are fewer above us now, and it means we can look down more comfortably.

Tiio and I act more like two kids finding treasures than men from different cultures. "Look at that tail," I point, pulling at Tiio's shirtsleeve. A red-tailed tropic bird sits on its egg under a suriana bush. It is white and fat with brown flakes of color on the tips of its wings and a striking tail with two red reeds sticking out twice as long as its body.

"Wow, look at those," Tiio says, pulling me along. Crawling along a low tree branch are two enormous hermit crabs. Each carries a studded shell the size of a large man's fist. It reminds me of a terribly simple children's book I loved as a kid, a story with a typical Scrooge ending where the orphan gets the hermit's unneeded treasures. With money, we'd learned, this child's life becomes forever better.

We make our way to the maneaba where Temuti has set up a lunch of fish, rice, and pandanus-milk porridge. I lean against a support pole and stretch my back. My feet and hands dig into the soft, cool sand. It feels wonderful.

Everyone else seems to have already eaten but Bio, Tiio, and me. Temuti takes the lids off the containers, then serves our plates—fish, rice, and pandanus fruit. The flies come with the food, as I've learned they always do on this atoll. I eat with one hand, the other swinging to protect both my fish and the dishes. Tiio and Bio make an occasional swat at a fly, but they don't seem as squeamish as I am.

We talk a bit about the Nature Conservation Unit. I tell Bio how jealous I am of his job. "You get to explore your island for a living," I say. "Sounds like a great job."

He shrugs, "It's a good job." He does not seem excited; content, perhaps. What is an environmental agency job when most of your food can be found steps from your door? It must all seem somewhat silly.

After our meal we relax, leaning against the support poles of the maneaba. I fall asleep.

When I wake up, a hermit crab is crawling across the sand. It has no shell.

I've never seen a hermit crab without its shell. It has girth at its plated head and claws, but is naked behind—a soft, thin, wet finger out its back. It looks feeble, helpless.

The hermit crab struggles along without the weight, its sticky end collecting sand. I look around to see if the others are watching. The boat driver is still asleep, and Tiio and Bio are leaning against a support pole sharing a tobacco cigarette rolled in dried pandanus leaf. Temuti and her friend are asleep too, but her daughter is sitting near me. The daughter picks up the crab and rubs the sticky end in the sand, then puts it down four feet behind where it had been.

"Did you pull it from its shell?" I ask her. I know nothing about how hermit crabs move from one shell to the next, only that they do when they become too big for their current home.

She is too shy to speak English and pretends she doesn't hear. Bio answers for her.

"Yes," he says, without changing his affable smile. He takes a light drag and passes the cigarette to Tiio.

I look at the path in front of the crab—fifteen yards to the end of the hut, then fifty more through thousands of watching, hungry birds before an ocean where I'd earlier seen two white-tipped reef sharks chasing fish. My eyes search for the shell, but I don't see it.

I reach over and grab the hermit crab before the girl can pull it back again. She looks at me as if I'm about to start a game with her. I'm holding it and don't know what to do. His shell is gone, probably left wherever she picked him up—somewhere down the beach, perhaps. I don't know what to do. I don't want to insult my new friends, or look silly. I don't want them to think I'm being rude.

"We use those for fishing bait," Bio, the representative for Wildlife Conservation tells me.

"You can eat them too," Tiio says, taking it from me.

Please, I think, do either of those, or give it a shell.

I don't know why I'm so frantic. I fish—for food and for fun. More often than not, I release those fish with a hole in their mouth and my fingerprints on their scales. I'm careful, but I don't doubt some have struggled or even died because of me. But I'm on a nature preserve, where nature is supposed to be protected. I wonder if I'd be this distressed if we were in someone's backyard, on their property.

Tiio puts the hermit on the ground behind him. It begins crawling toward the sea, a shorter distance in the direction he's faced it, ten yards to a narrow beach of rocks. As it limps away I wonder if Tiio faced it that way on purpose, to shorten its struggle.

A conversation starts up again and I force my eyes away from the hermit. I have trouble listening. I can't get him out of my mind. I wonder if he will find a new home, if he will find something to grow into, or, perhaps, if he will simply not make it through the day.

❖ ❖ ❖

Benjamin S. Grossberg

The Space Traveler Pities Us

Roy G. Biv is a friend, but only
one of many. Sound too in ranges
that jerk your dogs' heads sharply around,
a hard calligraphy on air to spring
the radar dishes of their ears. Listen
in whatever range you can, human—
it's not that you know dust only
in handfuls, but that the tools
by which you know it make it
only dust. Out here are creatures
who see in it the handiwork of God:
not in the cheesy metaphorical manner
of your evangelicals, but with beautiful
literalness: the fine-handling fingerprints
of the first cause smudging the glass
of each grain. So I don't blame you
if hearing silence where is music
beyond your range you nominate
nothing, or if you end after violet
the spectrum of visible light. But
even on your world, the least of you
discharges colors he can't see, his body
dispelling silence in nearly all registers.
Imagine yourselves as I see you—
even the reduced form looking back
from a bathroom mirror, woken
too early, when outside's a snowy
morning he has shortly to enter.
It is an odd irony—a ready excuse for
all your cynicism, even the chewed
aluminum of your politicians—that
you of all creatures are denied sense
of your own radiance.

Editor's Note: "Roy G. Biv" is an acronym for the seven conventional colors of the rainbow: red, orange, yellow, blue, green, and violet. The human eye perceives wavelengths of light in a manner that sorts a continuous spectrum into these limited color bands.

Benjamin S. Grossberg

The Space Traveler's Calculus

You? Your fate was sealed the moment
you set a ring of stones around a fire:
in some Neanderthal night, the collective
tremor of northern species, and global
air circulation pausing a moment
to apprehend change. I'd like to think
the stars, too, clarified in translucent
darkness, that for a moment all
burned blue, looked down
in an earnest convocation.
What to say, human? That generally
by the time a trajectory becomes clear,
it's essentially completed? That causes
swim in conclusions? Now you know.
Now I know, too. And though
from up here I'm unable to help you,
I will say—pondering your world—
no destination seems so important, no
work trumps my attention like your
gloved hands, tenderness conducted
through latex and scrub brush toward
all those small lives you have ruined.
Perhaps a few decades from now
an interstellar cavalry will arrive—
do-gooder species watching your
accelerating bleed, moved, will pull
you back from the ledge by the x
of your crossed suspenders, will deposit
you and such Earthly life as remains
on a pristine world. Imagine
the pods launching out like bees
from a flaming hive, the furious drones
cooling with distance, and then
the landing—chrome studs among
long grasses, a field wide as Kansas.
Fanciful? Had I been there, human,
I'd have poked the Neanderthal
on the shoulder, tapped my snappish
foot until he handed me that first rock.
Then I'd have clocked him with it.

Benjamin S. Grossberg

The Space Traveler's Missives

So many missives. And each an attempt
to say and not say, as if direct
statement had undone itself—
a candle melted flat into the table.
Do they reach you? Do you stroll
out to your mailbox to find the red
flag lowered, envelop hanging out
like a crab's fighting claw?
The stamp is from no Earthly polity.
You soak it off in water; take out
a magnifying glass to study
the alien flower, its stigma an eye
that winks at you. Do you read
the script? On warm nights, you ride
your V-max under the stars. I fly
my ship over eastern Ohio; make
a semaphore of the fins; toot
the engine fires in Morse Code.
Others take out cell phones, post
videos on the Internet. But the text
was for you: who keep your vision
level, your legs spread as wide
as if you were mounting a horse.
You know, when you ride
you look like the Marlboro Man:
it's the set of your jaw, the cool
hardness, as if your skin was a metal
just lifted from snow. You remove
your helmet; sparse blonde hairs
explode upward. I suddenly become
shy and zoom off behind the tree line.
Did you see me? Sometimes I think
you keep your understanding
to a studied minimum, limit the size
of its cage and what you feed it,
knowing how—if it got too large—
it might take over the house. Start
demanding walks. Want your bed.
You'd have to reckon with it then.
You'd have to follow it through to
troubling conclusions. Other times
I sit balanced on my ship's nose cone

like a spinning plate and pluck
flower petals, letting each float off
into space. Imagine them settling on
the surface of your world's atmosphere—
drifting down to the vitreous blue
of a mountain lake. He loves me?
I think not. If they fell far enough,
every petal would burn.

Benjamin S. Grossberg

The Space Traveler Falls in Love

Over dinner. This time it happened
between soup and entrée, when
the waitress came back
to ask if he wanted more
oyster crackers. I told a joke
and he insisted on guessing
the punch line for a full five minutes.
I watched his mouth spit out
possible puns, as if he was
in the blowing-bubbles phase
of learning to swim. He got
close. I went back to the salad bar
to clear my head. Scooped up
too many chick peas and grew
afraid he'd comment.
People behind me were waiting.
Dare I put a few back? Over coffee
he asked for details about
this space traveler's life. I assembled
a rocket ship out of asparagus
using his leftover mashed potatoes
to mount them upright. There's
no point falling in love with humans.
Sometimes (in movies) one of you,
the displaced one—the one we
feel sorry for—the teenager
whose terrible foster parents get
eaten—that one will end up
boarding, will take the hand of some
bipedal outline in light. Truth's
shabbier. Old Toyota, radio playing—
he and I pull up to my rocket ship,
hidden in a stand of pines. I promise
vistas, possibility, a willingness
to continue the conversation even if
it takes all night. Your species
has perfected the shrug. Then
maybe, I say, dinner next week?
But I'll be a million miles away
by then. Probably.
If not, I'll plan my day around it.

Ripe

The apricot needs to be sucked off;
ruddy half-moons wet the tablecloth,
shudder to sugar.

A black ant—astronaut on a third-story window—
peers into a dining room and understands:
Hunger brought me here, ripeness brings me home.

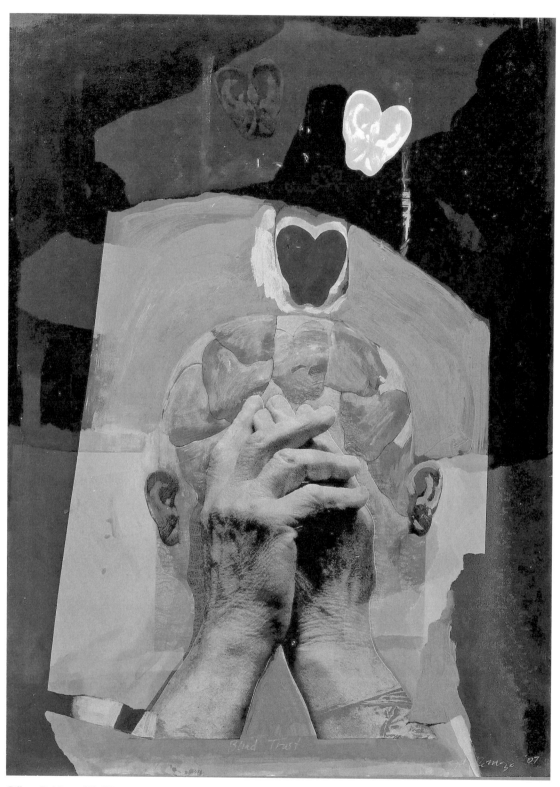

Gilbert DeMeza. *Blind Trust*. 2007. Silk screen monotype. 30 x 22 inches. Photo by J. M. Lennon.

Ph.D.

In reality they all lived in a kind of hieroglyphic world, where the real thing was never said or done or even thought, but only represented by a set of arbitrary signs.

-Edith Wharton, *The Age of Innocence*

Research

Thinking I might run into you at the library today, I stopped by your carrel. Empty except for a few, slim volumes. Don't you have a dissertation to finish? I thought of your fantasy: the cool cement walls, the occasional click of heels in the stacks. If you had come by, I would have lifted my skirt.

But you didn't come by, and I walked downtown feeling exposed. The weather was good, so I thought I might see you strolling in your t-shirt and shorts. I wandered through the farmers' market, bought five Brandy Wine tomatoes from that Amish beauty. She wore our favorite blue dress, surprisingly flattering for its prairie shape. Her blonde curls poked beneath the edges of her cap. *One hot bonnet*, you said when we spotted her last summer. I laughed: our little Amish joke.

Today in the crowd of people trawling for local produce, I saw a man who looked like you from a distance. He called to a woman buying peaches, very pregnant, carrying a basket of carrots, collards, and sunflowers. It's the kind of scene you would have made fun of—*self-satisfied, future baby-sling-wearing, hybrid-driving liberals*. And yet in teasing you would have revealed both how much you actually wanted that life and how you were not entirely sure you wanted it with me.

Knowing I shouldn't, I left the tomatoes on your porch swing. Your car was not in the driveway, and I walked home in a fluster, berating myself for being silly enough to want to buy you locally grown produce.

I returned hours later, concerned that an unmarked bag of tomatoes might look suspicious— or worse, like trash. The idea was to take them home with me, turn them into something useful, like a sane, summery salad with basil and mozzarella. The bag of tomatoes had disappeared. I saw a light in your office window, which got my hopes up, but it was only the glow from your screensaver. I looked for shadows. I listened for voices coming through an open window. I felt ill as I watched from behind a tree.

But I did not move until a dog-walker stopped nearby, then squatted to retrieve her poodle's tiny shit. A demeaning task, we agreed once, when we considered rescuing a greyhound together. And how embarrassing for the dog—no privacy! This woman did not even look away, but congratulated her pooch on its instinctive behavior. I'm quite glad we decided not to adopt. Who would walk the dog now? Who would feed it?

Standing in front of your apartment, I half-expected to see you traipsing home with Miriam. Before you moved out last month, you said you were ambivalent about her advances. She makes you crazy because she believes in the superiority of archaeology—(tangible objects!)—over your great passion, Medieval French poetry (so subjective and, frankly, a little too obsessed with martyrs and saints). Here is what I imagine: she has been calling you in the middle of the night from the Ancient Roman wing of the museum. Right now, she's probably giving you a private and illuminating tour of Etruscan vases. Miriam could be beautiful, but she refuses to moisturize and has poor fashion sense: saggy overalls and threadbare t-shirts. A person would never be able to make her see the benefits of a flattering wrap dress. Rumors in the Comp Lit and English crowd suggest that you have admitted she looks good naked, in spite of all the body hair.

I find Miriam's lack of vanity almost grotesque. But if I had met her separately from you, I imagine I might have liked her.

Preliminary Exams

I read for days without stopping to eat. *Faulk-nerEliotHardyJamesConradBrontesEliotWoolfAus-tenDickens*. We hadn't been dating long, and you stopped by my apartment when I didn't return your calls. You took one look at my graying skin and went right out the door for takeout, return-ing with chicken shwarma and lots of napkins, because you knew I would make a ravenous mess. You placed my foil-wrapped sandwich in my open palm, very gently.

"This will put the color back in your cheeks," you said. Lifting a sliver of meat from the sand-wich, you fed it to me as delicately as a mother bird.

Then you cast an eye over the storm of pa-pers and open texts on the living room floor. "Remember," you said, "you're not inventing the atomic bomb here." You turned on the TV and we watched hours of home improvement programming.

When I was down to a few hours before the exam, I resorted to Sparknotes. I'm embarrassed to admit it, but in my defense, it was all to fill in gaps in plot. I knew all there was to know about the characters and their motivations.

Title Page: Untitled

(OR Each Time You Happen to Me All Over Again)

Chapters 1-2: Obsession, the Better Self, and the Seven-Year Itch

To get your PhD in the humanities, you need an obsessive nature. One might even say the process of writing a dissertation requires the sensibility of a stalker. Why else would we all be working for so long on one topic when the chance of us getting tenure-track appointments is about as likely as getting discovered by a Hollywood scout in the food court at the mall?

A long time ago, I wanted to be an expert. In the third grade I had an accomplished imagi-nary friend called Marietta Divina. She sang opera all over the world, wrote bestselling nov-els, and dreamed of being awarded the Nobel Peace Prize before she turned twenty. In January of that year, just as my parents were divorcing, Marietta announced her intention to go back to school to get her PhD in anthropology. I never

saw her again but received letters from her in which she detailed her research in an undiscov-ered Amazon village. She'd fallen in love with the chief, would soon become a princess, and was being hailed by the villagers for her crystal-line voice and for her facility with their complex language, which contained over one hundred words for the verb "to do."

I decided to be *that* kind of doctor.

Nineteen years later when I started grad school, I thought I would enjoy stalking Edith Wharton around the globe. She reminded me of Marietta: born into privilege, financially in-dependent enough to write and travel. I feel a kinship with her that I've never felt with an-other modern writer. Her characters are com-plicated—worldly yet confused, calculating but unhappy, well-intentioned but often ruined. Recently discovered letters to Wharton's child-hood German governess profess effusive grate-fulness and loyalty. But in her autobiography the governess is barely a footnote.

At the beginning of the summer, when things were already going badly between us, I made the trip alone to The Mount to see the beauti-ful grounds. It made me very sad to see the run-down state of things and not be able to complain about it to anyone but the docents.

One of my advisors calls Edith the Jackie Collins of early twentieth century American lit-erature. He does not mean this in a good way, of course, but I'm interested in the idea of a self re-made for another time. Probably because I have to admit that watching for you, while good for an initial adrenaline rush, has become tiresome and isolating. I've started having dreams about trysts with Henry James and Graham Greene. I picture myself driving around old Havana in a '54 Chevy with Hemingway.

In one persistent fantasy, I'm snowed in at a New England bed and breakfast, and who serves me my eggs benedict but John Fucking Updike. He allows me just one bite before he pulls me from my captain's chair, leads me through the swinging door to the kitchen—all the guests at the dining table stare in shock—and screws me in the pantry, where I manage to pull down an entire shelf of beautifully canned peaches. As I pull up my stockings afterwards, John smoothes his red-striped apron. I suggest another round, but he's already putting together a tray of tea and biscuits for the couple in the Maple room;

they have requested room service. "The roads should be plowed by now," he says. "You'll be able to make check-out time."

Chapters 3-4: When Nothing Adds Up, or When Everything Does

I admit that I checked the garbage cans and the compost in back of your apartment. I can see how bringing a flashlight for the task might look like premeditation, the work of a mind unhinged. I saw tomatoes on the top the heap, but they looked too old to be the fresh heirlooms I had bought for you. As I caught myself reaching into the compost barrel, fingertips almost touching wrinkled, organic matter covered in coffee grounds, I drew back in horror at what I'd become. I resolved to engage in healthier leisure activities.

I trudged home and lay on my living room floor. Even when it gets hot outside, the hardwood remains cool. The last time I saw you—just last week, isn't that a kick!—we spent some time there. You lifted my dress with one hand as your other hand pushed my shoulder into the floorboards. It was a sharp, not unpleasant feeling. You had been so distant since our breakup, but here you were; my discomfort proved it. The front door was open, the screen door latched, and I heard the mailman's familiar shuffle on the porch, just before you finished.

And then you left so abruptly, mumbling about *being out of touch.*

You could have been more specific; that would have been useful.

And I could have been more direct: Tell me what the hell is going on: *Will you be out of touch while fucking Miriam? Does she honestly look good naked?*

And yet, I nodded you away without a *why?* or a *what?* It's been a genuinely difficult year for you. Your father has been ill, and you've considered taking off some time to be with him in Maine. Your advisor is having a fit, concerned you'll become a doctoral casualty, just another ABD. But he shouldn't worry; you're dedicated to completing (almost) everything you start.

You might even be back with your family now, too busy to remember me. And if you are home, you might see Carla, the high school sweetheart who haunts your dreams, wearing the sundress she had on the night you broke up with her. She recently found you on a popular social networking site that we all visit more than the library. Because she refuses to post a picture of herself, I still have no idea what she looks like. I have imagined the Buttercup-beauty you remember from childhood, but I suspect she has aged terribly—as women who never leave their hometowns tend to do—and this will grieve you. You could be at the pharmacy on old Main Street, picking up a prescription for your father, and she appears right in front of you, pushing a baby in a stroller, pulling a squirmy toddler by the wrist. *Unrecognizable,* you will say later about her puffy face. And yet you want to lean her against the shelves of band-aids. You would do it, too, except her husband shows up, a guy you used to drink with in high school.

Determined not to wallow in self-pity all night, I headed to the refrigerator for ingredients. I moved all the eggplants to the counter, where I sliced them with vicious precision. Roasted eggplant is not your favorite dish. I make it when I'm alone. Searching through the refrigerator for feta, I had to move aside almost-empty bottles of ketchup, hot sauce, and mustard. For some reason, each half-consumed condiment reminded me of you. Remember when you suggested I give up academia and write a cookbook? I should have been pissed, but you complimented my pork pozole, smoothed my hair back, and kissed my neck. You made me a midnight espresso, dark and creamy. Afterward, we watched late-night television until it was early. You always know how to ploy me: with sex, caffeine, and a live studio audience.

Remember how just before we started dating, you hooked up with Rebecca, the raven-haired Norwegian-Uruguayan Comp Lit student who dropped out to live with a Microsoft exec? You thought you were destined to marry her because she has the same last name, only spelled differently. Also, she looked a little like Carrie Fisher in her Princess Leia years. But she ran away, you mourned, and I got drunk at Zander's Halloween party. That was the first year, and apparently I didn't get the sexy memo; I came dressed as the Cowardly Lion. I had spent hours papier mâché-ing the head and painting it. But I took inaccurate measurements and the too-small mask made my face sweat. I had pinned the tail of yarn to my savannah-colored corduroys from the Salvation Army. You tugged on it to get my attention, and when you pulled the mask from my head, I could see my face reflected in your dark eyes: shiny with sweat and dizziness.

You debuted *The Naked Chef* that year. And now a Halloween party isn't complete unless you show up shirtless, in your apron and boxers. The irony is that you're a terrible cook. I never could say it to your face before, but it feels like the right time to tell you how much I always hated your overstuffed breakfast burritos.

Back then you had me fooled with the banana crepes you were passing out on compostable plates. (I found out later that your roommate had actually made the light and airy pancakes.) Also, I was lonely. I hate the Midwest. It's windy here and there are no hills, and as a pedestrian, I fear for my life; no one pays attention to traffic laws and everyone drives enormous cars.

Without you here to talk to, I have time to think about everything in frustrating detail. I should thank you for disappearing. For not answering your emails. For not returning my calls.

Of course, you might be at your father's funeral, weeping into your dear mother's shoulder.

Or, you might be dead, your face pressed against the windshield of Miriam's or Carla's car, the hood of the car crumpled up against a tree. For all I know.

While chopping garlic, I sliced my finger. Holding it above my head, pressed into a dirty dishtowel, I could not stop laughing. If you were here, you would have been running around, getting the hydrogen peroxide and sterile bandages. You can be thoughtful like that. You worry about germs.

Footnote: One Man's Thesis Is Another Man's Sore Spot

I never explained my theory about grad school. It's just like high school, but with more complicated words to describe the same emotional bullshit. I'm in the marching band, and you're in the popular crowd. Girls like you because you take your shirt off for Halloween and perform higher-education themed lyrics to popular songs—*All the literate ladies! All the literate ladies!*

At the end of the spring semester, we hosted what would be our last barbeque together. While talking to a group of first-years in Women's Studies, I pointed to you across the lawn. You

were playing cornhole, a game I will never understand the charm of, and one of these women looked at me jealously and called you a "humanities hottie."

When I told you later about your new fan and the title she'd bestowed on you, you were offended—not because she had objectified you but because she'd qualified your hotness. When I chuckled at your annoyance, you snapped, "It's not actually that funny."

I guess I should have realized it sooner: you have a sense of humor about everything but yourself.

Annotated Bibliography

Wharton, Edith. *Custom of the Country.*

It's easy to loathe Undine Spragg, Wharton's vain and beautiful social-climber. She advances through society and husbands by a process of imitation, not understanding. Her third husband, the French aristocrat Raymond de Chelles, is at first charmed, then finally horrified, by her designs: "You come among us speaking our language and not knowing what we mean; wanting the things we want, and not knowing why we want them; aping our weaknesses, exaggerating our follies, ignoring or ridiculing all we care about." (334)

I'm tired of people clamoring for "likeable" characters in fiction. I don't necessarily root for Undine, but neither do I want to look away. Of all of Wharton's female characters, she's the only one who isn't forced to die or live alone in misery as punishment for going after what she wants. And in her I see something of all of us academic wannabees: we learn to speak the language, we pretend to understand Foucault, to have strong opinions about obscure German philosophy, to have read (and adored!) *Ulysses*. But catch me at home on my couch, and you're more likely to see me poring over a weekly celebrity gossip magazine than the latest issue of *The Journal of Literary Criticism.*

Solomon, Isaac. *Get a Life, Get a Job, Get a Better Boyfriend: Implied Words of Wisdom from a Well-Meaning Father.*

When my dad called this weekend, I lied and said we were trying to work things out. Sometimes it's easier to invent stories than to actually look at things for real, especially when I am talking to a man who is always detecting signs that I'm unhappy: *Is graduate school worth it?* he'll say. *Are you getting enough sleep?* Or: *I hope they're teaching you something interesting because they sure aren't preparing you for the real world.*

He sends his regards, by the way. The funny thing is, even though he doesn't say it, I know he finds you unworthy. It's his tone of voice, a kind of icy distance he also adopts when he talks about Mom. For example, he'll tell me how he ran into her and Frank at the grocery store, how she seemed good and looked good and was buying a lot of ribs for a dinner party, but what he'll want to say is how hurtful it is to keep running into the love of his life—the woman who left him the second a more business savvy option came along—at the supermarket. I used to appreciate my father's diplomacy, the fact that he has never derided my mother or chided me for my poor choices in men. He should, though. His quiet acceptance of people's romantic failings is considerate, but it never got him anywhere in his own relationships.

Tilman, Helen. *A Few Things Are Illuminated.*

My mother has a PhD in marine biology, but she runs a daycare center. In her third year in graduate school, she fell in love with her advisor and moved with him for a summer to Mosquito Bay to research phosphorescent plankton. I find this period of her life entirely fascinating and romantic, but she claims she hates talking about it. "I was a cliché," she'll say after enough dry martinis. "Sleeping with my old and married professor. Skinny-dipping at night in the glow-in-the dark Caribbean. Kayaking through luminescent lagoons."

As it turns out, the dude was using her research and not giving her credit. She discovered something about the reproductive processes of dinoflagellates that he passed off as his own find. But she won't talk in detail about what she discovered, because to describe it, she says, would remind her all over again of that sequence of powerful sensations—the wonder of discovery followed by the wound of betrayal.

Roberts, Ralph. *Hard to Get: An Undergraduate Romance.*

Years before you, there was Ralph, the long-distance runner. He wasn't even my type—he was pre-law, wirey, clinical, and distant. We had some good banter going on initially, but our love life was lousy. He refused to kiss me during sex. In that way, he reminded me of a prostitute.

And yet I sat up at night wondering why he hadn't dropped by that day, I called him constantly, I obsessed over whether he thought I was as beautiful as the thin girls on the cross-country team. He never said anything, but I knew he compared. Years later, he married one of them, and I even attended their very lovely and meaningful wedding, but as they danced their first dance I still thought, *Well, fuck you, Ralph. Fuck you.*

Oral Defense

I've been planning what I'll say the next time I see you. I would like it to be something remarkable, something that will make you stagger backwards and put your hand over your eyes because it's just too much to bear.

But instead of eloquent declarations, I'm stuck on this utterly prosaic realization: after you know so much about a person, it's impossible to stop knowing it, no matter how much you wish you could.

Some of our friends have taken up smoking while they write their final chapters. I'm thinking of trying it out—break one horrendous habit with another. Also, I know that if I do start up, you will not try to kiss me again, because even though you like a good Cuban cigar now and then, you hate the taste of tobacco on other people.

By the time I'm on my pack-a-day routine, maybe you'll come over for a beer and we'll joke easily about old times and how I never actually thought you and I were meant to be together. While I dream of a childless, lakeside cottage in Slovenia, you secretly want a large and chaotic family that raises chickens and subsists off its own sustainable vegetable garden. You want to be adored by dozens of beautiful and well-read women who love you equally for your tight abs, your puns, and your scholarly articles. You still have a soft spot for the Grateful Dead, and yet you look terrible in tie-dye, and when you smoke pot you can't relax; you get tense and start worrying whether you should have gotten your MBA at Harvard like your father thought you would.

Maybe by the next time I see you I'll have decided to move to Italy to study the cooking traditions of a small northern village that has, so far, kept the foreign snoops out. And I'll write a book about my time there, how I really screw up the first batches of polenta, but that by the end of the first year people can't tell which dishes were made by my mentor and lover, and which were made by me. I'll write about winning over the people, about all the offers of marriage I receive, which I turn down of course, because by then I'll have seen how these guys are with their mothers. When the book is made into a blockbuster movie starring Sandra Bullock as me, you'll wish you weren't stuck teaching four sections of freshman composition and one section of introductory French in Grand Forks, North Dakota.

Maybe after I tell you my Italian plans, you'll bring up the Brandy Wine tomatoes you found on your porch swing months earlier. You'll even thank me for them—their fresh flavor will have helped you through a lonely evening. I'll pretend I don't know what you're referring to and suggest that—maybe—you should stop stopping by.

You'll advocate for a continued close friendship, by which you'll mean, let's spend the rest of the day in bed. After all my efforts, you'll overlook the cigarette in my hand because you know it's only a silly prop. And maybe I'll say no. No, we cannot be friends.

But probably I'll just let you lead me upstairs. You'll tug at my sleeve and tell me a joke. I'll be thinking murderous thoughts, but I'll start unbuttoning my blouse as I soften my voice and ask, "So, tell me, where have you been?"

❖ ❖ ❖

Gemenids

I've missed another
meteor shower, blind here
under the city lights, the
clouds like a smoky bar
where I sit alone and there
we have it—the street is
lined with stone horses
and planters bursting with
star-shaped flowers and
grapes, the walk like
houses falling down
around me like sparks
from the blacksmith, a halo
in the dark and all
the time.

Kendra Frorup. *One*. 2009. Mixed media. 48 x 48 inches. Photo by J. M. Lennon.

Laura Maylene Walter

Q & A at the Film Festival

When my brother Maurice and I were kids, we buried Pepsi bottles out in the woods and set off bottle rockets, convincing our sister Selma that they were landmines. Once I set one off too close to Maurice, without warning him, and the rocket struck him just below his right eye. I could have blinded him, but all he got was a raw-edged scar the shape of a star on his cheek. Instead of embracing it—a scar! Girls love scars!—he grew ashamed and shy, forever putting a hand to his face to hide it.

Now Maurice lives in a small city in upstate New York with a girlfriend named Rose and a black-and-white cat that snuck into the guest room my first night there to piss in my sheets. The big event that weekend was the international film fest, which Maurice could not have been more excited about. I've never been to a film fest before, international or not, and if the rest of the movies were anything like what we watched earlier this afternoon, I might be better off staying in and chancing the cat piss.

"You ready, Brian?" Maurice slipped into a leather jacket so worn it was practically orange. There were many things I wanted to say to my little brother, not just about his jacket but about his hobbies and his approach to life in general, but this weekend was no time to turn him against me. So instead I followed him mutely out the door and down the street to his car, which by the looks of it had become the target for every bird that had to take a shit in a twenty-mile radius.

❖ ❖ ❖

Our first movie of the evening was a Swedish drama. The plot went like this: For seven years, a young girl is sentenced to a kitchen to make the same vat of soup over and over. She never sees who she is feeding, and the ingredients never change: celery, chickpeas, carrots, onion. A little bit of salt. One bay leaf. That's it. When the girl is released on her sixteenth birthday, she walks outside and an old man hands her an orange. She stands looking at it for a long time, turning it over in her hands. Finally she throws it in a trashcan and walks off into the distance.

The lights came on in the theatre to reveal Maurice wiping his eyes. "Can you believe that?" he asked.

"I know, right? I thought that old man would at least try to hit on her or something."

Maurice put on his jacket. "No, the orange. She didn't even recognize it as food. Really got to me."

What got to me was how my brother turned into this gigantic douchebag without my even noticing.

On our way to the next theater, a film fest volunteer stepped in front of us. He looked exactly like every other volunteer there, male or female—nineteen years old with greasy hair, plastic-framed glasses, tattooed arms, tight jeans with wide cuffs, and a t-shirt with an ironic slogan. This one actually said, "Look at my ironic shirt." I can't make this up.

"Can't go in, fellas. Movie's been delayed."

"What?" Maurice frowned. "Start times are never delayed. Ever."

"I know," our hipster told us. He leaned in to confide something further, since he clearly recognized Maurice as a kindred spirit. "This is a Director's Spot movie. And the director? Is so not ready. He's in the back puking into a trash can."

"Get the hell out of here." Maurice started wringing his film fest booklet into a tight tube. "That's intense."

"So it's postponed," the volunteer concluded. "One hour."

"Awesome, we can eat." I grabbed Maurice by his jacket and steered him toward the exit. "Let's get a beer and burger at that Pear and Fag place or whatever."

"The Pear and Fig," Maurice said, struggling to look back as I ushered him out. "Don't you think we should hang around, just in case?"

"You heard the little dude. Director's puking his guts out. Leave him be."

We wove through the crowds to cross the street and enter the Pear and Fig. I ordered us both talls of the beer on special, something from the U.K. that I didn't recognize, but it looked like it would go down okay. I noticed the waitress checking out Maurice's scar, but he was oblivious and went on tapping his fingers against the table and then against the beer glass. He was always a tapper, even back in high school. I used to tell him he should take up track with me to let go of that energy instead of tapping on his desk like a goddamn nerd. But it only got worse—in his junior year, he started playing the French horn.

"So which movie is your favorite so far?" Maurice asked.

I closed my eyes and pretended to think. "The Mexican one," I said. That one at least had a hot actress.

"That final scene was a stunner," Maurice agreed. "The way the hoof prints just faded away in the sand like that."

"Definitely." I waved over the waitress and ordered the bleu cheese burger. Maurice got a ten-inch pizza with goat cheese. Didn't this place have any plain old American cheddar?

I took a long pull from my beer and signaled for another. What the hell. If I had to watch this next "film," which was Japanese and apparently "a revealing glimpse into the contradictions and unexpected joys of the human condition," I might as well be loaded.

"Drink up," I told Maurice, and watched as he brought the beer to his lips. He told me at Christmas two years ago that he prefers wine, for the antioxidants. If it weren't for that girlfriend of his, who had strawberry blonde hair and a little heart-shaped mouth, I might start to worry. Then I reminded myself to focus. This might be my best opportunity all weekend.

"So Maurice," I began, wondering if it was best to start with how I've had zero job leads since the foundry laid me off a couple of months ago, or if I should focus instead on the medical bills for my knee. Or maybe I should dive right into my idea for the brewpub. Maurice had always been a dreamer himself. Hell, maybe he'd want to be a full partner. He could move to Indianapolis and open the place with me. Might even be fun.

"Wait," he blurted out. "I have something to tell you."

I sat back in the booth and put my hand around my cold beer. A few more film fest types filtered into the pub. You could tell who they were by that dazed, I-just-saw-ten-movies-in-a-row look in their eyes. For people who claimed they wanted to discover the mysteries and wonder of life, you'd think they'd get outside a little more instead of cramming together in the dark to read dialogue tracking across the bottom of a screen.

"All right," I said, hoping he was about to tell me his life felt meaningless, the kind of void that could only be filled by a new and exciting business venture. "Shoot."

Maurice picked up his napkin and folded it in half, then in half again. "Um," he said.

"What? Spit it out."

"Mom's married."

"She's what?"

"She got married to this guy from D.C. They met online last year."

"Mom was on *dating sites*?" Holy shit, *I* go on dating sites.

"No, it wasn't like that. They met on some forum for people who want to learn how to prepare for big emergencies, like natural disasters, the end of the world. You know."

"Mom is worried about the *end of the world?*"

"What. Who isn't?"

"Jesus Christ, Maurice. So she married some random guy who thinks the world is going to end? That's great. Just fucking great."

"Settle down. He's not that bad."

"You met the motherfucker?"

The waitress arrived with our food. She gave me my burger and slid the pizza in front of Maurice and then got the hell out of there.

"Yeah," he said. "I was kind of at the wedding."

I took a few slow, deep breaths. They sounded more like wheezes. "Was Selma there?" Selma lived in Sacramento with her husband and three rescued pit bulls. She hated leaving those dogs for anything.

"Of course, Selma was there," Maurice said. Then he shut his mouth and reached for the salt. He shook it hard all over his pizza without looking up.

"Christ," I said. "I wanted to ask you to go into business with me. You know, open a restaurant. A brewpub, maybe. And now this."

Maurice looked up, surprised. "Why would I invest in that? You do know that new restaurants have something like a ninety percent failure rate, right? Besides," he went on, taking another sip of beer. He looked remarkably relaxed now. "Rose is pregnant."

At this point I slammed the rest of the second beer and, without even looking around for the waitress, shouted out for another one.

"We're not planning on getting married, at least not right away," Maurice said. I realized he'd been holding this in the whole time, just dying to blurt it out. "We want to focus on the baby for now. We're looking at houses." He reached into his messenger bag and pulled out a realty guide. "Rose wants a fenced yard. And a garage, and an extra room so she can have an art studio."

When the waitress came with my beer I told her I'd changed my mind and would take the check instead. I let Maurice pay, of course. As he slipped the credit card back in his wallet, he looked up at me. "You still want to see this movie?"

Obviously, I wanted to say no. But I also knew this might be the last year Maurice could enjoy the film fest without a screaming kid tying him down.

"Yeah," I said. "Let's go see it."

We eased out the booth. Maurice led the way. Maybe it was the beer, or the fact that he was going to be a father, but I noticed that maybe he walked a little taller, a little stronger than I remembered. And that only pissed me off more.

❖ ❖ ❖

Of all the weird shit I'd seen in my life, this Japanese movie took the grand prize. The director, a skinny, feminine-looking dude wearing what I swear was an ascot and pointy-toed shoes, stood up in front of the theater in the beginning to say in heavily accented English, "I made this movie for my brothers." He paused and looked around. His face was bright red and his neck, too, what we could see of it behind the ascot. "You are my brothers," he added lamely, and then he sat down and the theater lights dimmed.

The movie was full of characters that were half human, half something else. For example, it opened to show a man with an automatic bread-maker in his belly getting married to a woman with silver teaspoons for hair. Her head jingled whenever she moved, and in the sunlight she gave off halos and rainbows.

"You've got to be kidding me," I whispered to Maurice, but he ignored me. I slouched in my seat and resigned myself to the movie. There wasn't much dialogue, but I didn't bother much with the subtitles anyway. I needed to think.

In high school, I was always the one who got the girls. I was a track star, a basketball player, a swimmer, and I had the body to prove all of it. Somehow, I ended up unemployed in Indianapolis, and the single dream I could come up with—starting my own brewpub—died before it even had a chance. Now I was forced to finish out this weekend watching bullshit movies before getting in my car and making the long drive back to Indiana alone.

When the movie was over, the director held a Q&A, but the questions were ridiculously stupid. A couple of guys kept asking process questions, like "What kind of camera do you use and would you recommend I make my first movie with that same one?" or "Do you have to get releases from all the people who appear in the background of the street shots?" To make it worse, the director wasn't very fluent in English, so he had a hard time both understanding the questions and formulating responses. Of course, the film fest hadn't provided a Japanese-English translator. That would have made too much sense.

I was embarrassed for everyone involved. Maurice must have noticed, because ten minutes into the questions, he looked at me and said, "Let's get out of here."

We left the theater and headed straight home. When we walked into the apartment, we found Rose asleep on the couch with an afghan draped over her body. Goddamn Maurice, I hadn't gotten a girl like that in years. Rose stirred when she heard us come in. She sat up and rubbed her eyes. "I missed you," she told Maurice.

I rolled my eyes and walked into the kitchen. I opened the refrigerator and stared inside. Maurice and Rose had lots of eggs, all lined up neatly in the egg tray on the door. They also had a head of iceberg lettuce, organic peanut butter, sliced turkey, a half gallon of soy milk, and about a dozen containers of yogurt. I reached down to open the vegetable crisper and found asparagus, a red bell pepper, and a package of mushrooms. Even with the hum of the refrigerator, I could still hear Rose and Maurice talking in low tones in the next room.

I stood up and closed the refrigerator door, then leaned on it. Against my better judgment I found myself thinking of that crazy couple in the Japanese movie. When they made love on their wedding night, the spoon woman tilted her head back, sending a rain of tinkling sounds down her spine and into the sheets. Afterward, they lay side by side on the bed while steam crept from the man's breadmaker stomach. Later in the movie we learned a new life baked there, down below his heart.

I left the kitchen without a word to Maurice and Rose and headed into the guest bedroom. That little shitter Classy was sitting on my bed, looking at me.

"Jesus Christ," I told Classy. He just stared, his eyes huge and golden. It appeared he had not taken a piss, so that was nice. "Little asshole," I added. "You smell like ass. Anyone ever tell you that?"

Classy hesitated. Then he slid his eyes into a half-shut position, all relaxed and happy.

"You like that? You like being called a little asshole?" Without trying, I'd let my voice get softer and slower. "You little black-and-white douchebag. Aren't you? Aren't you a little douchebag?"

Classy started purring and kneading the blankets. I sat next to him, exhausted, and stroked his head. He leaned into my hand, encouraging me.

"Yeah," I said. "Same to you."

I got under the covers and let Classy nap by my head. I lay there in the dark until I heard Maurice and Rose go to bed across the hall. Then the apartment was silent. I reached down on the floor for my jeans and dug through the pockets for my cell phone.

It rang four times before my sister picked up.

"Brian?" She hesitated.

"Hey, Selma. How's the weather out there in good ol' Cali?"

Selma breathed into the phone. "Oh, same as always," she said, her voice taking on that careful, cheery tone I hated. "Sunny all weekend. You know. Ha-ha."

"Ha," I agreed. "Yeah, you sure love that California weather."

"You bet."

"I know how much you hate to leave it. Even for a weekend. Even if, say, your own mother got married. Am I right?"

"Shit. Maurice wasn't supposed to say anything."

"How in the hell did everyone neglect to tell me she was getting married?"

"You already know the answer to that question."

"Apparently I don't, Selma. Apparently I have no fucking clue why my entire family would conspire to keep me from our mother's wedding."

"Because you have a history. Remember Gilbert?" Gilbert was my mother's boyfriend a few years ago.

"Gilbert was an isolated incident," I said.

"You called him a son of a bitch."

"Yeah, so."

"On Christmas Eve."

"Hey, the guy was a creep. Someone has to look out for Mom."

"Brian." Selma was quiet for a moment. Then she sighed. "I'm sorry," she said quietly.

"Me too," I said, and then I hung up on her.

I dropped my phone on the bed and noticed that Classy was gone.

"Classy," I whispered. "Where are ya?" I made a couple "psst psst" sounds. "Come out, you little dumbass."

The bedroom door was cracked, so I got up and crept into the hallway. I tiptoed into the living room, expecting to see Classy perched on his Pet Apartment or maybe crouched by the food dish, but what I found instead was Rose. She was lying on the couch again, alone in the dark, holding her hands against her stomach. She didn't look pregnant to me—her stomach was practically flat—but she held her hands there like she was already nine months along and waiting for the baby to come. She looked up and then followed my gaze to her stomach.

"I couldn't sleep," Rose said.

"Me either." I walked over and sat in Maurice's armchair. "You're lucky you're skipping this film fest. It's pretty messed up. Like this Japanese movie we saw today? One of the characters was pregnant."

"Yeah?" Rose shifted a little on the couch.

"Yeah. Only it was a dude. And the baby was a loaf of bread. Baking in his breadmaker stomach."

Rose stared at me for a few seconds. Then she laughed. Her head tilted back and while she didn't have spoons for hair, I imagined she made those jangly metal sounds like in the movie.

"I guess I just don't get it," I told her.

We were quiet for a moment. "I came out here looking for the cat," I said, to fill the silence. "He was in my room and then just disappeared."

"He does that. Sometimes he goes in the laundry room and hides in the dryer. Or else he burrows under a big pile of clothes."

I linked my hands behind my head and made the recliner bounce a bit. "That reminds me of when Maurice and I were kids. We had this club, just him and me, and we dug a hideout in the woods."

Rose watched me. "How old were you?"

"I don't know. Nine years old. Ten. We'd be out there for hours."

Rose nodded, like I'd given her something to think about. "I won't be able to sleep for a while," she said. "You want to watch a movie? Maybe something a little more accessible?"

"Sounds good."

She got up and rummaged around their entertainment center, then held up a DVD case. *Weekend at Bernie's.*

"Perfect," I said.

Rose put the movie in and hit play. The recliner was making me feel a little seasick, so I got up and sat next to Rose on the couch. She grabbed another blanket and tossed it at me. "I haven't seen this in forever," she said.

"Me either."

We watched even though we knew how it would play out. Those boneheads would rig Bernie up to all sorts of ridiculous contraptions to make him look alive. And for one weekend, he would be. I thought back to those times Maurice and I played in the fort we built in the woods, the smell of rotting and dirt and decay. How in the evening, our mother would come outside looking for us. She hated walking through the scratchy undergrowth, and she'd remind us of that fact later. But for the time being, Maurice and I hid in our makeshift clubhouse, laughing. When her back was turned, we'd leap out and run up behind her. She never knew about the hideout, so to her, we just appeared like magic.

Or maybe, I reflected, she knew the whole time but let us believe that we were hidden.

When I glanced over at Rose again, she was crying. She caught me looking and wiped her face. I turned back to the TV and saw Bernie's hand, attached to fishing line, flapping around.

"I can't believe I'm saying this, but maybe the Japanese movie wasn't all that bad," I said.

Rose pushed off the afghan. "Tell me about it."

"The director was there to take questions afterward," I said. "He told us that he wanted to make a movie about marriage."

"That's all it was about? Marriage?"

"I guess so. He said that even though his characters were so unusual—breadmaker body parts and spoons for hair—they're really just like us."

Rose frowned, like she wasn't sure whether she should believe me.

"And then Maurice asked a question," I said.

"He did?"

"Of course he did. He asked, 'Did you make this for your wife?' And the director said yes, he did, but that every time he tries to make a film about his love for his wife, he fails. Just fails again and again, yet he can't stop trying. And Maurice? Maurice totally got it."

"Oh," Rose said.

"Exactly," I told her.

"You know what first attracted me to him?" Rose asked. She wasn't making eye contact anymore. "The scar on his face. And it wasn't because it made him look dangerous."

"Nothing could make Maurice look dangerous."

Rose smiled faintly. "It looked like he had a past. Like he needed someone to take care of him, and even though he didn't have that, he got by anyway."

"I was the one who gave him that scar," I said.

She nodded. "I know."

After a few moments of silence, Rose nestled into the couch in a way that brought her body a few inches closer to mine. I waited a couple more minutes and then reached out and put my hand on Rose's stomach, about where I imagined the baby might be. Rose didn't move.

I thought of my mother sitting with her husband in D.C., the two of them surrounded by stacks of canned food, flashlights, batteries, jug after jug of water. And then there was Selma, out in California with her slobbering pit bulls and her husband. And Maurice, asleep in the next room, sleeping with the scar side of his face against the pillow.

Rose was wearing just a thin cotton tank top, and it was easy enough to slide my hand under the shirt and onto her bare skin to feel her heat. In the heartbeat of her body I imagined the other life just beginning there. She reached up and touched my face, gently, in the place where

Maurice had his scar. Meanwhile, another life played out before us on a screen. Even after I closed my eyes I could still see the flickering movements of light from the TV, where people spoke from a script and had their whole lives mapped out.

My eyes were still closed when I heard footsteps and then Maurice's voice asking: "What the hell?"

Rose shot straight up on the couch as Maurice stared at me, clear-eyed and furious. The glow from the TV showed the smooth outline of his face and his eyes. His scar didn't exist in the dark. It was like we didn't even know each other, like we weren't brothers at all. I was just a stranger in his apartment, who had touched his pregnant girlfriend's stomach and, for a moment, wished something of his could be mine.

❖ ❖ ❖

"...the slightest orb" *(Merchant of Venice,* Act V, scene i)

He smokes on the terrace
watching the star between
the palms, the humming pearl
slipping through the long green
lashes as a breeze bends
the lines of sight then curls
across his face and chest.
Gently his sullenness
is shamed away,
he almost hears the music,
his muddy vesture of decay
not quite so grossly closed in.

Ina Kaur. *Certain Enigma.* 2010. Color etching, relief, and blind embossment. 24 x 18 inches.

Born in the Caul

He was explaining how his wife, hours after giving birth, still full-moon bellied and woozy with accomplishment, had been swiped off the planet. "A wild blood clot walloped her brain." His voice cracked—or was it our crappy phone connection?

"Awful," I said. "Just awful."

"Her name was Shira Marie."

"An angel name," I said.

"You have no idea. That woman made friends like some make empty promises."

From out my kitchen window, the inky night sky suspended a crescent moon. I wondered if he could see it waxing, too.

"Thing is, she's not gone to the co-op for squash, but gone, gone." A real whimper snagged his deep tenor and sent my heart south. "And me and baby Gwen, we're fumbling without her." Two deep breaths: him first, then me. "You can come by tomorrow?"

Minutes before, while flipping through the *Pennysaver* looking for a clunker Winnebago, I'd come across his want ad. There it was, his tidy plea sandwiched between *Washing Machine* and *Wurlitzer*:

> **WET NURSE:** Wanted immediately in that capacity, a young, healthful person of good character, with a fresh breast of milk. If from nearby, the more desirable. Thanks, Dyson Ledge sale-xbxtk-2120643589@pennysaver.org

After I emailed him my phone number, Dyson had called back immediately. I honestly hadn't expected to get a response. Thirty-one years old and I'd never answered a want ad in my life. I didn't believe anyone actually existed on the want end; always figured it was more a conspiracy of wanters giving seekers a false sense of emotional commerce—and hope.

"I can tell just from our quick conversation here that Gwen's gonna have no trouble taking to you." He forced a hollow laugh. Then something else from his end of the line: wispy double-time huffing easily mistaken for a struggle if I hadn't known, even then, that it was Gwen breathing for all of us.

❖ ❖ ❖

The next morning, I stood on Dyson's straw doormat. Any other day at 10 a.m., you'd find me manning the register at Cupettes—Yuma, Arizona's, first cupcake boutique. My neighbor Lauren owned the place and last year convinced me to resign my Director of HR post at Motorola. Okay, fine. Since my hubby, Ian, made decent enough money, I reasoned, here's my chance to taste entrepreneurship, put my rusty MBA through its paces, and eventually work up the nerve to commence my dream concept: a telescope-mobile. Like the Bookmobile, but instead of Dickens, my Winnebago cum stargazer would shuttle half a dozen Stellarvue 102mm White Refractor Telescopes into bad neighborhoods and give kids a view beyond their encroaching walls.

I knocked and shivered. The Arizona desert could be a cold, mean place in January. Where a doorbell once lived, desperate little wires reached out to reconnect and ping the air with sweet *ding-dongs* of visitors. Clutches of nappy fescue and ragweed littered his front yard and grew up and around a termite-riddled wagon wheel—a totem to indigenous defeat.

Finally, Dyson answered the door with Gwen casually cocked in one arm as if he'd been trained to hold helpless things. The honest morning light rendered this man, this tamer version of Mick Jagger, too old to be a new father and way too young to be a widower. His head almost touched the top of the weathered doorframe. His knees needed meat.

With his free hand reached out to mine, he started, "I'm Dyson. And you . . . shush, don't tell me . . . I know it beings with an 'A' . . . . dammit . . . my memory is shot. Please forgive me . . . Ash—?"

"Ashlyn," I said, wishing for something more substantial to appear in my mouth or hands: a blessing, hot soup, my address a hundred miles west of his mess.

The baby squirmed in his arms, perhaps smelling the breast milk leaching through my shirt. Dyson loosened the blanket cocoon. "This is Gwen. Two days new." He fixed his eyes on her, forgetting me.

"She's beautiful," I lied. She was wrinkled as wet linen, a mysterious rendering of humanness.

"You shoulda seen her mother."

We stood still; two high divers surveying liquid worlds about to be breached. I tried with no success to stop the muscles twitching in my temples. Then his eyes scanned my body, which I think made him uncomfortable, like an old habit he couldn't break, because he quickly switched Gwen to his other arm and with the reminder of her flawless flesh, seemed to regain his focus.

"My gosh, I'm sorry about making you stand out there in that cold like that. Come in. Please. By the way, sorry about the mess, Ashley-Lynn"

I didn't correct his mispronunciation. Coming from him, I saw the extra syllable as a gift. "Please don't apologize."

"So, you've done this before?" he asked after showing me to the leather couch in the family room, its cushions split with fault lines.

"You'll be—" I retraced the misstep. "Your daughter will be my first."

"I guess that's okay. It's not like a job skill. You either got the milk or you don't. Right?" He mussed with Gwen's blanket. "Any questions for my wife?"

My whole body recoiled. The blood in my head drained someplace safer.

"Hypothetically, Ashley-Lynn. This is all hypothetical; no pressure is what I'm saying. But just for me."

"I'm not a mother," I said. Warmth like bath water—hands? breath?— enveloped the empty swag at my gut. Some knee-jerk maternal reflex went to touch it before the reality of what was gone hit me. "I should have explained. I lost the baby three days ago, a month shy of her due date. Nature's sick joke that I get the milk, but not the baby."

"So sorry. I mean, you sure you're ready?"

"Never been one to throw away food in the refrigerator, and not sharing this milk seems a graver sin."

"And your husband, he's okay with this?"

His assumption was my own fault; I still wore my wedding band.

"Ian's gone, too." Suddenly, the air rippled like heat shimmying off summer's asphalt, and a succession of waves formed a vague shape, something as intimately familiar as habit, as Ian. I went to reach at the air and stopped myself, supposing Dyson would judge the move crazy. I jammed my hands between my knees.

"Oh jeez, I'm sorry. Truly." He spun an earring.

"Please, you couldn't have known." I turned away from the spectral glint to survey the house: beads on pillows, Indonesian rugs tacked to walls, and plum-colored velvet drapes weeping over windows, altogether refusing the light outside. But it'd been different one time. I could tell that sunlight had once ruled; the emeralds and turquoises were sun-bleached.

"What's the give in all this? You and me both, not bad people, far as I can tell," he said. His voice fell ten octaves and rediscovered the same empty timbre from last night's phone conversation. "And the world's not doing us no favors."

"Nope, no favors." Even as a guest in his house and sitting in the pith of his grief, I could only parrot his observation. I'd skimmed off most of my emotional flotsam and pitched it out the window onto the I-8 connecting my house in Yuma to his here in Gila Bend.

He turned toward the picture on the wall of his pregnant wife and revealed his own stunning profile. Head-on, too much was in disrepair, but from the side, with that jaw set like a sharp turn, he looked capable of digging himself out of hell.

"So, I just want to be real up-front," Dyson continued. "I promised myself I wouldn't do some chicken-shit dance around the truth. It's got nothing to do with you personally. Just something I got to say: You're not Gwen's mother."

"Never. No. Of course not." I searched the air for Ian, for one of his gentle, pragmatic retorts to use as my own, but he was gone.

With his pinkie, Dyson swiped white dribble off Gwen's mouth. "We'll set feeding times, and outside of that—point is, limit your time with her to feeding." He stood up, handed me Gwen. "Give her a taste. A test run." He politely turned away from us and hurried toward the kitchen.

"So is this a contractual thing? Or do we just shake on it?"

I looked down at Gwen's mouth sealed tightly to me as we'd have to be chiseled apart. A current of satiety flowed between us. Overcome with the urge to go bleary-eyed and proud, to preen and sniff in that mammalian momma way, I knew I was trespassing. My milk let down in a cosmic shower of analgesic stars, numbing my tongue.

Dyson pulled out Chapstick from his pocket and mashed it on his lips. "When you two are done Ashley-Lynn, I'll show you the spare bedroom."

❖ ❖ ❖

I put my house in Yuma up for rent, quit Cupettes, and with my laptop, camera, minimal clothes, and the six-year-old honeymoon picture of Ian clasping his arms around my wedding-whittled waist, I moved to Gila Bend.

First night in Dyson's house, under the fingernail clipping of a waning crescent, Dyson moved a bureau from his bedroom into the spare.

"You need a nightlight?" Dyson asked. "Since you'll be the one stumbling around at night."

"So, you're not joining?" I teased.

"Plans have changed in that department." Our laughs collided, and in the same instant we silenced them. He uncapped his Chapstick, studied its waxy bulb, then walked out.

The honeymoon picture looked nice on the bureau. Above my futon, I thumbtacked the *"Ooljee baa hané"* poster Ian had brought back from a professional astronomer's powwow on the Navajo reservation. He'd explained that of all the "Phases of the Moon," his favorite was *dah netuh gone*—when the moon is said to visit the sun.

The first month at Dyson's flew by in a purposeful whirl: I had both a hungry baby and an empty man to fill. But by month two, a dull sense of gravity returned. Gwen had gained enough weight for Dyson to stop watching us 24/7.

One quiet afternoon, the sun coming in at a slant, I set up a complicated online social network, reconnecting with college friends who I had nothing in common with except cataclysmic loneliness and memories of drunkenness. Within days, the novelty of instant chitchat wore off, and I began taking pictures of Gwen and posting them to my virtual wall. No captions. No explaining who she was, or who I was—and wasn't.

❖ ❖ ❖

My own mother would have sacrificed limbs if given the chance to renounce motherhood, its anchored weight and damp peculiarities. It was her curse, a condition best treated with Grey Goose and long bouts of pouting over her middling status among the tarts of Manhattan's art scene.

One Friday night, Mom's "Lips en Grosse" decoupage exhibit had been kyboshed, leaving her no choice but to keep me, her tragic high school outcast, company.

"I'm serious, schweetie, you were born in the dark." She was sitting on the couch mourning her empty snifter while I microwaved pizza. "You came out with the amniotic sack still sucked to you like a plastic produce bag."

I snapped open a Diet Rite.

"They busted it to get you air," she said. "You were born in the caul, Ash. Real good luck in some backwards tribal cultures, except ours, sweetheart, where apparently it's a sign of going nowhere, looking into walls your whole life."

"Screw you," I whispered. No need to shout. The condo was tiny; our lives had shrunk to accommodate Dad's departure.

"I'm only trying to help. Wouldn't you rather know what dark corners you're up against before you're up against them?"

❖ ❖ ❖

Moon waxing gibbous. I plugged in the star nightlight I bought for Gwen's room so she wouldn't have to interpret my shadows, and I wouldn't have to interpret hers. Soon as the room went dark, it blinked on.

Dyson had returned to work as the construction foreman on Gila Bend's first bowling alley. I joked he ought to be careful not to get arrested for climbing scaffolding, what with looking like a trick-or-treater in his tool belt and hardhat.

With all that physical labor, soon as Dyson's cheek hit the pillow, a deep snore snatched him up—my cue to sneak into Gwen's room, to rock and feed her outside the strict schedule he'd charted and taped to the refrigerator.

Next thing I knew, I was sneaking in every night for photos. I'd rearrange her in sweet Sears positions: hands in prayer, hands in a *hooray*, feet in the frog pose. I snapped enough pictures to paint an impression of full-blown family life.

One night, I arrived for our nightly off-schedule date with my iPod and introduced her to David Gray. As "Babylon" played, and Gwen and I swayed, the white linen curtains Dyson and I hung earlier that day shifted, letting in a flash of the full moon. I quickly got hot, as if Ian had wrapped himself around me, mummified me in his spirit. As if he'd come to watch me be a mother, to lean in and smell us and try to figure out where Gwen's scent ended and mine began.

My plan, if Dyson woke, was to move in close to him, to feel the hair on his arms bristle against mine, and with her between us I'd explain how sorry I was, but she sounded like she was trying to breathe underwater.

❖ ❖ ❖

Ian's plane crashed at dusk. No moon, no sun—the universe's changing of the guards, when the sun punches out and the moon punches in. It was a single-engine Cessna, owned and piloted by our friend Manny. Manny had a wife and three kids, the perfectly composed octagonal family Ian and I couldn't wait to start. After spending the weekend in San Diego for The Astronomers of America Conference, Manny and Ian took off from San Diego's Montgomery Field in a light, harmless fog. According to Manny's flight plan, they'd fly low up the coast to do a pier hop: from Pacific Beach to Huntington to Santa Monica, then head east back to Arizona, landing at Scottsdale Airpark.

The NTSB concluded it was a case of spatial disorientation. The dusky grey sky blended into grey ocean—what looked like ocean was actually sky, and what looked like sky was thousands of feet deep. In fact, once Manny and Ian lost their visual horizon, they also lost all sense of up or down, spinning or diving, and most likely entered a graveyard spiral, not wasting their final fistful of seconds on fear or futile prayer. They split through the Pacific probably midsentence in conversation about kids: Manny's oldest was headed to college and Ian's first was still safely swimming in my brackish womb.

❖ ❖ ❖

Saturday, July 1, temperatures hit triple digits before breakfast, and the moon was at perigee, so close to earth I could feel its pull

and promise of instability. There I was, six months into my informal one-year contract, and Gwen was looking more and more like me: green eyes, long lashes, a nose destined to do nothing but deflate her self-esteem. Seemed my milk was filling in the blanks, sort of overriding her prescribed DNA and having its way.

Despite the heat, I found Dyson in the backyard building a porch awning. The red Makita shirt I had bought him the day before lifted up to reveal a storm of masculinity. He had Gwen in a baby backpack, her face slathered in sun block, her head covered in a tulip hat. One of those sun-tea Saturdays.

"I need a picture of this," I said and ran inside to grab my camera.

When I returned, the sun shone on them like the eighth wonder.

"Smile," I said. The hammer fell to his side and he forced a grin. "I don't think so. Try again."

"I was just telling Gwen how you should book yourself a massage or something today. You're off the clock; Gwen's going to see Shira's parents in about an hour."

Off the clock. Shira's parents? I stared into the sun, let it brand my retinas in white spots.

"Didn't know her parents lived here," I finally said.

"Came as a shock to me, too." Dyson shaded his eyes with a gritty hand.

"They'll be moving from Chicago in the next month. They're out this week to finalize the purchase on a place." My hurt and confusion must have been obvious. He softened. "Sorry I couldn't give you more of a warning. I suck at breaking news. You know that. Sorry. Forgive me. They're entirely too pleasant—Frank and Sandy—nothing at all to hate about them. Shira was an only child, so they're coming out to be grandparents."

I steadied the camera and asked again for a smile, trying not to feel orphaned and betrayed.

Dyson cooperated, but the right side of his face drooped like I'd never noticed before. He looked thinner, too. But considering the past year, expecting equilibrium was silly. Another smile, I said, hoping to find the asymmetry corrected. No luck.

He lifted Gwen's arm for the camera and waved it. I made that arm, I thought. Forged it with my existence. Would Dylan argue for my place in Gwen's life, maybe explain to Shira's parents not just my physical necessity, but the bigger void I'd filled? Not the void of Shira herself, but the general maternal roosting and warming of the nest.

I posted the picture with a caption: "Daddy raises the roof."

❖ ❖ ❖

Summer reluctantly gave in to fall, and the baby bee costume I'd ordered online arrived and sat for days at the front door, waiting in the same spot I'd stood almost a year prior.

"Ashlyn, why you dressing her as a midget con-con-convict?" The high of Dyson getting my name right on a regular basis was blunted by the fact that he'd developed a horrible stutter. He'd recently fallen on the job and blamed the concussion. I pointed out that the stuttering had started well before the fall.

Weeks later, when the body jerking snuck into his limbs like a phantom ventriloquist, we connected the dots: His Dad, in his thirties, had died of Lou Gehrig's. We knew we were in for a long haul because we'd become we without trying; it'd happened as naturally as conception usually does. We were sun, moon, and earth lining up for a lunar eclipse.

❖ ❖ ❖

Dinner in scraps sat near the sink. I'd spent the first half of the day stringing holiday lights in a haphazard, artsy way I imagined Shira would approve. And while Gwen napped, I'd spent the latter part of the afternoon finalizing the purchase of a fifteen-year-old Winnebago. Dyson had no idea. The whole dream was far off, something slated to happen in a future he wouldn't see.

Exhausted and floating with buyer's excitement, I called Gwen over to the rocking chair, hoping nursing her would settle me. Eleven months now, she waddled to me for meals, saying, "Win hungry." "Win," in her language, certainly translated to Gwen *and* Ashlyn.

Shivering and wrapped in a blanket, Dyson had himself propped up on the couch, watching a PBS series on life after death.

"So you believe that fairytale, that we'll all be together again?" I said. "Some kind of family reunion on a cloud? God supplies the punch?"

He retrieved his Chapstick from the coffee table. His hand shook more than usual, and he ended up salving most of his chin as he spoke. "Don't assume. You know n-n-nothing about me."

Dyson could have sucker-punched me and I'd have recovered my breath quicker.

The air suddenly agitated again and a mash of molecules hovered. If I'd known it would be Ian's last visit, I'd have called him out: *You wise-ass hypocrite. You're an astronomer, Ian; you have proofs and algorithms to disprove this haunting hocus-pocus. Right? And yet, here you are, the undeniable, totally improbable umbral shadow between Dyson and me.*

I strained my focus on Dyson. "I know you love peanut butter straight from the jar; I've seen the spooned divots," I said. "I know you're reading *The Tommyknockers.* I know you prefer Makita power tools to Milwaukee. I know if you had your way, Shira would be sitting here, not me."

He stared mid-plane, perhaps mourning the pieces of him I'd scattered like buckshot. Or was Dyson watching Ian retreat too? "Bet you didn't know that David Gray is pl-pl-pl-playing in Phoenix next weekend?"

He'd found out mine and Gwen's secret, and I didn't care what level of snooping it had required: I was most thrilled by the idea of me maybe going down as his last discovery.

"We'll need a babysitter," I said.

"Overnight prob-probably. Call Frank and Sandy." I didn't call them to help, not ever; I waited for their polite intrusions. Now, what with Dyson smiling at me like that, I had no choice but to ask them to babysit.

My God, where was my camera? I wanted to post his luminous face, then write about how moments later he got up, staggered over to us, and while reaching to touch Gwen's cheek, accidently brushed my bare breast, confirming what it was to be father and mother, plug and socket, screw and driver, a yin-yang amalgam of talents and tics. More and more photos—I'd post every one, until I was a wall of pictures and all that mattered was a documented life with a man I'd known only for a year. But with Gwen acting the transponder between us, it felt as if Dyson and I had written a whole family history together. I supposed babies did that, spliced enough moments so that time could be pushed around your plate, so that dying almost never felt too empty. Perhaps the best argument for procreation I'd ever invented.

❖ ❖ ❖

Two days into the new year, well past midnight, during the most spectacular show of earthshine I'd ever seen, Dyson died. We were at home. The three of us holed up in Dyson's room, which had become in the last few months *our* room, the place where sleep graciously sloughed off reality. Gwen had fallen asleep beside him, her twiggy arm dangling off the side of the bed. Per Dyson's earlier request, the bedroom windows were cranked wide open, the lights turned off.

David Grey plinked ivory keys in the background, though I couldn't find his familiar melody. I heard nothing but the labored breathing of two people boarding two different battle ships: one leaving for battle, the other returning home, and I wasn't sure who was on what ship.

For most of the quiet night, I'd been staring at the strange lunar glow, so how I caught Dyson's last moments, I don't know. I turned back, and there he was blinking, again and again, about twenty times in succession, as if squeezing out the few remaining drops of his reflexes, exercising last rights to his body. After that effort, nothing opened or closed, gasped or inflated. A light on; then off. We're no more elaborate than rudimentary electricity.

I barely had the mental strength to orientate myself in our room, let alone define "us," what we'd been or who we'd become, but at that moment I had to make sense of something. I knew this: death is either a calamity far-off in the sky, a plane falling with artifacts of the real story trapped in a black box, or it is right here, right goddamned here and ever-present and splayed out to dissect until it all makes sense—though it never does. It's always the same mysterious thief.

I lifted Gwen off the bed and carried her outside.

With her warm, limp body propped in my lap, we sat in the same patio chair Dyson had sat in just days before to tell me that he'd signed over adoption rights to Shira's parents. "They've agreed to give you forty-eight hours after my death before coming to claim Gwen," he'd explained. "Claim her?" I'd laughed. "What is she, a winning lottery ticket? A flat screen on layaway?"

The pathetic jabs hollowed me. Dyson stood and used the pulp of his strength to hoist me up and stroke my head. His hairless face against mine felt boyish, his breath was odorless, spent.

He'd explained that it was Frank and Sandy's second shot at raising a girl and not outliving her. He hashed through legality and blood ties, how Gwen should be with family. All I thought was: I am the body and blood of Gwen. I am the measurable inches on her growth chart, the slush in her cells. Give me the shot.

The patio chairs were cheap and sagging with the weight of Gwen and me. Dyson had bought them on a whim one day outside a drugstore. He'd gone in for painkillers and come out with those plus a patio set. Never too late to start eating outside, he'd said. This January night was strangely mild, tempting balmy even. Exactly the weather for sitting almost naked in underwear and that faded red Makita t-shirt of Dyson's.

My body ached with the thought of having to move tonight, tomorrow. In forty-eight hours would my body perform the simple mechanics of letting go: arms extended, hands released? Would Frank and Sandy "claim" her outside or in, morning or afternoon, in churchy or plain clothes? Would they be responding to true love or some obligatory reflex? Would I have a bag packed for Gwen, a legend to help them decode her babble language? Would she and I be waiting graciously in summer skirts and sandals? Would Gwen and I even be here when they arrived? Would we?

I tickled Gwen's toes to rouse her. She whined weakly, until finally peering through half-open eyes, heavy as shades. I whispered in her ear another thing I knew: "This is an earthshine night," I said, taking her fisted hand and extracting a sweaty finger to point at the sky. She giggled, tucked her head into my throat. "The light from the sun is reflecting from the earth's surface, to the moon, and then back into our eyes."

She lifted her head and nodded. A giant yawn spawned a gush of stale breath I loved for its shameless exit. Her head flopped back on my shoulder.

"It's a double reflection of light," I said, still managing to silence the weep metastasizing in me. "We're sharing our light with the moon. And did you know that every day someone falls too deeply in love to back out?" Gradually her body succumbed to the sleep I'd interrupted, and she sank back into me, absorbed me. "And did you know, baby girl, it's the dark side of the moon we see glowing tonight?"

❖ ❖ ❖

Brook J. Sadler

Free-Range Chicken

I dig your feathers.
Your nakedness.
You peck corn like nobody's business.

You roam the open grasses,
groove on the liberty of sunshine.
High on wild air,

you remember the warm
squirm of the brown worm.
I wish I could be there

to see your bohemian glory,
your chicken freedom,
your utopian co-op, sans coop.

But I have only a short while
to stoop over the chilled aisle,
admire your thighs.

You ended up here
in the cellophane wrap
just the same,
but with an organic name.

J. M. Lennon / Lennon Media. *Fiona*. 2014. Photograph. 11 x 17 inches. ©2014 Lennon Media Inc. All rights reserved.

Gina P. Vozenilek

Tri-level

[Editor's note: *This essay, chosen by Kyoko Mori for an AWP 2012 Intro Journals Award, was printed in our last issue in a truncated form that omitted the third section of the piece. We apologize to the author for the inadvertent digital glitch that led to that mistake, and we are pleased to publish her winning essay here in its entirety.*]

I. *I try going downstairs*

I seem to have lost a scar that was on my hand since I was maybe seven years old. It had been right there, etched into my palm one summer day as I came up the concrete steps from the cantina in the basement of my Nonno's tri-level. I was clutching two slender bottles of 7 Up, running. Sunday's supper was upstairs on the table, waiting for the drinks and me. My sandal slipped on the edge of a step near the top and I went down hard, smashing the green glass and releasing a foaming sea of pop that washed down like a waterfall on me. I remember the suddenness of the fall, and a vague embarrassment, and the soft, sizzling sound of the frothing soda. Then I was in the bathroom, being tended by my parents and grandparents who had come running at the noise of the shattering glass, a sound I don't remember at all. I don't remember the pain, either.

This used to be a pretty good story. It was full of sharp detail, including, I believe, a vicious-looking carpet needle that was used to stitch up my cut. My dad is an engineer and believes he can fix most anything on his own. But maybe I'm wrong about the needle. The story has faded with the scar; I never noticed it disappearing. It was a white close-parenthesis about half an inch long that used to punctuate my right palm, there under the first knuckle. I'd trace its arc with my left index finger and narrate the accident that had printed it on my body. I sit here now, some 35 years later, and wiggle my finger slowly, summoning the scar. I stretch my hand out, extending the digits, reaching, searching for it. A hint of the old curved line suggests itself. Maybe that's it. But I'm not so sure. I have to ask my father if he remembers this story, and if he really came at me with a carpet needle. That can't be right.

It's not. Later, my father helps me with the memory as he cooks my birthday dinner in the kitchen of his bungalow in Park Ridge, the town where we both live. I'm forty-one years old today.

"No, you're mixing up that story with the one about your head and the obstetrician," he says. He doesn't even look up from the sink where he is cleaning shrimp for the pasta.

Ah: The scalp laceration that got sewn up at the kitchen table. That was one time my dad called in an expert. I'd taken a violent tumble off my sled one cold, starry night. After the world righted itself, I sat picking at what I thought were crusts of snow in my matted hair. The moonlight was bright but offered no color. I was slow to understand what had happened: It was the stickiness I realized first, and then, gradually, the fact of blood. My dad must have carried me into the house and called our neighbor, the obstetrician. And then under the light of the white milk-glass lamp in the kitchen, they all lied to me—my mother, my father, and the doctor. They told me that the pain I was feeling was only discomfort from something called—innocuously, enticingly—a butterfly bandage. They figured that I couldn't see the top of my own head, and that I could be tricked into accepting the necessary and graphic procedure if I didn't have to imagine a needle. Children are gullible that way, and adults feel that sometimes a falsehood serves their children better than the hard truth. The fiction worked; I sat still while the doctor pinched the torn flaps of skin and sewed them back together. My bravery in this scene was predicated entirely on my failure to have perceived what was really happening. It seems impossible now to believe that I could ever mistake the sensation of a needle pulling thread through my scalp.

Especially if it was a carpet needle. "But the neighbor didn't use a *carpet needle* on my head, did he?" I ask my father now, logic finally illuminating the stupidity of this question. A carpet needle's gauge is massive. Where did such a notion come from?

My father looks up from across the stainless steel-topped island, a slippery gray shrimp in his hand. He laughs. "No. You must have heard someone compare the needle to a carpet needle. It was curved like one."

"So then the cut on my hand that other time—did you just bandage it up?"

My father seems puzzled by these odd memories and my interest in revisiting them. He keeps his eyes on his work, but he tries to oblige me. "Yeah," he says, pulling off the shrimp's shell, releasing legs and tail in one translucent husk. "Probably a butterfly bandage."

This whole story—I mean *this* one, the bigger one I set out to tell—starts with my going down into that cantina. That was where I was headed, following a tendril of memory, when I got sidetracked by the sight of my own hand and its missing scar. I'd been thinking about my Nonno, my father's father, and how I will be visiting him soon in Florida. He lives there alone in a three-bedroom ranch without Nonna, who passed away almost two years ago, and without a cantina, because you can't dig a deep foundation in Florida's sandy soil. He is adrift there now without those two anchors, floating along in his beige Lay-Z-Boy through days uniformly sunny and warm.

When I go there I want him to tell me his stories about the old country again, all the ones I knew growing up. I've been struggling to write them; when I try to set them on paper, gaps and inconsistencies reveal themselves. Details I used to know have faded; others I thought I knew don't quite fit as pieces in a coherent whole. Then there are other things I never understood, never even thought to ask about. For these stories to *work*, that is, to be transformed into something more than fond family memories, I must track down details, timelines, contexts. Nonno is my best remaining source. And at eighty-nine years old, his memory is starting to fail.

When I think of my Nonno I try not to think about the diminished man who waits for me in his recliner. I want to think of him as the vital man who arrived in this country in 1956 with his wife

and young son and three hundred dollars. It's important that I get his stories right, not just because I am a nonfiction writer, but because I believe that understanding them will help me understand something deeper about my family. I'm not sure what that something is, but I feel driven to know it. I must start in his cantina—that small room in their tri-level house outside Chicago that seemed a portal to the mythical old country.

But to get to the cantina I have to go down those concrete steps, and those steps trip me into that memory of the exploding glass, the torrent of bubbles, the wound. And then the ligature to the other wound: where the thread of a deceitful but well-intended fiction helped stitch my head back together. I don't mean to write about fading scars and misremembered needles, but there they are—interposing themselves and their own metaphoric commentary about the way memory moves and morphs, about the organic and perspective-bound nature of truth, about what we don't know. Still, I started out writing about my Nonno's basement.

So, down the stairs I go again.

II. *to the basement of memory*

At the bottom of those stairs, down one half-level from the green shag carpeting of the family room where we watched Lawrence Welk, down to the foundation of their tri-level home, Nonno had built a storage cellar for his homemade wine. I loved going down there. The cantina's low ceiling, lit by a bare bulb, pressed the fruity, cool air close down around me. The ceiling of Nonno's father's cantina in the farmhouse in Italy, by contrast, had been hung with smoky prosciuttos and hard-rind cheeses. Nonno's was a suburban American adaptation. He'd built low shelves from planks and cinderblocks around the perimeter of the room to hold his purple-stained casks and soldier-rows of wine bottles and a couple six-packs of 7 Up. There were bins of dirt-dusted potatoes, sprouting fantastic, wormy eyes, long-haired onions, and a few other vegetables that had sprung from his backyard garden. The smell in the cantina was earthy and pungent, and, to a girl trying to know her grandparents' world, Italian. No one else I knew had a cantina.

It was my job to go down into the dank cantina to fetch the 7 Up. Nonno and Nonna mixed the sweet, clear pop with their heavy home-made wine to make a spritzer. We didn't call it a spritzer, though, and we didn't call 7 Up by its American name, either. My Zio Bepe, Nonno's brother, had come over from Italy for a visit and tried to read its name on the bottle: "Sette Oop." My brother and I knew *sette*, because Nonno taught us to count in Italian. We liked trying to speak Italian, and we liked the pale pink color of the Sette-Oop in our glasses after Nonno tinted it with some of his *vino*. Italian children grow up drinking wine, he explained. We would too.

Nonno had a distrust of certain Americanisms, such as eating breakfast cereal with cold milk and sleeping late. My brother Mike and I stayed with Nonno and Nonna often on weekends. On Saturday morning Nonno would wake us up early. As we groaned, he'd scold us: "When I was your age, I was already up two hours. I feed the chickens and I make the coffee and *polenta* for *my* Nonno!" His blue eyes sparkled merrily, but he meant it. He was afraid we'd grow up soft and lazy in America.

We learned how to do things at their house. Nonna taught me to crochet and hang wash on the line. Nonno showed me how to whittle sticks with his bone-handled pocketknife and also to use it to cut radicchio for our salad. Their house had a perpetually spotless kitchen on the ground floor where Nonna fixed coffee and maybe a sandwich. But there was a downstairs kitchen—the scene of great culinary labors—one half-level above the cantina. I was apprenticed there. Nonno cranked miles of fresh sausages and beat salt cod with a two-by-four to make tender, pungent *baccala*. Nonna daily churned out fresh, fat loaves of bread, which we ate hot from the oven and slathered with soft ricotta cheese. *Manicotti* were rolled and tucked into baking pans; meaty *sugo* and *minestra* with garden vegetables bubbled in pots; yellow *polenta* cakes sat quivering and cooling on a wooden board. I watched Nonno and Nonna dance past each other from sink to stove, fridge to counter, in a steamy choreography. It was easy to see (and smell and taste) that their cooking was akin to love, and that their food connected us to the old country.

Nonno used to take me by the hand to inspect the garden and teach me what was what. He liked to pluck a sage leaf, *salvia*, soft as a lamb's ear, and rub it on my cheek or on my neck like perfume.

"Smell," he commanded, and I drew that fragrance into my memory for good.

He grew all sorts of things in the yard, and they all bent to his will in tidy rows and clusters. With red begonias or bright yellow marigolds he planted a large G for me and an M for my brother. Our interests were well accounted for in his gardens.

One day a little cage appeared next to the porch. It contained a brown bunny. My parents had never allowed me to have a dog, even though I had begged them ceaselessly for something fluffy to love. Here, at last, Nonno had given me my own pet. I was elated.

Every time we'd visit, I would go bounding around the corner to the hutch and play with my bunny. It was all I had hoped for. I held it on my lap and stroked its long, soft ears. I fed it lettuce through the chicken wire when I wasn't able to take it out. We shared a season in that happy backyard where good things grew just for me.

And then one day as I rounded the corner to my bunny, I saw the cage door standing open. The bunny was gone.

"Nonno!" I shouted. "The bunny escaped!"

Nonna and he were ready for this. They knew I would be devastated and had planned what to say. "Oh, honey, I am so sorry," Nonno told me.

Nonna helped explain, rubbing my back with her large hand. "Your Nonno must have left the cage door a little loose and the rabbit jumped away. I'm sorry."

"It's my fault," Nonno agreed, shaking his head sadly.

I felt the cracking ache in my throat that comes before tears. I did not wish to make Nonno feel bad for his mistake. I walked urgently back over to the hutch and opened and closed the door to see how it must have happened. I looked for clues. I believed their story implicitly, but I didn't want to accept that my pet had just left me like that. I searched among the tomatoes and the begonias until dinner.

We had *polenta* that night—a dense, steaming cake of cornmeal mush. Nonno served this dish often, spooned over with glossy, braised meat chunks. I remember the gravy was especially savory, maybe the best I had ever tasted. I asked for seconds, sopping up the juicy plate with a crust of homemade bread. I never guessed what was on that table until a long time afterward. I was a teenager when the memory of my long lost bunny came to me, finally whole, the truth of it crystallizing in a sudden moment. And luckily for Nonno, it came to me when I was just old enough not to hate him for what he had done, or for his hooting laughter when I figured it out. He'd allowed me to enjoy the bunny while there was time to do so, thinking there was no harm in allowing me that pleasure—the idea of the bunny as mine. His action was based on a cultural logic that I had no right to judge. It was an old country thing that I should respect. But nothing about it just then seemed respectable. What's worse, it was true: the rabbit had been delicious.

III. *and find the place always changing.*

When my father and I surprise him in Florida on his ninetieth birthday, my Nonno is in a sweater vest and long sleeves. It is easily eighty-two degrees outside. He is eating his lunch, prepared by the Honduran woman who is hired to help him and be his companion. A Spanish soap opera blares in the kitchen.

"*Buon compleanno, Nonno!*" I shout at him. And then in English, "Happy birthday!" He smiles, his milky blue eyes brightening. When I hug him, I notice the compactness of his frame, his leanness. He has always been trim, but now he seems somehow taut.

I notice his fingernails are a little too long, that he could use a shave, and that he is missing another tooth. As he carefully chews his bread and cheese and drinks his glass of wine, I feel the weight of silence beneath the loud television. He refuses to wear a hearing aid, which makes conversation difficult. I sit right across the round table from him, yet I feel far away. It is clear, though, that in his quiet way he is happy we have come.

I have come because I love him and think he should not be alone on his ninetieth birthday. My father has come for the same reason. The Honduran woman, Ada, takes me aside and tells me that my grandfather always asks when I will visit. "He loves to you," she tells me in her quirky English, fixing her eyes on mine. "I tell him you comin', you comin'." He has been waiting for six months.

It is true that we have come to be with him for his birthday, but there are other reasons. It is the peak of hurricane season. My dad will make repairs to the air conditioner and assess a leak in the porch ceiling. The house must be kept up so that it retains its value. The tri-level house in Chicago was sold years ago to buy this one outright. It represents a lifetime of work towards the American dream, and it will be my father's inheritance.

My other reason for making this trip is research. I will try to get Nonno to talk about the old country. I want details. Those stories, if I can get them, will be my inheritance.

When my father was thirteen years old, he and his parents left Italy to come to America. That's true. In my mind, before I tried to write these things down, this opening scene always went something like this: I pictured my father as a boy at the rail of an ocean liner, scanning the western horizon for the upraised arm of Lady Liberty. That's false. They took a train from Trieste to Munich and flew to New York. I don't know how the image of the ship got spliced into this story—perhaps it is iconic of the immigrant experience; perhaps I saw such a picture in a history book. But no, there was no boat in my family's story, no ship's manifest to track down, and I have to admit I am sad to edit it out. It was what I *believed* to be true.

Some of what I believed to be true about my father's heritage turns out to be a matter of perspective. My father once posed a riddle to me: *How could I have been born in Italy, and your Nonno, too, but his father was born in the Austro-Hungarian Empire. And all of us were born in the same house, which is in Yugoslavia?*

The answer, of course, is easy once you know it. It goes like this: The ancestral house, not a stone of which has ever been moved, is located in a village called Padena, which in turn is located in a region called Istria. Istria's borders sway with the pressures of geopolitical change the way an amoeba advances and recoils on itself. At present the house rests within the borders of Slovenia (an update to the riddle since the disintegration of the former Yugoslavia). Cousins still live in the house. Because my father and his parents were born in Padena when it was part of Italy, and because they moved to Trieste, they are Italian. See? Easy.

Thus, for all of my childhood, I understood my father's family (and therefore myself) to be Italian. Thus the cantina. This is not untrue.

You would think that the occasion of this cute riddle would also have inspired my father to explain a bit further. Because as it turns out, the story is even more complex: Although they were Italian by birthright, my father's family was actually ethnically Slovenian. It was his first language. It seems the true solution to the riddle, the meaning on a deeper level, is that where you are from does not necessarily dictate who you are.

When the Yugoslavs invaded after Italy collapsed, they brought communism to Padena. True. They conscripted my Nonno, even though he hated communism. He deserted and was recaptured. True and true. And when he escaped again he made his way to his wife and baby who had already sneaked out of Yugoslavia with false papers and were waiting for him in Trieste. I think this is also true. Nonna explained this to me before she died. This is what I want to ascertain from him. I want to understand how he made the choice to leave Yugoslavia. I want details.

Here, today, on his ninetieth birthday. This man who can hardly hear me and who doesn't see me nearly often enough—I want to make him tell me about the day over half a century ago when he ran away from one life to start another while people hunted him with rifles. Yes, I want that story from him.

"I'm recording your voice," I shout at my Nonno, and place my iPhone on the table.

I ask what it was like in the Yugoslavian army. "I don't remember much, that old stuff," he says. His voice is breathy on the recording. It is obvious that this task will be virtually impossible. He once belonged to the army famous for switching sides halfway through the war, and then he was forced to put on a second uniform. Anyone would have trouble keeping it straight.

We talk for an hour. Well, I shout, and he struggles to answer.

After a time I see he is growing tired. I turn off the device and go to the closet where Nonna used to keep all the photo albums. They are still there, near the extra blankets. I pull them out and hand some to my father. There is one she labeled *le vecchie*, the old ones. We begin rifling through them. Nonno gets up from the table and goes to sit in his recliner. Every now and then I bring him one, ask him to identify this person or that. He shrugs. "They are all gone," he says.

I find the photo of him in a studio, one of the only formal portraits I have ever seen of him. He is posing steely-eyed in military jodhpurs, a cigarette in one hand and white gloves clutched in the other. I show him the picture and he seems not to recognize his old self.

❖ ❖ ❖

Matthew Lippman

Autumn Sonata in Backyard

If I drink anymore iced tea I am going to blow my brains out on fallen leaves.
I am going to get out my rake and build a pile of leaves so big
that when I climb to the top with my daughters
we will see Mexico City and Paris.
Here is the thing about Mexico City and Paris—
they both have the Eiffel Tower.
That's the thing about New England in October,
if you drink enough iced tea you can make The Tube in London
and The Great Barrier Reef of Australia
that disappears as we talk. No worries.
We can save Australia with our bent rakes.
We can save Greenland from becoming green
and sometimes we can save the kids in China from the ugly orphanages of Shanghai.
We can rake them up parents out of leaf piles,
give them bowls of hot soup, and blue jeans from The Gap.
It's all about the work, the sweat under our sweaters,
the long sweep followed by a succession of quick short sweeps
for the drought infected states of Iowa, Indiana, and Pakistan.
Sometimes when I blow my brains out in autumn
I go outside with my rake and don't do a thing.
I stand in the middle of the backyard and watch the leaves dance.
Sometimes they are Baryshnikov and sometimes they are Beyoncé.
Sometimes they come together in their own piles and forget they are leaves.
They assume the constitution of my wife, kids, parents, sisters, friends,
my best brother, Mike.
I stand in front of all that colorful decay and think, *this is love, this is love*
this has to be love
still trying to figure out that there is no way to know anything
and then everything blows apart again so that the next morning
I'm out there again, with my daughters,
and we're drinking iced tea, blowing our brains out,
making more piles so big we can see Israel and Peru,
and it's The Leaning Tower of Pisa in Israel and Peru.
The Leaning Tower of Pisa that steadies us straight
and so we make the next pile, and the one after that,
and the red and yellow one with a hint of green
that we jump into and grab and throw up into the air shouting:
the rain, the rain, the beautiful rain.

On Quietness

Sometimes the world of things has something to say. Randall Jarrell wrote that stream water made a sound that was like a spoon or glass breathing.

—Mary Kinzie

In fantasy I'm a hermit. I live in a hut and my poems are my prayers. But in life my "home office" buzzes and dings with computer and printer. I'm a person—writer, teacher, editor—who's too busy, overscheduled, often interrupted, and seldom caught up. Perhaps that explains why I crave quietness. Or could be it's a common human craving. I like the idea of quietly writing at a heavy oak desk, the oak heavy enough, thick enough, solid enough to emit quietness.

Quietness is simpler than silence. Or perhaps simple is not the word I want. It's more familiar, more homey. A quiet night at home might include washing the dishes and reading by the fire. It might include quiet music, quiet conversation, quietly sitting. A quiet day might be a day of cooking and gardening. It might include sweeping the sidewalk.

Silence is more forbidding, perhaps a bit fearsome. A silent night is a holy night. There is such a thing as getting the silent treatment. You can be greeted with a stony silence. To be silent means to refrain from speech. To be silenced is to be repressed, suppressed, censored, shut up.

To be quieted is to be calmed down. The Anglo-Norman and Middle French root of quiet (*quiete*) contains quietude—tranquility.

There are artists who capture quietness in their works, and gazing at their works quiets the mind. One reason I like going to art museums is to quiet my mind. I like going alone, and I may not stay for long.

Here at Seattle's Henry Gallery, I stand before a large-format photograph (four by five feet) of a dry West Texas landscape. A barnyard, fenced with a rough-stick coyote fence, gated with a wide-swinging barnyard gate. An expanse of gravel and dry grass. The vast Texas sky. Close-up, a truck fragment—tire, chrome fender, a blur of red. A shed, shot from ground level, with the rippled roof-edge evidence of corrugated tin. On this dry ground sits a tiny (life-sized) brown-capped bird. The sun is hot. It is quiet, very quiet. You have entered this quiet country, and you see it through the bird's eye. The photographer, Jean-Luc Mylayne, will spend two or three months to get such a picture. All twenty-three of these large-format "landscapes with human traces" include a small bird. Mylayne chooses a spot where birds flock, chooses a particular bird for his subject, and allows the flock to get used to his presence and equipage. He names his large-format photographs according to the time spent—"No. 198 January February 2004."

Is it Mylayne's long quiet days with the birds that communicate quietness to the image and through the image to me the viewer?

Another day in another museum I go looking for another quiet image. I am on a search for what a "quiet image" might mean. Alas, this is family day at the Seattle Art Museum, the day to "Rome the World." The museum is noisy, chattering and laughing, baby-crying, replete with running feet and parental reprimand. I look for quiet corners and quiet images, but nothing is quiet. Is it possible to find quietness amid noise? I believe it is, but not for me, not today. This quiet object I seek—does it exist? Is this quest for quiet entirely subjective, entirely in my head, my own emotional problem or psychological fixation?

No. I'm sure of it. Certain objects emit quietness: wooden spoons, diner mugs, a bowl of pears, old bones, thick books, rocking chairs creaking on old porches.

Wandering the museum, I feel agitated, dissatisfied, slightly lost. This entire museum contains not one quiet thing to look at. I wander about in a desultory manner and then go to lunch at the restaurant. The restaurant is loud like a school cafeteria. But I get seated and have a chicken-salad sandwich and a bowl of potato soup, and I begin to feel better.

Then I go up to the fourth floor, away from most everybody, and there I find a quiet object. It is an ancient figure carved in white marble, female, about a foot and a half high. Her head is oval, featureless except for a triangle nose, abstract-looking, modern-looking. She has small breasts, arms folded over her torso, long thighs, knees oddly bent at a slight angle, toes pointing straight down (was she once viewed from far below?). She dates from 2500 BCE, the Greek Cyclades period. Does her age—human hands carved her more than 4,500 years ago—contribute to the feel of quietness she emits? There's no ornament, no fuss, no striving, no name, little information. Was she a goddess, or was she a girl? Later I google "Cycladic Art" and discover that these were funerary figures, placed on their backs, face up. The stripped-to-essentials abstract-art look results in part from the fact that the paint has worn off.

Gazing at this ancient figure quiets me. Somehow, deep quietness is related to living a meaningful life. Or is "meaningful life" too heavy a term, too sweaty and forced, almost banal, leading to the uninteresting challenge: Meaningful how? Meaningful to whom? Say, rather, that quietness opens the door to a richer interior life. I cross the threshold into that quietest of rooms, and here are the muses in their simple garments. Will they be kind? Will they attend to my case? Will they help me compose a quiet sentence?

Is there such a thing as a quiet sentence? Writing emits sound like a tuba or like the wind, but only when it's read, whether silently or out loud. Bam! Bam! Eek! Don't shoot! Those are loud sentences.

So how would a quiet sentence sound?

Quiet sentences doze in somber shadows. They have sipped smooth Irish whiskey. They mosey along toward nowhere. Across their flat, white plain they softly sigh. They move so slow because they make their own meanings and keep their own time. Their words drift and curl like mist among the locust trees.

Our *Homo sapiens* brain needs the trees, needs to meditate while sitting under trees. Our neurons generate rhythmic electrical pulses (brain waves) including alpha waves (eight to twelve cycles per second) emitted during untroubled focused attention. Alpha waves pulse when we are aroused above sleep, but below anxiety, stress, and other states of being stirred-up, such as thinking and learning. I have a thick book titled *Zen and the Brain* (by James H. Austin), which states that it is not only alpha waves but the synchronicity of neurons thrumming in unison from different parts of the brain that characterizes mindful attention. Synchronous brain oscillations suggest quietness.

One more museum: Seattle's Asian Art Museum, Buddhas, Bodhisattvas (those saintly souls who forego Nirvana in order to stick around and help others attain enlightenment). I sit before a life-sized wooden female GuanYin, the Bodhisattva of Compassion, carved in tenth-century China. She is seated, meditating, one knee drawn up, one foot on the ground. Her mudras (hand positions) on the one hand touch the ground (steadfastness) and on the other hand, bless. I sit before her on the bench provided. I have my cynical thoughts: What temple was this sacred figure stolen from, when, and by whom? What is a tenth-century Chinese deity doing in twenty-first century Seattle?

I look up at her. I decide to stay here for twenty minutes, to take in her blessing. The artist who carved her must have felt her quietness. Many hours, many years of learning to carve so skillfully her robe, her benign face, her benevolence. I breathe. I feel quieter and quieter. I must ignore another museum patron entering the gallery. I do ignore. I sit alone with GuanYin. My breathing slows. I can almost feel my brain slowing to alpha. Now I'm really here, hushed, attentive—receptive to Guan Yin, her quietness, her eternal quietude.

❖ ❖ ❖

Dan O'Brien

The War Reporter Paul Watson Retiring

I'm still hoping to be found by the ghost
of my father. I get that. It doesn't
take much brains. I'm simply willing to go
where no sane person should. And I get praise
for it. Feels good. A colleague once called me,
Adventure Journalist! but the bad guys
who want to kill us aren't hanging out
at the hotel pool. But that's no excuse
for leaving a son without a father
or my wife without income. She begs me
every chance she gets, This is ruining you!
Ha ha ha. She wants to squeeze a promise
out of me. So I say, Okay, you're right,
I'm done. But the moment I get off Skype
I'm planning my next war. I was speaking
to my editor recently and she said,
We're going to have to close down the bureau
soon, at which point I don't know what we'll do
with you. And I was like, Sorry, what's that
supposed to mean? Well, I'm sure you're aware
you have a reputation for being
kind of this quirky reporter. Sucking
dirt in hellholes like Afghanistan, and
basically what she's saying is, You're not
useful anymore. Useful was her word
exactly. And it felt like a vacuum
sucking out my guts. And I blew—I blew
my top! First of all. I screamed and I hung
the phone up on her. I have some trouble
waking up still. After lunch I like to
go back to sleep. I'd like to resurrect
myself somehow, I'd love to feel the blood
flooding my veins. But instead the Devil's
got hold of me. Ha ha ha. I suppose
I just have zero tolerance now. The world's
disabused me, so I've simply begun
disabusing myself of the world.

Lew Harris. *Coming and Going at the U.S. Open.* Digital photograph. 2013. 36 x 48 inches.

Thomas M. Atkinson

Red, White & Blue

I saw Gwen under the Aqua-Mule sign, with a hoarfrost of powdered sugar caught in the fine hairs of her upper lip. She had her arm around Chief, steadying him, the fresh stump of his wrist resting lightly on her shoulder, cuffed in clean white gauze. Her little girl Amber was sneaking sips from the seven-ounce Little Kings dangling from his good arm, and when she smiled, her teeth were stained red with sno-cone.

Amber'd gotten a little honeybee painted on her face. And I wondered if she picked it out herself or if her mom told her, "That'd be cute." "Honeybee" is what I call Gwen. It popped into my mind the very first time I saw her, when Amber was just a baby, picking out off-brand diapers at the Dollar General. I think because she was so tiny, but not skin-and-bones like she is now. She had the same dirty blond hair and big, dark eyes and that hum just under her skin. That first time in she bought diapers and some little dime boxes of candy cigarettes we had leftover from broken bags of Halloween treats. They can't call them candy cigarettes anymore so they call them candy batons. I didn't say anything when I rang her up, but she opened up one of those boxes and worked one slender stick into her mouth and back out again. She had a white smudge down the center of both lips, with a faint streak of red from the painted ember, like one of those old Japanese geisha girls. She said, "I love these things." She smiled at me with teeth like so many sun-polished seashells and I tried to smile back with my lips together. One of my front teeth has a corner broken off, from a different kind of baton. She had a beautiful smile back then. She asked if I was new.

I didn't know it then, but I'd already met Chief, actually worked with him on a roofing crew my first job in town. Me and two local 'billies stripped the old roofs off with Number Two coal shovels and then grunted seventy-five-pound bundles of shingles up a ladder so Chief could tack them down with an air gun. I like him, always have, even when it'd be easier not to. He didn't care that I had tits, because I never held up the show, but the other two wouldn't let it alone. One day I guess Chief got as sick of hearing "dyke" as much as me and chased one of the 'billies across somebody's front yard shooting roofing nails at him with the air gun. He ducked down behind Chief's truck, and Chief let loose a half-dozen nails to rattle around inside the bed, just to let him know what was what. It seems like I might have even met Gwen when we'd all stop for a beer after work, but for some reason I can't remember. I got the job at Dollar General, which is a lot easier, and it wasn't long before the Mexicans put Chief out of business anyway. The money's not as good, but at least my knees and shoulders don't hurt all the time and I don't run through all the hot water in the trailer trying to get the shingle grit out of my hair. Less chance I'll need the health insurance I still don't have. That roof work'll make you old before your time. Chief got on over at Discount Tire with Billy and Grimace. At least he was.

When they started walking, I followed at a distance, between the square trailers selling cotton candy, corn dogs and nachos, funnel cakes and sno-cones. And layered over all of the other smells, a thin fog of manure from all the animals judged this morning. There were still a few black-faced sheep huddled in the corner of an unfamiliar pen, waiting on a truck or a trailer, and the girl who raised them up was flirting with a county deputy twice her age. Gwen's loose jeans started riding down her sharp hips and when she bent over to say something to Amber, I could see the tattoo across the small of her back.

Close behind me, somebody said, "She got herself a tramp stamp."

I turned and said, "Hey, Karl. What brings you out in the sun?"

Karl's my probation officer, but as long as I do

what I'm supposed to, he doesn't give me much crap.

Karl said, "Wife. Kids. Hereditary predisposition to fried food. Pick one."

I didn't think you could get Karl's fat ass out from behind his desk with a pop bottle full of gas and a match.

I said, "I didn't even know you had legs."

He considered his legs for a moment and twisted one foot in the sawdust.

He said, "I'm supposed to be getting more exercise. Beats getting whiplash on these rides." He pointed his chin toward Gwen and said, "When'd Skin 'n Bones get that?"

And I said, "It's been awhile."

I cried when she got it, and I don't cry too often, at least not in front of people. The small of her back was my favorite spot, those two dimples. I can't even find where they used to be now that she's wasted away to nothing.

Karl said, "What's it supposed to be?"

"She says it's 'tribal.' Whatever that means."

Chief's supposed to have some Shawnee in him and looks it, Indian or Scots-Irish, or maybe Melungeon, which is probably nothing more than the first two combined. Every time Gwen takes my big head in her hands and pushes her thin fingers through my hair until she's too weak to get in any deeper, she says, "You got the same hair. You could be kin." And Amber got it too.

Karl said, "'Tribal,' my ass. The closest any of her people got to an Indian was nailed to a lodge pole."

It's not that she was perfect before the tattoo, but she was perfect to me. She has a few scars from childhood, some scars not from childhood. But they're all honest—she didn't blow some greasy biker for any of them and have to pretend "tribal" means something.

Karl looked back over his shoulder and then back at Gwen.

He bunched his lips up to one side and said, "You know, that hand ain't gonna help that train wreck."

I thought about that for a minute and said, "No, I don't guess."

He said, "Well, back to the bosom of my loving family. If I start at the Scrambler and follow the trail of puke . . . "

He wandered off toward the rides. He walked backwards for a few steps and called, "Keep your nose clean."

They walked slowly, Gwen with her arm around Chief, Chief and Amber holding either end of the same small green beer bottle. When they got to the games, Amber shook the bottle and pointed to the Bozo Balloons booth and a stuffed animal up on the high "three wins" shelf. You're supposed to shoot a stream of water into a clown's mouth with a water-pistol, which fills up a balloon on his head. If you get enough water in there to blow up the biggest balloon, you win. But the water pressure goes up and down, so it's really hard to keep it going in the clown's mouth. Chief slapped down a five dollar bill and won two games in a row, drowning the purple clown without a wasted drop. Not too many dead drunks are a dead shot, but Chief didn't blink or waver, and Amber squealed encouragement behind him. Gwen looked at me with her dark eyes and smiled from behind her pale, blue-veined fist. She never used to do that, hide her mouth like that, not back before all the rot set in along the gumline. And I can't remember when her eyes started to look fake as a doll's. On the third game, the water pressure suddenly dropped, dropped enough to make Chief lose his aim and the game.

Chief slid a dollar of his change across the counter and pointed the white cap of his stump at the worker. He said, "Mess with that pressure pedal again, I'll shove this up your ass and break it off."

The worker took a step back with both hands up in surrender and said, "Like I'm getting paid."

Chief got his third win and Amber collected her unicorn with the glittery horn. Chief wandered off, and Gwen looked at me over the top of Amber once more before chasing after him and hooking onto one of his belt loops.

Behind me, Karl said, "You still here?"

He was eating a funnel cake off a limp paper plate and his shirt was dusted with powdered sugar.

I said, "Yeah, just watching the games."

He looked at the purple clown in the Bozo Balloons and said, "Damn if that don't look just like Grimace's shrunken head up there."

Grimace dropped the backhoe on Chief's hand Thursday when he was setting a jack-stand and nobody's seen him since. He wouldn't be hard to find if anybody was looking because he burned his whole head up a few years back when the batch of meth he was cooking blew up. He comes in the General with his senile mother and he wears a knit cap year around pulled down over the nubs of his ears and there's not enough nose left to hold up a pair of sunglasses. He cashes in all the change he steals out of customers' cupholders at Discount Tire and shoplifts eyeliner pencil to draw eyebrows on the violet, puckered skin. I look the other way. Somebody named him after that thing in the old McDonald's commercials. But nobody's looking.

I said, "He wouldn't be hard to find if anybody was looking."

Karl took the last bite of his funnel cake and said, "You're right about that, you surely are. 'If anybody was looking.'"

I said, "You know, we've got the same probation officer."

Karl worked on the greasy sugar stuck to the plate with one finger.

He said, "Why drag him back? Work at the freak show?"

I watched Gwen, still hooked onto Chief's belt loop.

I said, "They don't have freak shows anymore."

When I was a kid up north, my stepdad took me to see the Fish Man. On the poster out front he had scales and a tail, but he was really just an old WWII vet who'd lost his bottom jaw. They'd sewn a flap of skin across the opening and he wore dark blue mountain-climbing goggles, and a woman, maybe his wife, fed him with a turkey baster pushed into the back of his throat. I didn't sleep right for months.

Karl said, "No, I guess there's not much demand for tattooed men, fat ladies, and somebody with bolts jabbed through their johnson when you can see all that up at the Wal-Mart for free."

Gwen disappeared into the crowd, still haloed in Chief's black t-shirt.

I said, "He's alone out there somewhere."

Karl said, "'Alone.' That's what happens to you when you fuck up. I bet when you hooked your finger through that little college prick's ear and spun his head around like a bread bag, you never thought you'd be here, sniffing after some meth skank's ass through a county fair."

He wasn't being mean, just matter-of-fact. I didn't have to like it, but there wasn't much to

argue with. It was in a bar back home, before they asked me leave. I was playing eight-ball and some drunk college kid with big holes gauged in his earlobes said something, not about me, but about the boy I was shooting with. Turns out his dad was somebody, over in Youngstown I think, and drove a dusty rose Lincoln to the trial. There'd been some other trouble, but when that ear finally tore loose, it's like they cut the cord.

Karl said, "Don't worry about Paul."

And I said, "Who's Paul?"

Karl said, "Grimace. His name's Paul."

I'd heard his mother call that out in the General, but I never thought she was talking to him.

Karl said, "Better go see if my youngest lost an eye trying to pop a balloon with a dull dart."

I found them out in the bleachers, waiting for the demolition derby to start. I sat six rows behind them, a little to one side, far enough over to see her neck and the little crescent scar behind her left ear, the flat plane of her cheek, the yellow tint of her eye. Karl was sitting with his fat little wife, and she was holding a wet napkin to the neck of a fat little boy, and a fat little girl was hooting nonstop through a rolled-up poster. Johnny-On-The-Spot was standing between the bleachers and the concrete barricades with a girl in the shortest skirt I've ever seen, and everyone there was praying for a mosquito or a black fly or a light breeze.

Chief had caught Gwen with him even though he couldn't be seventeen, tracked them out to his grandmother's trailer. She's another regular at the General, with one of those little electric carts with a green oxygen tank in the basket up front. Chief kicked holes in the walls and stomped all Grandma's furniture to matchsticks. Then he pissed down the kid's back. That's why everybody calls him Johnny-On-The-Spot, after those green fiberglass toilets they truck out to the state park every summer. He looks a lot like a guy I liked back home, tall and thin like he'd been put on a taffy-puller, back when I still thought I might like guys. We used to shoot pool together, and once I cooked him breakfast after the bars closed, and when I drove him home, I put my arm across the back of the seat. When we got to his place, I leaned in to kiss him and he let me, but there was that little something in his eyes that let me know I had it wrong. Maybe I was just trying to make someone jealous. I guess Gwen must have let the cat out of the bag about the piss down his back since there was just the three of them in the room. Chief wouldn't be bragging his wife was with some high school kid, and god knows Johnny wouldn't be spreading that around. Grandma was passed out on oxy in the front room, probably with her tank still on and a menthol burning in the ashtray. I don't know what his real name is. It seems like Gwen might have told me, but I can't remember.

Gwen stood up and bent down to talk into Chief's ear, her hand resting on his shoulder. Then she said something to Amber before she side-stepped her way to the aisle and down the shallow steps. I watched her, and I watched Chief watching her, as she passed by Johnny and his girlfriend. He knew she was coming because he turned to talk to his sweetheart, so he could look casually past her ear to see Gwen. He looked away and a flicker of a smile, just at the corners, played over Gwen's face. I doubt if Chief saw it, not from where he was sitting, but he had to know it was there. It's not like I needed to see it.

I gave her another fifty yards before I got up to trail her to the restrooms. Amber turned to watch me go.

When she came out of the middle stall, I said, "Hey, Honeybee."

We were sitting side by side on the tongue of the funnel-cake trailer. The sweet grease smell hung over us like a veil and the faint warmth of her thigh found its way through two layers of denim to mine. And even though the second heat of the demolition derby had already started and the trailer was tucked up right against the back wall of the bleachers, the sound was far, far away, like high school boys racing way down the valley on a Friday night. I was brushing powdered sugar from Gwen's cheek with the edge of my pinkie when Amber found us. She stared at me and drug one finger through the paint on her cheek.

Amber said, "Daddy's gone crazy."

Gwen said, "What, Sweetie?"

Amber screwed her mouth to one side and said, "He couldn't find you. And now he's got it bleeding again."

I followed them at a distance, behind families with strollers and school kids holding hands, back through the rows of games and past the animals, out to the music stage across from the Aqua-Mule tank. Chief was up onstage with his shirt off, stomping around the amplifiers and mic stands, screaming wild-eyed and waving his bloody-bandaged stump at the gathering crowd.

Karl walked up and stood beside me. He watched Chief for a moment before he said, "Looks like the show's about to start."

Across the way, an old farmer led a dirty white mule between the rails of the ramp that switch-backed up fifteen feet to the platform above the tank. Gwen held Amber in front of her, one arm across her chest holding her back, the other between her shoulder blades pushing her forward. And with small, awkward steps, maybe from being so close, they worked their way toward the stage, the crowd parting and filling back in behind them.

I said, "Aren't you going to do something?"

Karl said, "Like I'm getting paid."

And I said, "You're some kind of half-assed cop. Don't you have a badge or something?"

Karl said, "Yeah, I got a badge. And I got a gun out in the car. But if I'm going to go all the way out there, I'll just see if I can't get Deputy Duane to stop hitting on the middle-schoolers in the parking lot long enough to come and sort this out."

The mule paused on his ramp, and the farmer whacked at the boards behind him with a switch to start him. Chief saw Gwen and pointed the ghost of his finger at her.

He said, "Why'm I always hunting you down?"

Gwen said something, but I couldn't hear what, and Chief shook his head sad and slow.

I looked at Karl and said, "You could stop this."

And Karl sighed and said, "Well, that makes two of us."

Chief pointed with his stump again, this time behind her, and said, "It's Aqua-Mule time."

Everyone turned at once to watch the mule trembling up on his high platform. Gwen worked Amber around behind her and they stood back to back, Gwen still watching Chief, and Amber, the Aqua-mule. Chief considered the empty space just beyond his wrist and slowly rolled his forearm from side to side, touching each invisible fingertip to his invisible thumb, lost in those infinite impossibilities. The old farmer growled and hit his switch against the side of the tank. The mule knelt and stretched his long neck down toward the blue-dyed water. He hit the tank again, but the mule wouldn't dive. Chief wiped the stump across one cheek, painting a broad red stripe with the wet bandage.

Gwen said, "No, baby, no." And Amber closed her eyes.

He painted the other cheek, then down the center of his face from his hairline to his chin. He began to howl softly and the old farmer yelled, "Don't make me come up there!"

Then he jumped, and everybody cheered.

❖ ❖ ❖

She'll come by tonight, tapping on my trailer door, so softly it's like something you're remembering, like a dream when you think you're awake. And I'll open the door, just enough to let her slip in, and fold her inside my flannel shirt for as long as I can, her rotting breath warm against my breasts.

But I wish she wouldn't. I wish she'd stay home. Just this once. Just tonight.

❖ ❖ ❖

Hurt

You are the beautiful half
Of a golden hurt.

　　　　–Gwendolyn Brooks

It's always me
that brings
the ugly—
the afghan, the fat
grey cat
in the way,
the back
of my head—
Not tonight,
honey—pressed
to a man's face.

Few have grace
enough to try
and change it,
to love it down.

Cause I
am the girl
who rode her bike
to a world
ten miles
over the state line
at thirteen
to kiss a boy.

That day,
on my way
back into Florida,
all I wanted
was to say, *Yes!*
I have something
to declare
from Georgia—
the boy I love
bruised my neck
like a peach

with his teeth.
I ought to be
inspected,
officer,
detained even.
I am
water-wild,
beach baby,
I am the yes
kind of girl,
not the maybe.

But I had seen
something else—
if you trust,
if you lean
into something
impossible,
it'll drop you flat
on your ass,
on the banana seat
of a hot pink
Huffy, your legs
pedaling the
seasick air
for the next
thirteen years.

Habemus Papam

O goodum!   *Habemus Papam*
who'll soon intone
the usual crapam

and the poor poor will weepum

and the rich will yawn
and eatem
like pablum

Gianna Russo

Way Out West: Sonny Rollins, 1955

He holds his saxophone like
an oasis and within it, a mirage
of desert gold, pink oranges and prickly
pear. Las Vegas reflects
itself up and down the finger
stops, coins of sunset, and when
he hits the Desert Inn that club will
swing, man, to his ever-living
breath, his fingers
flicking off those notes like
champagne bubbles that tickle
the nose of his audience, held rapt,
swayin' in their seats, in love
with that sound, man, he can blow
sweet jesus on that thing and
only the black pitch in his eyes and
the wooly arm of the Joshua tree
remind you that, like Sammy Davis,
he'll be using the back door
to all that town's glitter and God knows,
they don't let colored boys swim in the pools.

based on the photograph by William Claxton

Catherine M. Chastain-Elliott. *My Father's View*. 2012. Acrylics and Georgia red clay. 18 x 24 inches. Photo by J. M. Lennon.

Bark Beetles

THEY LIVED on a cul-de-sac. The mother, graceful as she was, spent her days pouring tapwater into floral arrangements while the Magnavox hummed through the wall, dramatic music telegraphing moments she would never experience firsthand. There were too many rooms, a bed no longer slept in though she made sure the sheets were always fresh. Packages were left conspicuously on the doorstep, even when a signature was required. The son, obedient as he was, attended Sunday school at the Methodist Church, solved Ten Commandments find-a-word puzzles in a portable behind the chapel. He leaned his bike against streetlamps, knocked on doors to houses that looked similar to his own only to find out that no one was home due to the neverending pull of teams, lessons, vacations. The big news—if you could call it news—was the neighbor's potting shed washed into the creek during a freak October storm, but they were able to salvage the jars of blackberry jam and still give them out at Christmas with little bells tied to the bow.

The mother, however, never complained. This was the contract she entered into, her compensation for a life of comfort, safety. The luxury to budget her own time, read magazines after her chores were complete while others squirreled away behind too-small desks answering phones for men who they would eventually have to rebuff. There was no renegotiating. Such was the nature of contracts in that day and age. The son didn't watch this unfold, rather absorbed it like gas fumes from a balky pump. He discerned the fine print using other senses—a twisted gut, tingling at the base of his skull—and there was an everpresent feeling that someday the whole accord might make the mother sick, but he felt unqualified to express this at such a young age. The son, through no fault of his own, was born intuitive. Not smart, rather an antenna for the refracted energy that bounced around in the mother's life—invisible wavelengths of ambi-

tion as she prepared dinner while her husband did push-ups after work, half-smiles illuminating prison break fantasies as she stood on a chair and dusted cobwebs from the exposed beams above the flagstone fireplace. If she felt trapped, she would never admit it, not even to the son. A cage with golden bars, perhaps, but a nice life in a nice town.

If there was one blemish on their otherwise pleasant slice of nirvana, it was the spur line of the Southern Pacific railroad that ran behind their quarter acre. Nirvana. That's what the father called it. *How was your day, son?* He would say as he pulled his briefcase out of the Buick. *Nirvana treating you right?*

The train did its best to temper any suggestion of paradise, rumbling by every day during the mother's favorite soap opera. The conductor was required by law to sound his horn at the nearby school crossing, and the mother, hanging on every word, refused to miss a single confession of love or murder from her favorite stars, who went by names such as Brent and Tad and Jacqueline. Her solution was to move the television to an unlikely spot as far from the tracks as possible, a nook in the foyer protected from the white noise of the encroaching world. It proved a worthy fix.

After unloading its cargo, the train would return shortly after school ended, just in time for the son to sit on the back fence and watch it pass. He imagined throwing a rock at the boxcar once he was sure the conductor could no longer see, but if he did this he was certain the train would screech to a halt and armed guards would jump off, taking him into custody. The son's only solace came from knowing he was a good hider and their yard possessed many good hiding spots, the most prominent being the Trees.

They were Monterey Pines. Big and indestructible, the trees were a world unto themselves. With branches crisscrossing under their own weight, they would drop cones that felt like hand grenades, and the son would use them to play fetch with their border collie Princess, that is until the vet said she was ingesting too much sap. The father intervened at this point, insisting the son collect the pine cones in a bucket and dump them in the trash. It always seemed to happen this way. Just when things got going, they came to an end. The balloon only stayed afloat so long. It would sag, then lie on the ground motionless, refusing to pop. But that was about to change.

❖ ❖ ❖

It was Monday night. The mother cooked Hungarian goulash, providing the disclaimer she only had smoked paprika so the flavor might be a little challenging. Cooking was the closest she could get to visiting exotic locales, which explained the tacos and corned beef and manicotti. The family sat at a round table, the one with a chip taken out of it where the father had demonstrated a proper baseball swing but misjudged the distance. The table could accommodate four, but there were only three now and the chances of another place setting being laid out were dwindling.

"They're moving the vanpool," the father said, sipping skim milk, "down to St. Mary's. I'll have to carve out another ten minutes."

"I'll set the alarm," the mother said.

"You still playing ball after school?" the father asked the son.

"A little bit," the son said.

"When they pick teams, get on the one with that Ellis kid and watch what he does—it'll help your game."

"Okay," said the son.

The mother passed the chopped iceberg in a bowl so large it was difficult to lift. She always made too much salad and the father would shake his head, make comments about feeding the Red Army.

"Rode with this guy, works for Hextel," the father said as he switched hands with his fork, a habit the son watched with keen interest. "Told me the darnedest thing. Said they had a five-year contract to build the airport in Bombay and four years into it these geniuses realize the planes are getting bigger so—*bam*—they have to start over. Government hires them back for five more years so they can build longer runways. Isn't that just something? What a racket."

The mother liked this story, not for its caution-ary tale about the inefficiency of government, rather for its far-flung locale.

"I remember when we landed in Waikiki," she said, "flying over those houses right by the beach, but they still had swimming pools. You wouldn't think they'd need swimming pools with such beautiful ocean all around—"

"That was forever ago. You should see the planes now. They're like cities in the sky. Things are changing so fast you can't keep track. Which reminds me—I hired a crew."

"A crew?" the mother seemed surprised.

"The pine trees. They're infested."

"What do you mean *infested*?" the mother said.

The son could tell she didn't like this word. He felt his fingertips buzz, an itch on the sole of his foot.

"Bark beetles," the father said. "Tom recommended these guys. Definitely the right price for such a big job."

"What about the hydrangeas and camellias? They need shade."

"Don't worry, we'll kick it up a notch in the spring. Stuff that loves the heat."

"What about my fort?" the son asked.

"I'll make you a deal," the father whispered as his fork jumped from his left hand to his right. "You let me take out these trees, and next year I'll build you a swimming pool just like the ones in Waikiki, only bigger. How does that sound? A couple cannonballs and you won't give a hoot about your dusty old fort."

❖ ❖ ❖

The work crew drove up in a truck with ply-wood siding. The neighbor across the street called to make sure everything was okay, but the mother was busy peeking out from behind the curtain in her sewing room and couldn't get to the phone. She watched as a group of six men, Latinos wearing flannel workshirts and scuffed boots, made their way to the front door. They were greeted with a sign the father had taped up that read *do not knock/side gate open*. The men returned to the truck and collected their things—chainsaws, ropes, dented garbage cans, and bags full of what appeared to be their lunches. The mother was confused by the fact they didn't have ladders. The trees were easily sixty feet tall, some rising higher. How would they get up there? Then a second car pulled up and a man got out—slender, handsome with cropped hair and wine-red cowboy boots. He kept a large knife on his belt, and the mother wondered if that was even legal. The man spoke confidently to the crew in Spanish, and they immediately picked up their pace, marched around the side of the house.

The man did not follow them. He opened the passenger door and replaced his cowboy boots with work boots, then grabbed what looked like a pair of ice skates and slung them over his shoulder. He glanced up at the house, his eyes stopping briefly at the sewing room window. Startled, the mother dropped to her knees and crawled into the bathroom hoping he hadn't seen her. She could feel the cool tile on her skin, wondered how she could have been in this house so long and never seen it from this point of view. She noticed some mold forming on the grout, made a mental note to scrub it when a loud knock jolted her back to the moment and her head banged the lip of the sink. *Can't he read the sign?* The mother held her breath, but he knocked again. Realizing this man was nothing if not persistent, she checked her make-up in the mirror, brushed out the crease in her blouse, and went to the door. She took a deep breath, then opened it.

"Hello, m'am, my name is Roque Diaz. I'm here for the trees."

"Yes, of course," the mother replied. He had light brown eyes and a cut on his cheek that was healing. She was surprised a man this young could run his own business, let alone one this involved.

"It can be alot of . . . *commotion* . . . so if there is anything you prefer we do differently, then please tell me."

"Thank you," the mother said, embarrassed as she removed the do-not-knock sign.

"Why don't you come this way—the trees are out back."

"Your floors," the man said pointing to his dirty boots.

"They're all scuffed anyway," she said, noticing that what she first thought were ice skates were something else altogether. Carved out of dark wood and polished by hand, they were laced with a brightly woven piece of red and orange rope. On the side were the initials R.D. inlaid with the muted rainbow of mother of pearl. Driven through each toe were two large spikes, their freshly sharpened tips reflecting the sun-

light like a prism onto the ceiling. Roque realized she was studying them.

"My fangs," he said.

"Oh," the mother said, slightly confused.

"For climbing. I make them myself. That way if I fall, I know it's my own fault."

Roque smiled, gave a little bow, then walked around the house to join his crew.

❖ ❖ ❖

When the son returned from school he was startled. Jutting skyward were two massive trunks cut clear of all limbs, like knights stripped of their armor. There were huge branches dangling from ropes, men yelling at each other in a language he didn't understand while others scrambled like ants over the tangled heaps, chainsaws roaring so loud they rattled the windows.

The son looked up and saw, high atop the tree, a man moving effortlessly with a spinning blade just inches from his leg. He would inspect, cut, then move swiftly to the next limb. It reminded the son of the time he went to the river and jumped from rock to rock without stopping, confident he would make it across without falling in.

Beneath the man there were no nets. He would yell down and someone on the ground would snap to attention, perform whatever task was demanded. The son realized that out of the entire crew, this man was the only one allowed to climb. His expertise commanded complete respect, almost like a god. That's when this man, the climber, saw the boy.

"Ah, we've been waiting for you. Did you bring your saw?" Roque yelled down, smiling.

The son became embarrassed and ran into the house. He immediately noticed something different—the television was off. Instead of finding his mother pouring distilled water into the iron or sorting a stack of bills, she stood in the kitchen window watching the flurry of activity outside, sipping a glass of wine.

"They're from El Salvador," she said. "They drink orange soda for breakfast."

"Oh," the boy responded, but he could feel his mother was someplace else.

"So much light," she said, almost to herself.

It was unclear if that was a good thing or a bad thing.

❖ ❖ ❖

At the end of the day, Roque directed his crew to stow their gear beneath a blue tarp along the fence. The son watched from a safe distance, his bicycle turned upside down as he did his best to tune it up. He checked the wheel to see if it was spinning true, then tugged the chain to make sure it was properly tightened. Roque jogged over as though he still had all the energy in the world. He pulled a tin of saw oil out of his back pocket.

"The bike shop wouldn't use this stuff, but chains are chains, sí? Sometimes we make do."

He showed the son how to apply it to each roller, then pedal backwards wiping gently with a rag.

"I think it's working," the boy said.

"You take care of things *before* they give you trouble," Roque said approvingly, "that's half the fight."

"What can you see from up there?" the son asked, pointing to the treetops.

"Oh, not much. There's a meadow in those hills over there," Roque said.

"A meadow?"

"You know, the one where the bears play chess."

"Bears can't play chess."

"And past the meadow I saw a boy . . . how old are you?"

"Seven."

"I saw a boy just your age toss a penny into the Grand Canyon."

"The Grand Canyon? That's the desert."

"Yes, it is. And if I squeezed my eyes like this . . . I could see the Empire State Building."

"You mean New York?"

"It's nighttime there. All the lights are blinking."

The mother walked out, curious about what she had missed.

"Mom, he says bears can play chess."

"Is that right?" she smiled.

"I didn't say they were good at it! I also saw something else. . . . I'm not sure if I should tell you," Roque winked at the mother, then bent down to whisper to the son. "Do you know about El Duende?"

"No," said the son with concern.

"They are little people who live in the trees. How do you say . . . gnomes? Sometimes they're your friend, sometimes they trick you. They like to steal things and hide them on the highest branch. Today, I found this."

Roque handed the boy a toy submarine, the kind you wind up and the propeller spins.

"If your mother says it's okay, you can have it."

The son smiled and looked to his mother, who nodded. He said thank you, then bounded away.

Roque turned around but his crew had returned to the truck. He stood there alone with the mother in the near dark, a warm wind sending a little cloud of pollen swirling to the east over the railroad tracks.

❖ ❖ ❖

The next morning the son was late for school as he waited on the front porch for Roque to arrive. The mother, realizing the uniqueness of the opportunity, did not rush him out the door, rather had the son put out a tray of orange juice and some deck chairs so the workers could get a fresh start. The crew showed up in their truck, but no Roque. The mother, hiding her disappointment, ushered them out back and wrote an office note for the son.

Nearly an hour had passed when Roque sped into the cul-de-sac, made a u-turn, and stopped just shy of the mailbox. The mother watched as he hurriedly changed into his work clothes, then noticed a bandage on his hand. She came out to see what happened.

"There were police this morning," Roque confessed. "Someone took a . . . *prisoner* . . . at the bank across the street. They used my window to set up rifles."

"Oh, my god, I heard that on the news. You live there?"

"I told them I had to work, but they wouldn't let me out so I climbed down the fire escape in the back."

"Roque, that's crazy."

"I reached down, there was a broken bottle. It's not a big deal."

"My god, we need to get you to the hospital," the mother insisted, noticing blood seeping through his bandage.

"No, no. I'm fine."

The mother didn't want to admit it, but she was excited by Roque's willingness to defy authority, to test the messy space between what we accept as right and wrong. She was fascinated by what it must be like to have no choice in the matter, to push ahead not because you should, but because you have to as a matter of survival. She had always wrestled with the idea that the ends justify the means, even wrote a letter to the editor once defending the actions of a local janitor who resorted to growing marijuana in order to pay for his daughter's dialysis.

Then the mother realized that while Roque was busy eluding the police during a hostage standoff, she was home washing her husband's coffee mug, placing it upside down on the stove to dry like she did every morning. As she considered this, Roque surprised her with a bag filled with some sort of treat.

"Pupusas," he said. "We ran out of pork, so I brought chicken." He sounded almost apologetic.

"What? After all you've been through?"

She felt the warmth through the bag, started to ask where he got them, but stopped herself when she noticed they were clearly homemade, each one wrapped carefully with the ends of the paper fanned out like a flower. Definitely a woman's touch.

"The jobs in the city, we have to rent equipment. All the permits. Out here is a blessing—we can do it the old-fashioned way."

"It's refreshing to find someone so content with what they have."

"You know how that is," Roque said.

"Well, some of us put on a good face."

Roque seemed confused by this, an awkward confession that veered into unfamiliar territory. He quickly changed the subject.

"I have something for your son," he said, pulling out a toy dragon.

"Please, you don't have to keep doing this. He's got enough toys."

"Not me," said Roque, "El Duende."

❖ ❖ ❖

The students sat down well before the recess bell rang. Their parents had made it clear if they wanted to get into top colleges they would need to start now, establish an aptitude for core subjects while at the same time maintaining an appropriate degree of civility on the playground. The first step was catching the teacher's eye. She was a perky Princeton grad who sounded like she was asking a question when in fact she was making a statement. She always wore a tight ponytail and jogged around the man-made lake on weekends. The teacher was incapable of putting

her foot down, but that wasn't necessary at this school. The kids policed themselves. Some even ate avocado on their sandwiches.

During show-and-tell the son raised his hand first. The teacher was surprised. The son never volunteered for these types of things, and she wanted to encourage the quiet ones to take initiative, so she picked him immediately. He walked to the front of the class and without looking up removed a piece of wood from his bag, peeled the bark away carefully revealing an elaborate network of tunnels that had been bored along its surface. The tunnels snaked in oblong patterns like contours on a topographical map. He explained they were the result of an infestation, that the culprits were five millimeters long, black with six legs. There was a beauty to the destruction, a painterly repetition of detail that the son understood on some level, though he could not express this to the class.

"So where are the they?" one of his classmates asked.

"Where are who?" the son responded.

"The beetles."

"They hide from people. That's why we didn't know they were there until it was too late."

"Do lumberjacks really yell *timber* when they chop down a tree?" another student asked.

"I'm not sure. They speak Spanish."

"If this is show-and-tell," the first classmate said, unable to let the matter go, "and you don't *show* beetles, then I think that's false advertising."

The class began to laugh. The son's face turned red.

"That's enough," the teacher intervened.

The son quickly returned the wood to his bag. His heart raced. He couldn't feel the floor as he walked back to his seat. As the class continued to laugh, he felt like a fool. He didn't even know what false advertising was.

❖ ❖ ❖

The son walked on the highway instead of the railroad tracks, avoiding his classmates. He took his time, creeping closer to the white line until he could feel the blast of air from oncoming traffic, taste the metallic dust of antifreeze. The car horns didn't phase him as they blared past. In fact, they gave him strength.

When he finally made it home and opened the side gate, his spirits were lifted. The mother had laid out a picnic blanket in the far corner of the yard, a safe distance from the crashing branches yet the perfect vantage for viewing the progress. She had put the pupusas in a floral bowl and covered them with an embroidered napkin. There was a pitcher of milk and slices of freshly baked sherry cake. She made three cakes in all, setting the other two on a card table for the workers. The son sat down next to his mother and noticed she was wearing sandals. Her toenails were painted bright red and she was wearing frosty eye make-up. She seemed excited, like the time they went on the roller coaster together at the fair.

"I want your opinion on something," she said to the son. It was as though he was much older, her equal. "You know I trust your opinion more than anyone in the world."

"Okay," said the son.

"I'm thinking of volunteering this summer. There's a festival in the Italian Alps where they make these amazing puppets. Bigger than both of us if you were to stand on my shoulders. They speak a language that's only found in a few remote villages, and they dance and do these rituals to give thanks for their harvest. The language is dying, so they want to bring it back. Do you think that sounds like a good idea?"

The son considered all she told him.

"Are the puppets those mean ones with scrunched-up faces?"

"I imagine some are, but they probably have sweet ones, too."

"If they're so big, then how do they make the puppets dance?"

"That's a good question," the mother smiled.

"Maybe giants," the boy said, "but they'd need really long strings."

The mother pulled her son close and kissed the top of his head. She held him there as they watched Roque grab one of the ropes and rappel to the ground. He took off his spikes, told his men to break for lunch. They made a beeline for the cake. Roque walked over to the mother and son.

"We're getting there," he said, wiping the sweat from his forehead with a handkerchief. "Three more days and we should be done."

"Can Roque have a picnic with us?" the boy interrupted.

"Well, that's up to Roque," the mother said.

He was caught off-guard by the invitation.

"Oh, no, that's okay," he assured them.

"There's plenty of room," the son was excited. He made a place for Roque to sit.

"Really, I should eat with the crew."

"They can eat here, too," the son was excited.

"I don't think you're going to win this battle," the mother laughed.

Roque reluctantly sat down on the far end of the blanket. His easy charm evaporated in such intimate quarters. He became like a child himself, which the mother didn't mind at all. Her confidence was growing. She became inquisitive, eloquent, like the late night talk show host she would watch on tv after the father went to bed.

"Tell me, Roque, what you think of this. Recently there was a man who went up in a weather balloon. It was tiny, the size of a tin can. And he jumped. Broke the record for human freefall."

"You mean a . . . *sky diver*?" Roque said.

"Much higher. He was in the stratosphere and had to wear a space suit. You know, the ones with oxygen inside."

"That sounds impossible," Roque said.

"Well that's only half of it," the mother continued. "He landed safely, only a few scrapes. But when they interviewed him afterwards, he said as he was falling he heard a voice. In his helmet."

"Was it the space station?" the son asked.

"That's the strange part. There was no microphone in his helmet. Nothing at all. The interviewers noticed he couldn't stop smiling, that he had this calm over him. Doctors measured his pulse—it was as low as ours sitting right here."

"Then who was it?" the son was getting spooked.

"He said the voice he was hearing, it was God."

Roque looked puzzled, unsure of where this was going.

"Of course, they asked what God had said but he couldn't be certain, only that the voice was . . . a woman's voice."

"So God is a woman?" the son asked.

The mother smiled at the son, shrugged her shoulders. She never pretended to have an answer when she didn't know for sure.

"What do you think, Roque?" the mother asked.

"I've learned to not take sides when it's girls versus boys."

The mother laughed, looked down at her brightly painted toenails, then took a deep, satisfying breath of freshly cut pine.

"But I will say," Roque continued, "to go so high and see the earth below, that must change you forever."

The son flicked an ant off the lip of his glass. It landed on his mother's leg, but she just let it find its way back to the ground.

"So when did you come here? To America, I mean," the mother asked.

"Eleven years ago," Roque said, having to think about it. "Chicago first, then California."

Princess, the border collie, sat politely by Roque, hoping he was unfamiliar with the household rules about table scraps.

"Do you still have family in El Salvador?"

"No," Roque said. He reached into his wallet and pulled out a picture of two girls.

"On the left, that's Rosa. The other is Tonietta, my oldest. Ten already."

The mother inspected the photo. The girls smiled brightly, looked so carefree.

"They're beautiful," the mother said.

"I'm already worried about boyfriends."

"Must have been hard, picking up and leaving when Tonietta was just a baby."

"We didn't have a choice," Roque said, "we needed to move."

The mother waited for him to share the reason why, but it never came. Princess inched closer and began to lick the salt off Roque's arm. The son tried to shoo her away, but Roque let him know it was okay.

"Back home we had a . . . mutt. I was the oldest so I got to name him, and my favorite movie was *Sandokan, The Tiger of Malaysia*, about a pirate who fights the powers of Britain. I named him Sandokan and everyone laughed because the dog was so gentle, not a cutthroat at all. When we left, we had everything on the bus, but Sandokan couldn't come. He ran after us several kilometers until we reached the bridge. Then he stopped. It was like a movie, but in the movies he would have found us."

The mother nodded, letting Roque know she understood. He looked away, admiring the progress they had made on the trees.

"My daughter, the oldest one, she's at private school. Their class flies to Washington, D.C., next week. They're going to the Lincoln Memorial. She says she wants to find out if Lincoln's eyes really do follow you no matter where you stand."

❖ ❖ ❖

That night, on a whim, the mother hired a babysitter so she and her husband could go to the Moroccan restaurant in the next town over. They sat at a communal table with several other couples, then were called onstage to participate in the sword dance while everyone clapped in time. At the end of the song, the father twirled the mother, then dipped her, harkening back to the ballroom dance classes they took before the son was born. The staff was delighted and introduced the couple from the microphone, then brought out a pot of sweet mint tea on the house. Before dessert came, the wife grabbed the husband by the hand and guided him past the women's bathroom into an alcove by the kitchen. She pushed him against the wall and kissed him deeply. When he realized the clanging of pots and nearby voices were not going to deter her, the father responded in kind. He pulled aside her blouse just enough to expose the cabled muscles of her neck. As she closed her eyes, gravity zeroed out. She became weightless, relinquishing all control to some unseen caregiver. She felt herself plunging through the blue-black echo of the stratosphere, the force against her body intensifying with the speed of her fall. She could taste sugar spilled on flame, hear the unwavering voice of a woman assuring her the language would not die. A wire-hot confidence expanded outward. She plummeted with blinding speed, certain the record was hers at last. Just before impact, the mother opened her eyes.

She was back in the dining room. Her husband was eating ice cream and talking to the others about the rising price of real estate in the suburbs of Phoenix. He reached under the table and squeezed her hand. A sign, she was convinced, that what just happened was real.

❖ ❖ ❖

Lying in bed, the son heard the garage door open and the Buick pull in. The mother and father stayed in the car for several minutes, the radio playing a cheerful song with lots of horns. When they finally entered the house, the son immediately felt something different—the weight of their footsteps down the hall, the cadence of their words, how the mother would start talking before the father had stopped. The son was startled when they staggered through his door wearing plastic visors with flashing lights on the brim that lit up the name of a bar. McInerny's. The mother tripped over the dresser and fell to the ground laughing. Rather than help her up, the father put his foot on her stomach like a big game hunter posing for the camera and said keep calm and carry on in British accent, which caused the mother to laugh so hard she let out a little fart.

"Is that all you got?" the father scolded her playfully. "Mom?" the boy called out.

"Nope," she giggled, "My name's Carol. Carol Colgate."

"I thought it was Lana," the father said as though he'd been duped. "Lana from Tiajuana."

"Why are you home so late?" the boy asked.

"Making sure you haven't been abducted by aliens," she said, trying to hold back her laughter.

The boy just stared at them. "Well?" the father asked.

"Well what?" the boy said, confused. "Were you abducted or not?"

"But I'm right here."

"Are you?" the father said, hoisting the mother over his shoulder. She pounded his back and pretended to beg for her release as they staggered down the hall, knocking the family portrait—the one taken at Knott's Berry Farm—clear off the wall.

❖ ❖ ❖

The son returned from school the next day to see if El Duende had hidden something on the highest branch. Anticipation turned to confusion when he saw—instead of the battered old truck—a gleaming rig with the name of another tree service emblazoned upon the door. The son raced inside to find his mother watching her soap opera as she ironed the father's handkerchiefs.

"Where's Roque?" the son asked, winded. The mother didn't respond. Her eyes were red as though she'd been crying. They were locked on the tv where Brent or Ted or Jacqueline paused in the doorway of the fake boudoir, turned to the camera, and revealed a deep, dark secret just as the music swelled.

The son repeated the question, but the mother ignored him again. He began to panic. He ran outside and saw a group of men, maybe ten or more, working in silence with matching orange vests and hard-hats. There was a large cooler filled with ice-water on a folding table, and paper cups printed with the company logo stacked neatly by its side. Then he saw it. A crane so large they had to knock out a section of fence to get it into the yard. In the basket of this colossal machine, way up high, was a heavyset man wearing sunglasses. He reached awkwardly over the rail with his saw, made a few spastic cuts, then fingered some little gadget, and the basket lurched forward to the next limb. The workers beneath him seemed indifferent. He commanded no respect. He had no aura of a god. When he spotted the son, the man turned off his saw and—unable to hide his annoyance—spat over his shoulder.

"You can't be out here, kid" he yelled. "It's too dangerous."

❖ ❖ ❖

The mother served pot roast with mashed potatoes that night. The father complimented her on the salad being a manageable size, then stated matter-of-factly that he discovered Roque and his crew were unlicensed. The father could not continue to use them in good conscience.

"God forbid one of them got hurt," he said.

The mother nodded in agreement and refilled his glass of skim milk from a pitcher with hand-painted flowers on the side. The son remained quiet as the refracted energy bounced around the room with nowhere to land.

"All it takes is a lawsuit and—bam—there goes the farm. Next thing you know we're working elbow-to-elbow in Chinese shoelace factory."

The son pondered this, what the inside of that factory would look like, whether people told jokes and if they wore different colored laces, like purple or red just for variety. Maybe they got so sick of shoelaces they wore slippers, the same way his uncle became a vegetarian after working in McDonald's.

It was at that moment the son looked over and noticed his mother had put out an extra place setting.

❖ ❖ ❖

The father kept his promise. A swimming pool became the focal point of the yard. Heat-loving lilies replaced the hydrangeas and a perfectly manicured lawn stretched toward what seemed like infinity. The railroad consolidated and stopped running behind the house. The tracks were paved over, replaced with a bike path that attracted smiling families who could now ride from one town to the next, ringing little bells when they crossed the intersection. Hummingbirds darted around the plastic feeder, enjoying it so much they wintered-over and sat four abreast even in the deepest frost. The baseball diamond at the grammar school was renovated and a professional p.a. system was installed. Cheers erupted as players' names were announced, and if the wind was just right you could hear the slap of leather.

The mother cut her hair. She expanded her repertoire, cooking such exotic dishes as curried lamb, teriyaki chicken, and mahi mahi. She read spy novels after the father went to bed, drank homemade Kahlua from a coffee mug, and even discussed politics when the moment presented itself. She encouraged the son to venture off by himself—down to the creek with his army men, up into the hills where middle-schoolers hung a rope swing from a huge oak. She even allowed him to put blankets in the rubber raft and sleep in the swimming pool.

Had the other parents known, they would have thought her reckless, but the mother possessed a confidence that lightning would never strike twice, that sometimes the water is too much for the dam and the river should be allowed to run where it may. She knew her son would continue the search long after her time was up. With this faith at his back, the son learned to navigate not by the stars but by the satellites passing overhead. Floating in a rubber raft in a nice pool in a nice town, he would fall asleep to the sound of a dog barking in the distance and wonder if Sandokan, the Tiger of Malaysia, had finally crossed that bridge.

Such was nirvana.

❖ ❖ ❖

James Davis May

Fields and Ledges

How sweet the pleasures we can't afford
but still pursue. Now that three of them
are finally divorced, four friends
decide to rent a cabin for the weekend.

The one who's never been married thinks
about how fall in north Georgia is not that different
from fall in Pittsburgh. Blackberries, the coat
you have to wear but feel comfortable in,

the smell—it's more of a rumor, really—
of burning leaves drifting through the bright day,
the reassurance of knowing that someone
still burns them. The wind that brings the sudden

and not quite harmless tantrum of acorns.
Gathering wood for the night's fire, he thinks of his lover,
how at times like the night before,
collapsed and breathing heavily just after sex,

they enter a space where all their jokes,
irony, and default fights don't exist
and all thoughts fail, silently, the way
the hive's worth of huge bees had died that afternoon

in the cold field—he felt some hit against him
(they were heavier than he thought, muscular)
and drop as if they had just needed the suggestion
of death. Later that night, the woman

who's not his lover drinks gin with five lime wedges
wrung out into the ice cubes crowded
as the stars above them. Her glass
balances on the ledge of the hot tub

like a lighthouse overlooking a green turbulence;
and the three of them, beautiful, naked, and happy
invite him into the water they all call perfect
though no one can stay in it for very long.

Bill Christophersen

Autumn Haiku

Cliff Notes version: The
black locust's gold upstages
summer's green machine.

*

Night's gambit: the moon--
a blood orange, hovering;
a gauntlet thrown down.

*

Late-October wind
rattles the turkey oak's dry
boughs: a smoker's cough.

Jeff Worley

The Death of Chang Eng

*"Eng . . . continued to lie there in a stupor
for an hour more. And then he died."*

—*The Two: The Story of the Original Siamese Twins*
by Irving and Amy Wallace

When I ask William, *How is your
Uncle Chang?* he looks at the floor

and speaks through the mounting heat:
Uncle Chang is cold . . . Our eyes meet

and he runs to find Adelaine, who let herself
be courted into this strange life,

took me, and turned taboo to love.
I won't look at Chang and won't forgive

his rotgut whisky, squealing women
he took from behind, yang and yin

locked in lust, while I gazed at the lantern,
distracting myself, the women

he'd hired again disappointed
by my pocketed hand, my steel-clad

resolution to stay limp. I ate
from the leafy green garden, meat

never bled from my plate.
But I couldn't stop him—profligate

of opium and spices, raw flank-steak
drenched with fu-yung. Bones broke

under the knife his left hand wielded.
I'd have signed my name ten times in blood

to end this coupling, the appendix
that connects us like a sword. Mix

of flesh and shadow, ego and other.
. . . *Uncle Chang is dead*. My brother,

what could I have said when William
told me this, my heart slowing? That I'm

forgiving you for all of it? I hated you
is the truth. Amazing: you never knew.

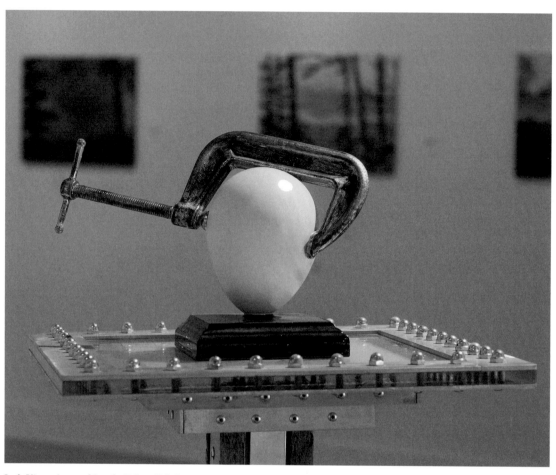

Jack King. *Approaching the Point of No Return*. 2008. Wood, steel, Plexiglas, and polyester. 48 x 12 x 12 inches. Photo by J. M. Lennon.

My Father and the Hair Grafter

No inventor can be a man of business, you know.

–Charles Dickens, *Little Dorrit*

When my father's life was on the skids—after he quit his job, and my mother filed for divorce, and he got arrested for shoplifting steaks in Jordano's Grocery Store—he moved to a shack on El Sueño Road, out past the Earl Warren Show Grounds. A few weeks later, he volunteered for a series of experimental transplants, in pursuit of a head of hair. The transplants cost nothing, for Dr. Lucas, the dermatologist who treated him, hoped to make my father his star exhibit and thus recoup his time and effort; but they were painful, requiring more than twenty injections of Novocain a day in the crown of my father's head. Eventually, some of the grafts took; in the short run, however, the procedure left bleeding scabs. Their ugliness embarrassed my father, made it awkward to apply for jobs, and complicated what was already the nadir of his life.

❖ ❖ ❖

One Christmas, my sister Laurie and I were sitting on the twin bed in my old yellow bedroom in Santa Barbara. We had closed the door for privacy, and my Marantz tape recorder lay between us on the faded yellow and brown patchwork quilt. As was our custom during family gatherings, Laurie and I were recording memories of our father—how he would awaken us before dawn to take our breakfast to Leadbetter Beach while it was cold and deserted in the darkness; how he delighted in names such as "Popcorn and Pink," the colors of the paints on my sisters' bedroom walls; and how he loved creating things for us kids: building me a desk in the living-room coat closet and making me a magician's hat from a Quaker Oats box, painted black and sprayed with glitter, when I was in my magician phase. In Minnesota, he had made us a playground in the backyard: transforming an old oak ladder into monkey bars, swathing the rungs in glossy yellow and blue tape to prevent splinters and add a touch of glamor; and erecting parallel bars and two wooden swings, one for standing and pumping, the other for sitting and singing, while we dragged our feet in the dirt.

My youngest sister and I were always trying to remember and analyze our father's life. Sometimes my brother and my other sister joined in this effort, but my mother rejected such discussions as a waste of time. "Life is forward!" she would say, like a soldier giving a command, or, in a frustrated tone, lament: "Why do we *always* have to live in the past?"

Only Laurie seemed to share my need to make sense of our father's downward spiral. We would sit for hours in that small front bedroom, recording discussions of him, struggling to grasp why a life that once held great promise had ended so sadly. During this particular session, Laurie suggested I try to interview the hair grafter. "You might gain some valuable insights," she said. "You shouldn't let the opportunity pass."

In theory, she was right, but I really didn't want to meet Dr. Lucas. My whole family regarded him as sleazy, because he had experimented on my father when he was mentally disturbed, unable to distinguish friends from enemies or make decisions in his own best interest. When my mother overheard what my sister and I were contemplating, she shuddered. "I don't want anything to do with that!" she said, before leaving the room. After a while, Laurie made my decision easier by offering to drive me to the doctor's house, provided that she would not have to meet him, but could wait for me in the car. At that point, I dutifully made the call, half hoping to find that Dr. Lucas had passed away. But he answered on the second ring and readily agreed to talk with me in his Montecito home.

❖ ❖ ❖

On the day of our appointment, in the middle of the afternoon, I climbed into the passenger side of Laurie's car and set off on my reluctant adventure. It was five days after Christmas, and the weather was typical of California in winter: clear and sunny, with a vivid sky overhead. The blue of the sky was more intense than most of the colors on the ground. Without rain, the vegetation had faded to dull gold or died altogether; the earth was pale chocolate and so dry that dust blew off its surface at the slightest whisper of air. I had forgotten to take the doctor's address, and I knocked on the door of an empty house before finally stumbling on his actual residence.

The door was opened by a woman with grayish-blond hair, dressed in a pink cotton housecoat and accompanied by a mud-spattered white poodle she called Cinderella. "My husband will be with you soon," she said. "He's checking his stocks on the Internet." Then she and the poodle retreated to the back of the house.

Dr. Lucas kept me waiting twenty minutes, and I used the time to examine the living room. It was decorated with artificial flowers and hanging plants. A mirror covered one entire wall, and oriental rugs overlapped each other on the living room carpet. On the coffee table stood ceramic panthers and a ceramic stage coach drawn by ceramic horses.

At last, Dr. Lucas appeared—a liver-spotted, elderly man, wearing a thin, embroidered blue shirt and khaki pants. He sat down on the damask-covered chair opposite me, in front of the bar, and apologized for making me wait. From our phone conversation, he knew that I wanted to write a book about my father, and he began by asking: "How much writing have you done?"

I hesitated, not knowing what to say.

"Because I'm looking for someone to write my autobiography," he said. As the doctor leaned forward, his skin emitted the fruity fragrance of his aftershave. The smell was cloying to me, and I moved my chair slightly backward in what I hoped was an unobtrusive gesture. I told him I was only visiting in Santa Barbara, and he said in that case, it "wouldn't work" for me to become his biographer. Grateful for the quick reprieve, I changed the subject, asking how he and my father had met.

"Your father called on me as a salesman for a pharmaceutical company," he said. "And we became friendly. He was a pleasant man to talk to. I called him 'Dick' instead of 'Richard,' and we exchanged personal thoughts. Later, he quit his job and moved to a shack on El Sueño Road, and he had me over to lunch now and then. I don't recall any other friends that he had, so he looked forward to my visits." Interrupting his narrative, Dr. Lucas whistled several times, in what seemed to be a signal, glancing back toward the hall from which he had emerged. After a few whistles, his wife appeared, an annoyed expression on her face. He asked her to bring us some water, and she did so quickly, then left the room.

"He was a mechanical genius," Dr. Lucas said, dangling his water glass in the air. "That jade bead processor was brilliant!" At the time of my parents' divorce, my father had been perfecting a more efficient way to transform jade stones into beads. The jade he used was not the valuable emerald-green or white variety but a more common kind of jade, from the mountains of California's Central Coast: creamy-green, rather dull in hue, with uneven intensity. Despite its flaws, my father found it beautiful. Maybe he was intrigued by the gem's cloudy swirls, the mysterious veins that appear to flow beneath the hard, green surface.

❖ ❖ ❖

Dr. Lucas's voice grew louder with enthusiasm as he remembered more and more details of his friendship with my father. "I would say to him: 'You know you can't live in this damn shack forever,'" the doctor recalled. "And he would say: 'I know, I know, but one of these ideas will come through.'" The words sounded just like my father, and it was pleasant to hear his way of speaking again after all this time.

Dreamer though he may have been, my father had reason to believe that one of his ideas would come through. After all, it had happened before. Along with his unfinished efforts, such as the tape gun and the jade bead processor, and his outright failures, such as the "olfactory nerve theory" and the "individual flying machine," my father had also achieved one great success as an inventor. It was called the "Magic Bow Machine." He invented it in his own garage on his own time, while employed as a ribbon salesman for the Minnesota Mining and

Manufacturing Company (3M). A moderately dangerous Rube Goldberg contraption, with exposed razor blades, my father's machine was the first to make the "Magic Bow." That was the name 3M had given to its version of the ornamental pompon bow, the one with all the loops, which is still used in gift-wrapping. Before my father's invention, the elegant bow could be made by hand, but only by those nimble enough to do so. His machine made it possible for every salesgirl in every department store throughout the country to make the Magic Bow. Netting a million dollars for 3M, the invention led to my father's promotion from salesman to "Idea Man" and his transfer to the Company's headquarters in Saint Paul.

And at first, things went well for my father in his new job. Upon his arrival, co-workers, knowing of the Magic Bow Machine, greeted him with admiration and high expectations, and his boss, because of my father's presumed genius, gave him freedom to create in his own good time.

However, my father's inchoate ideas were sometimes met with doubts and criticisms, which angered him. And nothing at 3M seemed to catch his fancy after the Bow Machine—certainly not the project in which his boss tried to engage him: an attempt to use "waste" from the ribbon-making process to improve "journal boxes"—those boxes that sit on the hubs of rail car wheels, dripping oil onto the axles.

Most likely he was already disillusioned when, in the autumn of our third year in St. Paul, my father accompanied his co-workers on a field trip to a railroad factory. There, he smelled some liquid foam that he came to believe had poisoned him. Soon after this trip, he quit going to work at the Lab. Afraid that he was not getting enough fresh air in his lungs, he stayed in his bedroom with the windows open throughout the Minnesota winter.

❖ ❖ ❖

"I knew he was off-base by his delusions," Dr. Lucas continued. "He thought someone would come after him at night, and he kept a shotgun. I keep a shotgun too, but not at my *elbow*." He took a drink of water and then wiped his mouth with the back of his hand.

"Another example," Dr. Lucas said, "is that in the mountains above Morro Bay, your father found a big chunk of jade, and he was convinced

it was the skull of a man. It was a delusion on his part. A delusion. I told him a fact: that people never turn into jade when they die. But he believed it was an ancient skull, so he was off-base there. He wouldn't accept my fact, as a physician, that when people die, they don't turn into jade."

"He called it 'Yorick,'" I said. The museum where my father took the stone had rejected out of hand that it was anything but a rock; nevertheless, my father's notion, and his excitement about it, floated through our lives for some time.

My father had many projects over the years that now strike me as strange, though during my childhood, they were simply part of the normal ambience of our lives. That last spring in Minnesota, for instance, he acquired a belief in flying saucers and kept vigil for them until late at night in our back yard. He also became interested in the Old Testament book of Ezekiel and devoted himself to its study with his usual enthusiasm. I still have our old Bible with its maroon cover and my father's red-penciled stars and reckonings in the margins of Ezekiel: 40-48. There, the Hebrew prophet, during the Babylonian exile of the sixth century BCE, narrates his mystical vision of a new temple in Jerusalem. My mother tells me that my father was converting Ezekiel's measurements from cubits and reeds into feet and yards. He thought he had discovered—in the writings of this ancient seer—the blueprint he needed to build an individual flying machine.

❖ ❖ ❖

"Could you tell me about the hair transplants?" I asked, glancing curiously at the doctor's own hair. Sparse and ash-colored, it appeared to be slicked back with gel, like the coifs of teenage movie stars from the nineteen-fifties.

The poodle named Cinderella had wandered back into the room and now stood between the doctor's knees. As he leaned forward to stroke her, I wondered how his hands had felt on my father's head. "Your father was prematurely balding," he said. "Doing a great deal of grafting was entirely justified in his case. He was very brave about it. You stick a needle in somebody's head and inject fluid, and it hurts, and he handled it like a soldier."

The image of the injection made me cringe, but at the same time I felt a flicker of pride. "What was motivating him?"

I had framed my question broadly on purpose, but he evidently considered it stupid and replied in a sarcastic tone: "To get hair on his head." Then he added: "Most men handle it well. They want hair desperately. They are of the opinion that the girls will like them better, which is not an opinion I share, because it isn't the truth. They like the man's personality, his kindness and warmth. But you can't teach a young man this. I couldn't make him see the light, and I never made anybody see the light on this, and I made a lot of money out of it, so why bother?" I wondered at his calling my father, who had been in his early forties at the time, a "young man."

"How did he reach his demise?" he asked after a moment.

"He committed suicide."

He sat silently, taking it in. "Well, I didn't see that coming. If I had still been in touch with him, I might have been able to prevent it, but I hadn't spoken to Dick in some time. After he moved up north, it was out of sight, out of mind." In that instant, I felt close to the dermatologist. Even he, I thought, had truly cared about my father and regretted the way he died.

❖ ❖ ❖

It was late afternoon when I walked down the path from Dr. Lucas's house to the car where Laurie sat waiting for me. She had parked underneath a lemon eucalyptus tree whose leaves exuded a fresh, pungent, lemony scent as I approached. On the drive back to our mother's house—past the old cemetery on the hill, past the Bird Refuge, where western grebes swam in the lake—I thought of how my father used to wake me in the morning when I was in high school. "Time to get up, Beautycute!" he would say, switching on a lamp away from my bed, so the sudden brightness wouldn't hurt my eyes. Minutes later, walking down the hall to wash my face, I would see him at the kitchen table, his head silhouetted in the eastern light. With slender fingers holding a cigarette in one hand, a pen in the other, he would jot down a few words on a white paper napkin and then look up, his dark brown eyes gazing into space.

No doubt he was trying to fathom some deep enigma or outlining the steps of a new invention, for those were the things he loved to do. My father's approach to life can be summed up in the two maxims he gave me to live by: "We were put on earth to solve problems" and "You have to do something great!" In keeping with these maxims, one of his favorite books was *The Creative Process*, edited by Brewster Ghiselin. He owned it in the 1952 Mentor edition, with the picture of an eye, a hand, and a head on its blood-orange cover. As with all his cherished books, my father had made the volume his own, fashioning index tabs from adhesive tape and scoring passages with wavy red lines. I remember the book's bright presence on our living room shelves, next to Winston Churchill's *The Gathering Storm* and my mother's Agatha Christies. From time to time, I would take down *The Creative Process* and read Coleridge's account of writing "Kubla Khan" in an opium-induced reverie, or Poincaré's story of discovering the solution to a mathematical problem while stepping onto a bus.

❖ ❖ ❖

When I glanced out the car window again, Laurie and I were driving on Cabrillo Boulevard, alongside East Beach. The day was remarkably clear. Looking out across the water, we could see the nearest of the Channel Islands, Anacapa and Santa Cruz, looming above the horizon. At Leadbetter Point, we turned away from the sea and ascended the hill leading up to Cliff Drive; a pink glow already suffused the sky behind the houses on the Mesa. As we drove, I tried to tell my sister that the hair grafter wasn't as bad as we had thought. "He appreciated our father's genius," I said. "He went out of his way to provide companionship when he was terribly alone."

But Laurie scoffed at this. "He shouldn't have let him go through all that pain," she said. Arguing with me throughout the ride, my sister remained firm in her position, while I soon began to waver. By the time the car crunched on the gravel in our mother's yard, my judgment of Dr. Lucas had hardened again, and I had lost all conviction about what I had learned.

A few nights later, Laurie and I watched the movie *A Man for All Seasons*, about the life of the martyr Thomas More. I had seen the movie many times and always cried passionately during the scene when Sir Thomas, awaiting death in the Tower, bids his family goodbye. I identified with Margaret, More's daughter and soulmate. She understands, better than his wife, the secret recesses of his heart. At the end of the movie, after More's execution, King Henry VIII commands that Sir Thomas's head be displayed on a pole to warn other would-be traitors. A month later, Margaret takes down her father's head and keeps it with her until her death.

The next morning, just before waking, I dreamed that my father was still alive and that we still lived in our first home in Santa Barbara, a small maroon and cream-colored tract house on Santa Catalina Street, just a few blocks from the cliffs jutting out over the sea. It was a sunny afternoon, and, in the dream, my father, brother, and I were shooting baskets on the driveway. My father and brother played gracefully, usually making their shots, whereas I was a poor player, rarely getting the ball through the hoop. My mother had called us for supper, and we were about to go in when I accidentally hit my father on the crown of his head with the ball. Then I hurried to his side, took his shiny bald head in my hands, and cradled it long and lovingly.

When I woke up, it took me a few seconds to realize that I was not in our first house, on Santa Catalina Street, but in the house on La Marina, which my father had built out of California Redwoods, high on the Mesa's convex bulge, where the sun rises over the Pacific. With a jolt of pain I remembered that my father was dead and had been dead for many years. What hurt me most was the knowledge that, during all this time, I had gone on with my life: earning degrees, building a career, falling in and out of love, as if I had forgotten him, his suffering, and early death. And now, too, there was nothing for it but to get up on that cold, limpid morning, look out at the silver ocean's vast expanse, and try to go on without him.

❖ ❖ ❖

Two Universal Truths and a Lie
(in no particular order)

I

The peas were not properly supported.
As they grew they looked around for what
Could hold them up, help their vines straighten.
The trellis I'd made was too far
And none could stretch a tendril so taut
To reach the weathered bits of string and wood.
Instead, they clung, each vine to the others
Until I could not tell where one began.
July's continual long march toward heat
Will push them all down to the ground. Show
No pity when the bottom leaves turn brown.
The weakest ones will hold tighter then,
Still hoping the few strong can hold them up.
But by August, all are dry and done.

II

You Tree-Of-Heaven, called ailanthus,
Outside my flower bed but spreading fast.
History records your presence,
tight and tangled, tropical,
In early China's dawn.
They treated you with honor, gave you a home
In royal palaces and fields alike,
Your sucker roots outlasting dynasties.
Now Ohio calls you pest, invasive plant.
I will have you out by Independence Day.
The resurrection lilies growing near
Will not protect you, they'll be dug up too,
If that's the only way: Destroying
This garden to get to you.

III

He thinks I must be something I'm not.
My hair: fragrant August goldenrod.
My lips: a rose blooming throughout the year.
These hands of mine are moving gently,
Swaying blossom laden branches.
When he hovers over me I sense
His soft caressing tarsus on my arm,
Looking for pollen waiting only for him.
His two compounding eyes cannot yet tell,
My hair's just stringy achromatic strands
That seem an ultra-violet look-a-like
To flowers, not the scent but the sight.
And I, I'm just a woman on her porch
With chips and apple juice, baloney for lunch.

John Drury

Honeymoon in Venice

A bottle of prosecco greeted us
in *La Calcina*, our front room with a view
of the wide canal, the island of Giudecca.
John Ruskin's room was right next door to ours,
but we fared better on our honeymoon.
His pheromones were triggered by the Gothic
arches and foils, not hardcore fleshiness
of a real woman with real body hair,
his wedding surprise, while ours got us in trouble
we couldn't resist, artists and models both
who plunged into romantic complications,
years of my dithering, a legal slough
we likened to the slow process in *Bleak House*.

But when we made love, that first afternoon,
feeling a sea breeze, hearing the boats and waves,
each other's odalisques, we were incensed
that baggage handlers or airport security
inspected our vibrator so hard it broke.
It hummed like a power drill but didn't shimmy.
It figured, since our love affair and friendship
had always been tempestuous, not calm.

She needed medicine, so I took a walk,
looking for the nearest *farmacia*,
but the shop at San Trovaso wasn't open.
I kept on looking for green neon crosses,
stopping on bridges, gazing at canals
where someone sloshed a mop on a boat's deck
and workers hoisted paving stones from barges.

Near Byron's palace on the Grand Canal,
blue screens kept off the cruising *paparazzi*
who trolled in boats, lusting for a shot
of Angelina Jolie. But my LaWanda
raged at the arrogance of stardom, swore
she'd never see *The Tourist*, in production
while we were honeymooning in the city.
I said I'd never pay to see the movie,
but still, it was a record of our stay,
and if we could ignore the silly thriller
it might become a kind of photo album:
sunny nostalgia, tinged with a bitter edge.

Scornful of cars, I didn't want to sully
our honeymoon by going to the Lido,
but she insisted we couldn't miss the beach,
sorry it wasn't warm enough to swim.
We took a bus—after the waterbus—
and got off at the Grand Hotel des Bains,
closed for the season, despite the ghosts of Mann
and Aschenbach. We walked past the cabanas
and men who were playing soccer on the beach
so she could wade in the Adriatic Sea.
I knew how wrong I'd been to discourage her
from joy that made her radiant as the wave tips
dizzy with sunlight, cresting with tidal surges.
Love wasn't rigid but resilient,
open to change, eager to divorce
anything impeding its energy.

The whole time we were there, she wouldn't visit
a single church, despite the Tintorettos,
but wouldn't miss the shrine of Harry's Bar,
savoring martinis, popping olives
in our mouths. The high point of the trip
came when the suave proprietor, named for the bar,
approached from behind, holding her chair to help
her from the table—Arrigo Cipriani
smiling and flirting with my vibrant bride.

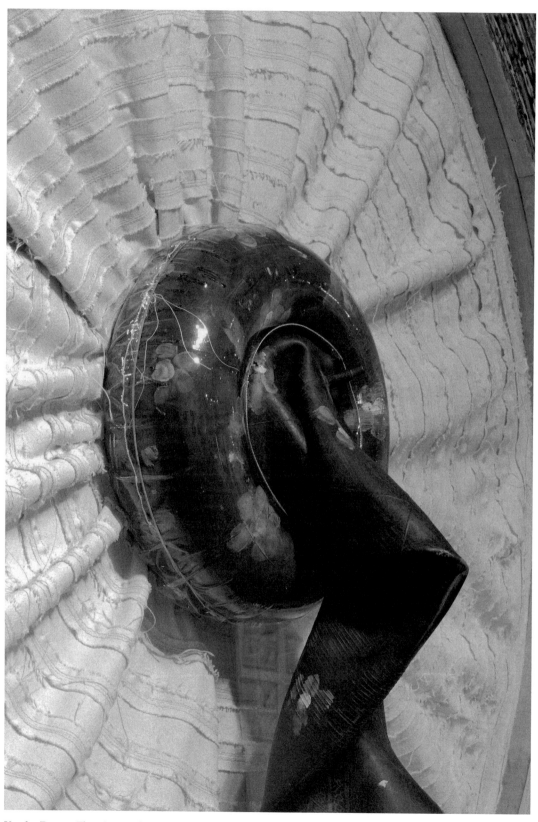

Kendra Frorup. *Three Score and Ten*. 2009. Mixed media. 60 x 60 inches. Photo by J. M. Lennon.

R. C. Neighbors

Easy Rider

When our daughter Chloe was born, my wife, Rebecca, and I bought a scooter. We needed a second vehicle, something reliable, and we had been burned by too many used cars to buy another. Above all, we needed something cheap. At the time, Rebecca was a preschool teacher at an area Head Start. I worked as a stay-at-home dad and graduate student during the day and, at night, taught as an adjunct at a community college. With Chloe, we became a family of three, with four college degrees between us, on a yearly budget less than twenty-five thousand dollars. A scooter seemed the perfect option. It was cheaper than a motorcycle and, at over a hundred miles-per-gallon, got twice the gas mileage. Its small size also made it easier to handle, so Rebecca wouldn't need to wrestle something several times her weight when she rode.

We decided on a Honda Metropolitan, a gunmetal grey one with black trim and a plastic trunk for my books. It came with a 49cc engine that rumbled between my legs . . .

. . . Okay, there's little rumbling, and it's more like under my ass, since I don't straddle the thing. But the innuendos for having something powerful "between my legs" versus "under my ass" are very different. Either way, those ponies max out around forty miles per hour. Downhill. With the wind at my back. Uphill, the speed tops anywhere from twenty miles per hour to the-speed-of-my-feet-pushing, depending on how steep the incline.

Rebecca and I decided that whichever one of us had Chloe would drive the car, and the other would take the scooter. But the plan had a problem: after we bought the thing, Rebecca refused to ride it. She tried once, though, shortly after we brought it home. She climbed on behind me, her arms around my waist, to get a feel for the bike—which, I must admit, made me feel pretty manly. But as we drove off, she buried her face between my shoulder blades and squeezed her

eyes shut. "Stop," she said. "Stop the scooter."

"We haven't even left the parking lot."

"Just pull over," she said.

"We're only going ten miles-per-hour."

"I want to get off!"

She did and has never gotten back on. Now, she takes the car, and I drive the scooter. Unless I have Chloe, in which case I drop Rebecca off and pick her up, as if we have only one vehicle. Our plan vanished, and in its place, I gained the inexplicable stigma that comes with being a scooterist.

❖ ❖ ❖

Based solely on appearance, I could be a biker, like the kind of guy who might've starred opposite Peter Fonda and Dennis Hopper in *Easy Rider*, except without all the leather. I'm broad-shouldered. I have a full beard that I could grow at the age of twelve, and my chest has resembled a shag carpet since the beard's debut. I'm also quiet. That, combined with my size, I'm told, makes me seem intimidating.

But I'm no Peter Fonda. My silence comes from social awkwardness more than anything else. Plus, I enjoy Taylor Swift. I've read *Twilight* more than once (Team Guy-who-almost-hit-Bella-with-a-van). And I've seen *Titanic* several times, sometimes even without a woman in the room. My glasses and affinity for schoolwork always helped me fill the role of nerdy intellectual better than countercultural biker.

In that way, it makes sense I would drive the most emasculating option for a single-person transportation device, even now, in the strange land of Texas. A state where you can drive for hours without seeing another human being. Where the heat feels like a hair dryer blowing in your face as you scoot down the road. And where you can pass a truck on the street, a shotgun in its back glass and a ridiculous sticker on its bumper ("Guns don't kill people, I kill people"), then discover a little, old lady behind the wheel.

In another way, it makes no sense whatsoever. As I mentioned, I'm not a small guy. I stand six-foot-two. And as for my weight, well, once I strap on my helmet and my very masculine satchel, I'm no longer operating the scooter under the manufacturer's stated terms of use. I imagine I look something like a clown riding a miniature bike under the big top, except there's no big top. And I'm dressed kind of like a hipster. I still picture the clown, though, because complete strangers have said as much.

One day I stood outside my office by a row of motorcycles. I slung my not-purse over my shoulder and mounted my hog, but before I could leave, some guy hobbled over—himself not unlike the Kool-Aid Man. He stared at me, sweat sliding off him like condensation from a pitcher, and I'm sure he laughed and pointed his finger, too, while a group of college girls surrounded us and joined in. "How do you fit on that thing?" he said.

"How does your head fit on your shoulders?" I responded.

Okay, I didn't say that. I may have given him a tight-lipped smile and driven off.

But I thought it, loud enough for him to hear.

❖ ❖ ❖

During my time as a scooterist, I've gotten mixed reactions from other motorists. For instance, I've conducted a completely scientific, in-no-way-made-up study of vehicles at traffic lights. The study shows that, while stopped at intersections, drivers laugh seventy percent more often next to my scooter than my silver Honda Fit. Which, in case you didn't know, is the Harley of subcompact sedans. The figure jumps to eighty percent if a man sits behind the wheel, and it leaps to ninety percent, if the vehicle in question is a truck with either a Confederate flag or "Don't Mess with Texas" sticker. In other words, most vehicles I encounter in Texas.

But I'm confident that bikers don't receive the same ridicule. They even form a sort of club, a brotherhood hostile to scooterists, with rules and secret hand gestures like "the wave." Before the scooter, I never knew such a thing existed, but motorcycle etiquette apparently requires bikers to wave when they pass each other. It involves the left hand, lowered toward the asphalt at a forty-five-degree angle, with any number of fingers extended like an infielder calling the

number of outs.

While scooting, I have received the wave from only a handful of bikers. Some stared me down, making sure I knew they saw me, and kept their hand firmly on the handlebar. Others have initiated the wave, but gotten to only about twenty degrees before noticing my hog and returning their hand to the clutch. This inevitably leads to one of my ambiguous-hand-motion-turned-hip-scratch-seriously-I-wasn't-really-waving-at-you non-waves. And once a biker waved with only a single finger. The asshat.

Other scooterists, however, are a different story. I don't see them often in Texas, but when I do, they always give the wave. It's too quick, though, too enthusiastic. Like in high school, when I would see a girl I liked across the supermarket and would twitch my hand at her before she averted her eyes and hurried the other direction. Like they need someone to acknowledge their existence.

It's sad, really.

❖ ❖ ❖

Depending on the state, motorists may gain scooterhood in their early teens, they may need only a car license, or they must obtain a motorcycle license. When I moved to Texas—the bastion of conservative ideology and limited government—I was required to take a written exam, shell out a few hundred bucks for a motorcycle safety class, and ritualistically sacrifice my firstborn, even though I'd been riding for years. I had to learn to drive a motorcycle, with its clutching, shifting, and leather-chaps-ing, before I could drive my scooter with its two controls—go and stop.

I signed up for a Saturday class in mid-September, when east central Texas was still afflicted by temperatures over a hundred degrees and one of the worst droughts in its history. That didn't matter, though. The training required "appropriate" bike wear—long sleeves, pants, gloves, and high-top shoes, at a minimum. I couldn't wear my usual scooter gear—a t-shirt, shorts, flip-flops, and a flagrant disregard for personal safety. We spent the second day of class swerving around cones in a high school parking lot, evoking memories of high school driver's ed—Coach read the sports page while my friends and I wedged cones into the wheel wells of a used Ford Taurus. After a full day on the bike, my gray clothes had turned damp black, and I was so dehydrated I couldn't pee the rest of the weekend.

The first day of class, however, we spent in a warehouse for the classroom portion of training. Inside, the air was stale. There were no decorations—the walls only bare Sheetrock, except gaps where lumber and insulation showed through—and interspersed along the floor were twenty folding chairs filled with students. A few college guys in Aggie maroon were getting licensed for the first time. Several good ol' boys, who had been riding for years and recently moved to Texas, were getting their motorcycle endorsement in the state. And only one woman sat in the room, there to ride with her husband.

Before class, a guy with at least one rebel flag on his person told me about a wreck he had while driving across the state. "I was cruising along, and some goddamn bastard pulled out in front of me," he said. "I had to lay 'er down. I slid on my ass across that asphalt a good fifty yards, too, till the seat of my britches was smoking." He shook his head wistfully. "Nothing I could do but lay 'er down."

The instructor—a local motorcycle cop, who resembled a middle-aged Wilford Brimley—twitched his immense, orange mustache at the man. "We call that crashing," he said.

"I had to lay 'er down," Rebel-flag repeated. "Sometimes you have to lay 'er down."

When class officially began, Brimley stood at the front of the room and asked us why we were there and what we drove. Each student discussed his or her make and model of bike—Harleys, Suzukis, Yamahas, etc. And then there was me.

"A Honda Metro," I said.

Brimley's mustache twitched. "I don't know that model."

"A Honda Metropolitan?"

He shook his head.

"A scooter."

"Oh," he said, the disapproval as thick as his drawl. "Bikers like me hate people who drive scooters."

"Then, it's a good thing," I said, "my self-esteem doesn't hinge on someone whose facial hair went out of style in the eighties."

Okay, I didn't say that. I may have given him a tight-lipped smile and avoided eye contact.

But I thought it, loud enough for him to hear.

"We'll convert you," he said, with the conviction of a missionary on a doorstep. "We'll convert you."

I haven't driven a motorcycle since the training. Who needs that much horsepower? The acceptance of one's peers? Acceleration?

I definitely showed him.

❖ ❖ ❖

Despite all my humiliation, Rebecca still refuses to ride the Metro. But when I drive home in the evenings, Chloe meets me in the parking lot—now three years old, with dimples and Shirley-Temple curls—for what she calls our "scooter adventures." I help her fasten her pink helmet, and she climbs on the seat between my knees. Then, we drive the loop of our apartment lot, to the mailboxes and back. Our neighbors, almost none of whom we know, gawk at us as Chloe announces each yellow speed bump we dodge.

"Faster," she tells me, her arms outstretched and eyes closed against our wind. "Faster, Daddy."

And I realize that I don't care what our onlookers think, as they smirk or scowl, feet firmly on the ground. I'm comfortable with who I am. I may not be Peter Fonda. Or even Wilford Brimley. But with Chloe, I'm king of the world, at twenty miles per hour.

❖ ❖ ❖

Douglas Basford

Beach Bums of the Buffalo Southtowns

The sun engenders bathers on the beach.
Or just the one. To land his kind of leather,
stretched taut around middle-aged flesh, you either
have to heave your bod way south of here or teach

it to sit still for months on end, a cooler in reach.
Pale strains of "Margaritaville" and "Seether"
traverse the autumn air and tint our leisure.
Perhaps his radio would have found a niche

audience in the wind-tossed octet out rehearsing
on sand flat a bleach-mop soon-groom-dude's notion
of how maids and gents meeting by the ocean

(Lake Erie) weave up front, order reversing.
Jeans'd, jacketed, sandaled, stiff, everyone laughs
and shuffle-jogs through what he choreographs.

Looking toward South Bristol

O impermanent tide, low or high,
where does your deed fall?
Does it waddle to and fro,
skimming the headless seal
that bangs against rocks? Does it
cover the purple tourmaline so blue
beach glass must be scraped free?

Hauling fields of fog across their backs,
waves collapse against the shore.
Minks slither over rocks to check
what the crows forgot to catch.
We can't even see Inner Heron island
or the toy lobster boats pulling traps
trolling from this float of mist.

Does the tide take the ferry to New Brunswick
or funnel along Tecumseh Way to meet
the notary who performs marriages and
dowsings? Does it resist stopping
at all the coves people from Connecticut
have bought up? Doesn't it know
the coast has always brought people

like us to their knees, bending to the view,
digging in sand and seaweed so that
there haven't been any starfish here
for years but the few deformed by glue,
propped on the mantles of cottages,
begetting the fog fixing the sand,
beached-up prows, houses that once were ships.

Matthew J. Spireng

Black Creek, Mississippi

Back home there's a Black Creek
that flows northeast to the Hudson—
small stream where herring run
in the spring and people dip nets
to haul them in. And recently
in a whole other part of the county
two signs have cropped up
along a road that crosses between two cornfields
announcing another Black Creek,
though there's no stream there, not even
a sign of a gully, and all I can think is
that once long ago a stream flowed there
that was diverted and someone has petitioned
the county to memorialize it with signs.
Two signs along a road in the middle
of fields, one facing traffic going north,
the other facing traffic going south, signs
bound to confuse more than just me. And now
what I wonder as we cross a small stream
on Route 59 in Mississippi called Black Creek
is whether somewhere there's a Black Creek
named when first seen because the water was
darkened by an upstream fall of nuts whose husks
would stain. I picture it as a stream whose water
is clear but dark, like tea steeped a very long time.
Black Creek in Mississippi might be
such a stream. Or the one back home
in New York that flows to the Hudson. All I've seen
of either is a flash of water shaded by trees
as I quickly drove past, and the signs, like those
in the field, announcing that this, this is Black Creek.

Daniel Saalfeld

Ballet

Waking from a doze on a white couch,
I see black and white posters of her

leaping on unknown stages with her legs
parallel to the floor and her arms out

as far as they'll go. It's another dream
I've wanted to wake up in: a dimly lit flat

with white carpet below a red Persian rug,
a Siamese cat named Pushkin

curiously looking at me, December rain
falling outside, and one long muscle,

a fancy fountain pen, having coaxed me
into this state with her Russian yes's.

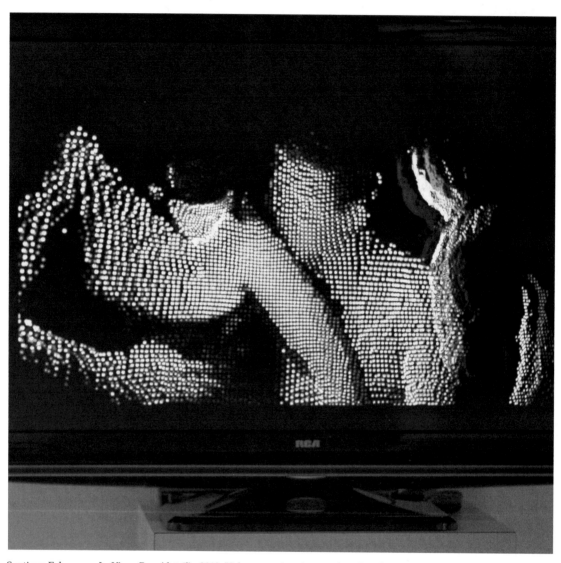

Santiago Echeverry. *La Vie en Rose* (detail). 2013. Videoart, animation produced with Kinect and Processing. 4 minutes, 45 seconds.

Minecraft

"Why are you still here?" my brother Caleb asks.

I have been sitting next to him on the couch for exactly four minutes—long enough to try three times to log him into his online high school courses and get shut out by the program. I will have to email his online mentor to get the password reset.

"I'm just checking my email," I say. Our mother is working and I have him today.

"Yes, but why are you still here?"

"Because I am comfortable," I say. "This will only take a few minutes, then I'll go."

"Yes," he repeats, pushing his glasses up on his face, already immersed in a video game that's loading. "It's just that," he says, "you know, I like to be by myself when I play. You're kind of in my bubble."

"I know," I say. I move over a few inches and look up at the television. "What's this called?"

My brother is seventeen and he has a repertoire of four or five video games that are his favorites. I know their names, but have actually only watched him play one or two. Runescape, Gears of War. Modern Warfare.

"This is Minecraft," he says.

❖ ❖ ❖

Oh. I had always thought Minecraft must be another shooter game, given what I'd seen of his other favorites. Mines, blowing things up, blasting other people to pieces. Actually, the zombie shooter game that he plays looks fun, but I have no talent for these things, and my singular attempt at playing with him was met by him simply removing the controller from my hands just as I was trying to double-tap a crawler zombie and saying, "You suck. I'm sorry but you can't play." But that's the way he is. He means no offense.

❖ ❖ ❖

It's a beautiful, sparse, cube-shaped world on the screen in front of us.

"This is my house," he says. "I built it myself."

It has three stories and is made out of wood. I'm impressed. It is stunning. Three-storied, spare, expansive windows, Taliesin-esqe except that he has no idea who Frank Lloyd Wright was. Probably. Or maybe he does. He surprises sometimes. The house is all form and function, except for a single tapestry on the wall. Which is also surprising. He refuses to let anyone decorate his room in any way. Art doesn't interest me, was what he said.

"I made that," he says now.

"Of what?"

"Wool and sticks. I dyed the wool with those flowers in the field."

Before I can ask how, he swings away from the wall hanging and his avatar looks out the window.

"Uh-oh", he says, "the sun is setting." A perfect cube of sun is slowly sinking in the sky.

"There are light cycles, here", he says, "just like in our world, but they are faster. Stay here a minute," he says, eyes glued on the screen, "and the moon will rise.

❖ ❖ ❖

I wait. I'm impatient today. I have midterms in a week and Abnormal Psych, which certainly shouldn't be kicking my ass, is. I really should be working on my own things if I can't supervise him with his schoolwork today. I have twelve credits left until I graduate at the technical college and it has been maddeningly slow with my responsibilities here but there is nothing else to be done. My mother is half dead from working night shifts and I am his sister. He will always need us, one or the other. It is as simple as that.

❖ ❖ ❖

A glowing moon cube rises on the screen and pixelated stars twinkle. I find myself looking for familiar constellations.

"If you watch closely, Caleb says, "you can see them move, because time moves faster here." A simple piano sonata plays.

"The music is beautiful," I say. "It's very calming."

"Yeah," he says, "I like it."

I sit back into the couch.

"I've got to get inside my house," he says, "it's dark, and that's when the monsters come out."

"Really?" I say. That makes sense. The pixels are deepening in this cubed world as he reaches his house and I see that he's put torches on the outside of it.

"Mmm hmm", he murmurs, closing doors behind him. "The first night I stayed here I left my door open and a skeleton thing came in and I lost a life. You gotta close the doors at night."

❖ ❖ ❖

Of course, I am thinking. Not that that keeps him in. Caleb wanders. The last time was a month ago; a call from the police in the middle of the night. He had walked away on an adventure, armed with a slingshot and flashlight. Our mother was working and it was me that drove to get him, me that told the police on the phone, "Please be gentle, he has Autism, this happens." When I drove to the park he was standing head down, pale and shaking under the yellow mercury lights. The officer released him to me. "We told him to stop and he ran," he said, as if it was my fault that I hadn't taught him not to. "He's lucky something worse didn't happen. It's dark and we didn't know what was in his hand." My mother and I cleaned and put salve on his knees for a week where the skin came off when they tackled him. I look at my brother. He is nearly six feet tall now, and appears completely normal from a distance, which is the most dangerous way to be.

❖ ❖ ❖

"It was a skeleton thing," he continues, "and the next morning when I woke up there was a zombie guy looking in my window. I went over there and he grabbed me and shook me and I lost a lot of life." His fingers fly over the buttons on the controller. "I'm going to build a fence. First you cut wood, then, you take it to your crafting table and make planks. If you stack the planks high enough the monsters can't get in."

"Any of them?" I ask.

"Any of them." The square stars are twinkling outside and he is standing looking out the large windows on the third floor of his house. Then he clicks on the bed with its red blanket. It's time to sleep.

After twenty seconds the sky is bright with a rising right-angled sun and rhomboid clouds floating by.

He has clicked on "wake," accelerating his night.

"Wow," I say, "that's fast." Just like real life. He sleeps half the hours the rest of us do.

I watch his avatar leave the house he built. A few blocky sheep are grazing outside and Caleb is heading into the hillside around his house. It's amazing how after a while you start to forget that everything here is made out of squares, how your mind starts to build in the curves, I am thinking, to soften things even though it's not real. None of this is real.

"I have a tame wolf here somewhere," Caleb says, "but I think I might have lost him.

"If you get a bone and lead a wolf into your house, he becomes tame and then he sticks around your house." His avatar turns right and left, looking around stiffly. "Oh! There he is!"

A large white cuboidal wolf/dog appears, wandering around the square hills outside his house.

Caleb turns to head back to his house. I notice that he returns there often.

"Does your wolf need to be fed?" I ask.

"Oh, I forgot!" he says.

He goes to a large box in his house where he keeps all of his items. "You can feed him raw pork chops," he says. And clicks and carries one outside his house. His tame wolf is wandering outside.

"If he gets sick or too hungry his tail droops," my brother says, feeding him the pork chop.

I notice that the tame wolf's tail is rather low.

"One pork chop didn't do much," I say. Caleb feeds him six more, which still leaves quite a large stock of raw pork chops in his box and the tame wolf, tail held slightly higher, wanders off again.

"I'm wondering what I should do now," Caleb says. His hair is falling in his face and I think that we are going to have to try to get him out of the house for a haircut soon. "Oh," he says, "I think I'll build that fence. I have to go to the forest."

As we walk, he points out each particular tree that he has planted. There are lots of others around that have simply sprung up on their own. Spawned, he calls it. He is particularly proud of a eucalyptus, and how tall it has grown. They all look exactly the same to me. How is he able to remember which ones he planted?

I ask about the large thing that is looming in the distance.

"That's one of my cows," he says.

"You have cows?"

"Yup," he says, "but I don't have any buckets yet to milk them. You have to mine ore first. If you get milk, you can make a lot of different things to eat, like cake." My brother has a sweet tooth. "Two stalks of wheat, an egg and milk," he says. He approaches the cow and swings at it rather savagely which disturbs me quite a bit but when the cubed beef drops, he's nonchalant.

"There." he says. "Another leather. I need twenty more before I can make a leather armor for myself."

"To protect yourself from monsters?" I say. I'm still a little shocked that this cow just abruptly changed into finely tanned leather.

"Not really," he says. "It just adds to your general health."

I'm thinking, PETA would disagree. And not be too happy about those raw pork chops, either. He interrupts my thoughts:

"I found an egg! Cool!"

I'd wondered what the odd clucking was.

"You have chickens." I see one hop by on rectangled legs.

"Sort of. They just spawn." He whacks at one.

"Wait!" I say. "You have to kill them to get an egg?!"

"Well," he says, "you can get feathers, and sometimes an egg. Sometimes they just leave the eggs on the ground." His avatar checks the sky. "Sun's going down, better get home." Every time he says that, my own heart rate trips up, a switch to my own fears. My brother walks along the cliffs overlooking his cerulean sea. Suddenly, he disappears.

"What happened to you?!" I say, bolting upright. He's gone, and the screen flashes YOU DIED. Just like that. My heart is flipping. It's just a video game, I think, calm down.

"Big spider," he says, offhandedly.

He clicks again and he's back, another life.

We're back again at the home he's built, this beautiful house overlooking the sea with the trees he planted and its tame wolf and a box full of raw pork chops. I look at him and I'm thinking something about the future that I have no words for.

I want to ask, "Are there any other people living here," but I know it really doesn't matter very much to him. I love his house, and this world, and he's let me watch, and today, that is enough. We are upstairs now looking out his third story and I'm there next to him even though you can't see me, and his tame wolf is ambling aimlessly around in the hills, staying close to his house.

❖ ❖ ❖

Lois Lane in Bronze

Illinois, your windmills can suck
golf balls through straws, your

tornados turn the world the color
of easy condiments. Let's mustard

and relish ourselves, pick the poppy
seeds from our navels with tooth

and nail—which is to say: tongue,
which is to say: language. Illinois,

you've always lionized
the proper heroes: women in

bronze over men of steel. Here,
even an Ohio River town of 6,000

can be called *Metropolis*.

Let's pretend my uncle found the girl
face-down in Boneyard Creek. Let's

say she was a squeeze to a superhero.
Let's pretend the wind carried her

there—flying like a balloon, Lindbergh's
grasshopper fetish, Santos Dumont,

the college boys tossing in groupie-dom
their underpants into her hands,

fingers glowing with coals. Let's pretend
Uncle Paul wasn't late to his third

wedding for gigging frogs in Peoria,
the beasts deflating beneath

his spear, the air dribbling over
the wings of the horseflies still

caught like hair in the backs
of their throats. Let's remember

how the sky flashed as we kissed
ourselves muddy, cooked the legs

in lemon and butter, stunned the poor
animals with bright light, so unexpected

in so much downstate dark. Let's
remember that home is where

the Nazi Buzz Bomb can spilt
a Steak 'n' Shake extra thick

with Sonny Bono's
Bobcat Vest. This is my old

house. This is unincorporated
Normal. Let's remember how

we once loved each other so much
in this state, our clothes flew

from our bodies, even without
the tornado. In our pockets, always

extra batteries. For longer life.
For flashlights that illuminate

as they blind.

Dede Wilson

To the Poet Writing of Wings

How can muse be piqued to quiddle with quills?
Backs are lustrous to the touch, skin unruffled,

yet you speak of *feathers, molt, preen,*
as though with wings we'd live

the easeful lives of dragonflies,
as though we'd drift along in dream, feeding

on the wind. No more
battering tattered rings around

some lustrous core. I mock
your feathers, dragging dust, your blades

that ache to flutter and soar, would *beg*
for wings if wings would lift us.

Desert

The arroyo twists its sand hips
at the thought of rain, tip
of DNA at the center of grey
spotlights, first clause

in the program read and re-read,
as if sky had the same memory
as land, as if the last
full moon and its cohort stars

were too faulty to draw
a ten-year rain from their well.
The sidewinders know full well
how tightly the springs of dust

are wound each night for the tiny
lives, roots never quite dead,
the ghostly subsistence that rises
from each corpse, the vultures off

track, and the heat's immovable
bubbles for all the amateur
ticket-holders to ponder. Scorpions
muscle the front row seats

like clowns or tumblers, sawdust
springs for the first intimations
of water. The grandstands lean
forward when the ringmaster

appears. Vendors hawk shredded
cactus for sparklers. Look,
the sky darkens, one cloud
wavers over center ring.

Chris Valle. *Between Love and Madness Lies Obsession.* 2013. Oil and acrlyllic. 40 x 45 inches.

The World Brought Close

All church basements looked the same: white drywall, fluorescent lights, metal folding chairs. Shepard went directly to the coffee urn and levered his dose of bitter liquid, felt the familiar crunch of Styrofoam between his teeth. There were no special effects down here: no carved wood crucifixes, golden chalices, stained glass or gilt—down here it was just guilt. He took a seat on a metal chair and watched the waves in the linoleum.

It was a small meeting with a new-agey theme: Sober Awakenings. The moderator had six years and called herself Mother Kai. Shepard had been sober ten; this was his first trip away from his family on Long Island in almost as much time. The Casualty Insurance Conference kept participants on a rigorous schedule. After hours of lectures on risk numbers and land acquisitions, everybody headed for the bars like lepers wading into the Ganges; Shepard headed for a meeting.

The Unitarian church was just a four-block walk from his hotel in suburban Boston. One guy was sharing about climbing telephone poles with a flask of Jack Daniels. He wore a denim shirt with Verizon Tech Support stitched across the pocket. The laces of his work boots were untied. Every time he moved his foot, they clicked on the floor. "One day, I touched the wrong wires and BAM." He bumped his fists together. "Ten milli-amps right through me. Fell off the pole. Broke my collar, my wrist and dislocated my shoulder."

A ripple of surprise floated through the group: chairs squeaked back in consolation, bodies repositioned themselves. Shepard had heard worse. Mother Kai shook her head; her feather earrings oscillated in sympathy. He wondered what she'd be like in the sack. Not that he was remotely attracted to her tangle of grey hair or doughy body, but AA meetings were always good to pick up some strange. For the past several weeks the idea of this trip

had hovered in his mind as possibly his last great adventure. However, Mother Kai's long sweat-shirt and black leggings placed her as far outside the sexual world as a nun's habit with wings. Women like that had given up on sex. For them, it was all about aromatherapy and banana bread.

His wife Trixie had become an expert in baked goods. She had twenty pounds on Mother Kai, yet, thankfully, still remained a bottle blonde. She had a pie for every problem, and a cookie for each catastrophe. She'd stuck with him through the bad years: the arrests, the car wrecks, the different jobs, kneading and frosting her way through all of his fuckups. Finally, he was glad to give her some stability. And though they hadn't had sex in years, he still felt a kind of loyalty. Not something he would easily break for just any piece of tail.

Around the room, other people were sharing. He focused on the scars on his knuckles and listened. Over the years, people in pain had become his music. Testimonies of addiction and remorse were songs from his youth he never grew tired of hearing.

One kid started speaking, and the room vibrated with his froggy voice. He looked like a teenager, but Shepard figured from his story he must be in his early twenties. The kid spoke as if underwater, speaking from swamps, from mud, from someplace deep where sound doesn't reach. Each word seemed to be pulled out of him with a hook.

It was a familiar tale about a father with a belt and a mother with a handkerchief. His name was Farley. He had been sober a year, but had recently relapsed. Shepard could tell he'd just come off a bender. His hair fell in black strings over his eyes, and he kept tucking it behind his ears. A tall kid, he sat hunched over and crossed his leg at the knee. Shepard stared at the kid's dirty tennis shoe tapping the air. He avoided his eyes, which were such a faded blue they could almost be gray. They were eyes that had seen terrible things and were still seeing them, even while looking into a Styrofoam cup.

Farley was having trouble finishing sentences. His words sputtered like a lawnmower with a broken choke.

"This kid's wasted," said Verizon guy, and looked to Mother Kai.

"You can't come to meetings intoxicated. It's one of our rules."

Farley took a sip of coffee. "No. I. I'm not. I mean I am. Sober. Pretty much."

Shepard thought he had to say something. "Hey. I've been to lots of meetings where guys passed out drunk on the floor in a puddle of their own piss."

"We have rules here, see." Verizon guy was getting all stern in the face.

Shepard didn't like that "see" and the pointed finger that accompanied it. The old adrenalin surge started pumping through his neck. He spent years sizing up guys in bars. He knew in three seconds who he could beat and who would beat him. Verizon guy had some upper body strength, but was short. Shep could clear his reach and land one on his jaw if it came to that. The dislocated shoulder and collar bone were weak spots to concentrate on.

"Fuck your rules. Let the boy stay." Shepard moved to the edge of his seat. It was all coming back now: the rush of air through his lungs, the heat in his face, that unexpected knuckle-sting contact of bone on bone. He kept thinking: this is my adventure. But under the fluorescent lights of sobriety, his bravado appeared boorish. He was too aware of everything else in the room: the bags of off-brand Oreos on the folding table, the soccer goalie nets stacked in the corner, the message board advertising piano lessons and pottery classes. He would keep an eye on Verizon guy all the same.

"It's all right, honey," said Mother Kai. "You can stay. Next time, come to us clean."

"You get the urge to drink, call me." Verizon guy handed him a card.

Mother Kai brushed off some cat hairs from her sweat-shirt. "Does anyone else have something to share?"

People talked about the customary things: booze; family; God. Shepard thought about his boys back home. He felt closer to them in this circle of strangers than he ever had sitting in his plaid-cushioned living room. With the buzz of caffeine and these supportive smiles around him, he could almost imagine his wife and children as benevolent beings, always forgiving, persisting in a foggy addict's memory as guiding lights and reasons for recovery.

His oldest, Jason, had just turned fifteen and was becoming a stoner. He recognized all the signs: the red eyes; the snacking; hysterical laughter coming from the garage at one o'clock in the morning. Jay was barely in kindergarten when Shepard's drinking hit its peak. He couldn't have forgotten the TV flying through the picture window; or daddy's broken fingers after a bar fight. When Shepard talked about his alcoholism, Jay would turn all solemn and respectful, asking "How much did you puke after?" "How fast were you going when you knocked down the fence?" For a teenage boy, bar fights and car crashes held a defiant glamour. And telling a son not to be like his father was a sure invitation for him to do the opposite.

Trixie's solution was to keep baking pies: apple; peach; and pumpkin. She rolled the dough on the counter until it was thin as paper. In summers, she made lemon meringue and coconut something. Their younger son Patrick devoured them. He and Trixie would sit at the kitchen table with The National Enquirer, a thin wedge of pie between them on a china plate. They would take turns as if they couldn't eat a whole slice each. Then they would flip the page and cut another piece. They could pass a whole afternoon like this.

The day before he left for Boston, he overheard Patrick talking to his mother in the kitchen: "Oh my God, Trixie. Look. This one's having another baby."

"She's your mother." Shepard stood in back of them. "Call her mom."

"Shep. You know Paddy and I don't have that kind of relationship."

"Fine." He slammed a spoon in the sink. "But just remember, I'm Dad. You understand?"

Patrick stared at his lemon meringue pie. His mother rubbed his back and turned the page. "Look at that one, Paddy. She thinks she's twenty-five again."

"Her hips are way too big for that dress," Patrick said. "She needs something cut on the bias. Like your blue dress, Trixie. You should send it to her, air mail."

He looked down at his pudgy wife and his even pudgier son, sitting in their matching aqua hoodies. They seemed like ill-formed stuffed animals. The kind of cartoon characters who always get hit in the face with a rake. And he wasn't the only one who thought this. Patrick was coming home every day from school with a bruise or a missing book. Shepard had tried to teach him how to fight: how to throw a punch; to swing with the weight of his body. But Patrick didn't want to fight. He stood with his little fists pressed into his pelvis and looked like he wanted to cry.

The day he left, Trixie asked for his contact numbers: the hotel phone, the conference coordinator's phone, and the cell numbers of three of his co-workers. "In case there's an emergency at home," she said. But he knew she was worried about his being alone. Packing his briefcase, he noticed she had slipped in a list of all the AA meetings within a five-mile radius of his hotel. For a man whose drinking had first started on company business trips, this was going to be a test.

He loaded his garment bag into the trunk, set his briefcase within easy reach on the passenger floor; it was twenty minutes past the time he told everyone he was leaving, and no one had come to say goodbye. He flipped on the wipers and washed the windshield. There was nothing stopping him from turning on the engine and backing out of the driveway.

From his position in the car, the house looked makeshift and neglected. The aluminum siding was coming loose around the upstairs dormer. There were dark patches on the roof where they had repaired a leak last year. The shrubs needed trimming. He imagined his family staring at him from behind the windows, waiting for him to leave, glad to be finally rid of him.

He slammed the car door and went inside his house. From Jay's room, he heard the crashes and gunshots of computer games. The laundry room was where Trixie spent most of her time when upset, and that was just where he located her; he could hear the dryer tumbling and Patrick singing from the basement. When he walked downstairs, he saw Trixie folding towels and Patrick with a pillowcase wrapped around his head singing: "They try to make me go to rehab. I say no no no."

He stood there watching his wife folding towels in perfect eight inch squares, and his son imitating a dead female heroin addict, and wondered how many ways he had fucked up his family. When they saw him, they both stopped. Patrick threw the pillowcase on a pile of laundry.

"I'm not going to rehab, son. You know that."

"I wasn't singing about you," Patrick said. He picked up a towel and started folding the same little squares as his mother.

Trixie reminded him to call when he arrived, then returned to her towels.

He wanted to do something fatherly, something husbandly: a kiss, a hug, make some lame joke. But the towels were stacking up in front of him. Looks were passing from Trixie to Patrick. It seemed like they wanted him gone. They wanted him not to leave and they wanted him gone at the same time. There was a pane of glass between him and his family; they stood behind it watching him, waiting for him to break through or disappear entirely.

"The car's all packed," he said. "I'm taking off."

"Okay. Bye, Shep." Trixie tapped Patrick on the shoulder. "Say goodbye to your father, Paddy."

Patrick stared at the towels. "Bye," he said.

He stood there trying to find his son's eyes, as if something could pass between them—a look that would say, take care of the house and your mother. But Patrick kept folding.

"Just go, Shep. You're already twenty minutes late."

He walked to the laundry table, grabbed a washcloth and tucked it into his pocket, as if it were just the thing he needed for his trip. As if his wife and son had been preparing this very item for him.

In the church basement, he took out the washcloth and wiped the sweat from his forehead. He had carried it in his suit pocket through a whole day of lectures. When things got really dull, he'd reach in and rub the terrycloth between his fingers. After he wiped his face, he folded the cloth into the same small square and put it back in his pocket.

When the meeting ended, the kid introduced himself. "Thanks for sticking up for me back there."

"That guy's a douche." He was still clocking Verizon guy, waiting for him to step out of line.

"So I got about two hours sober. Any advice?"

"Well, try for three, then four. And every time you feel you want a drink—do a meeting."

They huddled next to the coffee urn. The kid needed to talk, and Shepard didn't have anything better to do. He stood there and nodded, repeated all the AA bullshit. Eventually Mother Kai closed fellowship time, and everybody maneuvered their jittery legs up the staircase.

Outside, he couldn't shake the kid. Farley kept dropping hints about being hungry, so they went to a diner down the street. He bought him a hamburger; the kid had spent all his money on booze and was obviously starving. Shepard got a plate of fries which he didn't touch.

While wolfing down his burger, Farley told the rest of his story. He ran away at sixteen, lived on the streets until the police found him in Harvard Square and carted him back home. As punishment, his father made him paint the garage, and, when he dripped paint on the driveway, beat him with the long wooden handle of the paint roller. By eighteen, he was in and out of jail for stealing and dealing and had been scraping by ever since. He had recently lost his job as a shipping clerk and took that opportunity to go on a binge.

Farley spoke about his guitar. He'd taught himself to play in rehab and wanted to become a singer-songwriter like Bob Dylan.

"Kids still listen to Dylan?" Shepard asked.

"I do." Farley swiped a fry from Shepard's plate. "He's like the master."

"Blood on the Tracks. I listened to that a million times."

"Me too. A gazillion times."

They talked about music for a while: Springstein, Dylan, The Police, Bob Segar. Shepard was surprised at the kid's taste. It had been a long time since he'd thought about music. It didn't affect him the same way it used to. He could remember opening up his Firebird on The Northern Parkway, Badlands cranked on the radio, thinking he could just drive right over the lawns and pools and industrial parks into some cool blue future.

"So how'd you stop?" Farley asked. "What made you hit rock bottom?"

"Christ. I hit rock bottom so many times my ass must be made out of lead."

Farley laughed. He pulled some napkins out of the dispenser and wiped his mouth. "Seriously. What made you stop?"

"I don't know. Life."

"Yeah."

"Death. I don't know." Shepard looked out the window. In the glass, he saw an outline of himself that he didn't recognize: an old man with beard stubble and bushy eyebrows.

"You're not going to tell me how you did it?" Farley balled up his paper napkin.

Shepard pushed his plate of fries over to Farley. "Nah. It's all bullshit. Right?"

"So why you still at meetings then?"

"It works. For me."

"So you saying it can't work for me?"

It looked like Farley was about to get mad. Or maybe cry. Drunks after a bender were emotional wrecks. "Listen. I've seen a lot of kids like you. And you got no reason to get sober. And no one to get sober for. What? Are you gonna sober up to work another day in the stock room? Gonna get straight for dear ol' Dad with his paint roller? Or some God who could give a shit? You have ten more years of hard living. And if you survive—if you don't choke on your own vomit or get shot in some drug bust—than maybe, maybe you'll be ready. But until then. Drink up."

Farley threw his head back and contemplated the ceiling. "Maybe I'll do that."

"Hell. I'll take you to a bar right now. Buy your first shot. What d'you say?"

"Fuck you."

Shepard pointed to the plate. "Eat your fries."

"I don't want your goddamn fries." He picked up the plate and dumped the fries on the floor. Shepard thought he was going to hurl the plate at him; instead, he tapped it on the edge of the table, in a series of menacing thuds.

This was why he never became a sponsor.

In these situations, it was best to walk away. He was just about to stand up when the kid locked those horrible eyes on him.

"So. What did you have that made it work?"

Farley's hands were twitching on the table. Shepard pushed the plates to the far end. "I suppose losing my job was a big blow. I had a reputation, and finding work again was difficult. I was letting my family down—more than usual. It's one thing to wreck a few cars and vomit into the punch bowl at some cousin's wedding, but when your wife is working a second job at Applebee's and your kids are getting their clothes from the Goodwill, you realize you're not just hurting yourself."

"You have kids?"

"Two boys."

"How old?"

"One fifteen. One eleven."

"So you did it for them." The kid was bug-eyed with awe.

"Funny how that goes." Shepard put his hands flat on the table. "Now I can't stand the bastards."

"Come on."

"Yeah." He gazed into the dark hole of his coffee cup. "I really don't like them." It felt good to say it. Finally. To someone he'd never have to see again. "I'm sure they don't care much for me either, poor fucked-up sons of bitches."

"If they're fucked up it's because you made them that way."

"Oh, I take full responsibility. Doesn't mean I like them any better."

Farley was twitching and tapping his fingers on the table.

"We're all supposed to love our kids, right? Everybody deserves love? Right?" Shepard drained his coffee. "Sometimes you look at these weirdoes. These losers. These . . . strangers. And think, no. I can't do it. I can't be part of this."

"I don't believe that."

"You think your old man loved you?"

Farley took a breath and looked at the ceiling. "I don't know. Maybe."

"Maybe he wanted a basketball player, or a concert pianist, or just some good ol' boy he could take hunting. Instead, he got you. And every time you walked in the room there was disappointment. Every time you stubbed your toe or dropped the ball he had to look at his own faults and failures."

"And. And. He was right to beat me because of that?"

"No. He was wrong to beat you. But that's why he did it."

On the street, the sun was lowering beneath the trees. People walked past with bags swinging at their heels and the breeze blowing through their hair. He wondered where all these people were going. Home. Most likely.

Farley finally spoke. "I just want to know what an eleven-year-old boy can do to make you not like him?"

"Well, he can be a fat sissy that gets his ass kicked every day at school then comes crying home to momma."

"That's not his fault."

"Maybe you like fat sissies. I don't."

Farley put his head on the table. Shepard wondered if he'd gone too far. Pushed his awful truth on the kid. Then he realized Farley was sleeping. Typical addict behavior. In another five minutes, he'd wake up and forget everything that had been said.

He could just walk away now and be back in his hotel room with the king-size bed and a flat screen TV. Maybe even call home. All this talk about how much he hated his sons actually made him want to talk to them. When they were out of sight, he could always muster up some faint trace of affection. For the idea of them. The reality was walls of towels and video games and silence. He couldn't remember the last time he had touched his children. When they were little he'd pick them up from their cribs, cradle them in his arms. But he always worried he might be infecting them, communicating his disease and failures as a man. As they grew, their round baby eyes narrowed in accusation. He needed to be half in the bag before he came near them. Now sober, he felt they were strangers, dropped into his life with their own histories and experiences completely alien to him.

Farley raised his head and rubbed his face. "Sorry. I must've . . . passed out."

Shepard ordered him another coffee. Farley stirred in three tubs of cream, and Shepard asked if he had other interests.

"My songs."

"Well, that's something."

"Yeah. Sometimes I jam out all night on the guitar."

"That's something to stay sober for. You can't write songs when you're loaded."

"You wanna hear them?"

"The songs?"

"I got my guitar. Back at my place. It's only a few blocks from here."

"Naw. I got papers to read for tomorrow's meetings."

Farley's head started shaking to his own personal music. "Okay. Sure. Papers."

This was not a good situation. Leaving the kid here. Alone. In this state. "I'll come for one song. But then I gotta go."

They left the diner for Farley's apartment. While walking, Farley kept bumping him with his shoulder, stepping on the sides of his shoes. He talked about his songs, which all seemed to be about heroic suffering. Shepard had long ago given up such sentiments. For him, suffering was the most ordinary aspect of life, like brushing your teeth.

His apartment was a sectioned-off basement in a large house. A plastic curtain was stapled to the rafters as a makeshift shower; a nozzle hung over a drain on the floor. They sat on a broken-down couch in front of a huge flat screen TV. A Playstation with dual controls and snakes of wires was laid out on a coffee table. Shepard banished the thought that Farley might have stolen these things.

"Nice TV."

"I just got it. I'm addicted to Grand Theft Auto."

"I think Jay has that."

"You wanna play? I'll teach you. It's super easy."

Farley put in the game, and the room lit up with color from the giant TV. Shepard watched his car move through the streets. His screen character, Roman, a small-time gangster from Serbia, got beaten up by some thugs. He expected something futuristic, but this looked like nineteen-eighties New York. Maybe history always became the future. He played a mission where Roman had to escape from a bunch of loan sharks. He could see how Jay liked it.

Farley was really into it: cursing at the screen and laughing whenever he ran over someone. He made all the gunshot noises along with the soundtrack. They hadn't even finished the first level when he jumped up and said: "I gotta play you this song. It's about getting run over."

He brought out his guitar and sat on the back of the couch with his sneakers on the seat. He fumbled with some chords and had a few false starts, but once he found his rhythm, he locked into a trance. The room vibrated with his monotone croak. The song's chorus was: run me down, run me down, roll your tires over my skull, which Farley sang with eyes closed and brow crinkled in earnest intent. It was awful.

As soon as he finished that song, he launched into another. Something about black flag heart. It was hard to tell where the first song closed and the new one opened. Shepard didn't think he could endure another. He asked if Farley knew any Dylan tunes, and Farley began strumming "Buckets of Rain."

Farley's voice was better suited to this folky tune, and Shepard couldn't help singing along:

I been meek. And hard like an oak. I've seen pretty people disappear like smoke. It was a happy song about misery—Dylan obviously drunk on his own pain. What alcoholic couldn't understand that.

They drew out the last note with Shepard reaching for the harmony. By that time, Farley was standing on the couch strumming away. Shepard clapped as Farley finished his final chords.

"And now, I have to leave," he said.

"No. Not yet."

"I'll stop buy tomorrow night. We'll get a burger."

"Okay. Okay." Farley wiped his nose on his sleeve. There was panic in his eyes.

"This was fun, kid. You lie down and sleep. You've had a big day."

Farley backed towards the stairs and blocked the way. "Will you do one thing? Before you leave?"

"What is it?"

Farley pulled out from underneath his bed a wide brown belt. He laid the belt across his arms and brought it to Shepard.

"Beat me with it," he said.

Shepard looked down at the belt suspended across Farley's arms like some religious offering. The boy's flannel shirt was frayed around the collar; a little globe of snot pulsed in his nose. He visualized the boy painting the garage, packing his bags, stealing the car, wiping his terrible eyes in a jail cell. Across the kid's skinny arms, the belt looked thick and heavy.

"Do it," the boy said. "So I can sleep."

Shepard thought about his own boys. How he was always watching them walk out of rooms. How the hair on the back of their heads formed little swirls and knots, and hung thickly down their necks; he imagined he could part the hair and find their faces—blank faces that would look at him without accusation, without wanting something. He took the belt in his hands and pulled it from fist to fist.

Farley leaned against the wall and pulled up his shirt. His back was a map of fine white scars, little roads going in every direction, leading off the edges of his body. Shepard guessed his father had started the job, but wondered how many others had added their marks. There were fine thread-like lines crosshatched over thicker lines—scars trying to erase other scars.

"Do it," the kid said. His waist looked thin as a stalk.

How many times had Shepard wanted to hit his own kids but refrained? How many times did he want to slap the smirk off Jay's face? Punch Patrick in his fat stomach and say, be a man? How many times had he stood behind them while they watched TV, wanting to put a hand on their shoulder?

The sound of the first crack filled the room like a large branch breaking from a tree. The boy took a deep breath but didn't cry out. Shepard brought the belt down again. The boy braced himself with hands on his knees. The shirt fell over his head.

The skin on his back was getting red and mottled. His ribs trembled and shoulder blades sawed the air. He hated how the kid just took it without a cry of protest. No one deserved this. No one deserved this life.

"Again," said the boy.

He reached his hands around the kid's flat stomach. It was fluttering like a trapped insect. Shepard tried to pull him up and around.

"Again." The kid unbuckled his pants and dropped them to the floor. His skinny haunches bucked up against Shepard.

Just when he believed the worst was over, Farley was grinding against him—a blind man feeling for a hand in the dark—as if someone had plucked the worst thought from his head and said: now you must do this.

"Again." The kid moved his little ass around, two dents on each side like punched-in fenders. He could feel the boy through his pants. He didn't want to feel the boy this way. He was ashamed. Ashamed for the whole human race. He pictured Trixie watching him, rolling out her pie dough and spitting into the flour.

Shepard looked down on the back, flaming hot with his handiwork. The fine white roads rising up from the redness.

Farley bucked against him. "Come on, man."

Again, Shepard was doing the wrong thing. He was disappointing someone—disappointing himself. He didn't want to fuck this kid. He didn't want to beat him.

He grabbed the kid by the back of the neck and tried to pull him around. He needed to see a face. The kid resisted, pushing his head down and grinding his ass. Shepard tightened his grip and pulled him up. He couldn't have weighed more than a hundred and thirty pounds. Lighter than Trixie. The kid struggled and tried to turn away. He shook him, lifting him off his feet, tightening his grip around his throat.

"What's the matter with you," Shepard shouted.

The kid's face was bouncing in his hands, getting redder by the second, eyes wide and ecstatic. His Adam's apple moved up and down through Shepard's fingers; his cock slapped against Shepard's leg. He felt the bristly neck—a surprise. The kid had a light beard that didn't show on the skin.

He wanted to say something important, but the words became shakes. He held the kid by the throat and shook him with everything he had. Those eyes looked back at him, sick of looking at the world yet still looking.

He loosened his grip. The kid gulped. Water started pooling in his eyes, and ran down his cheeks. He cried silent sobs. Then not-so-silent sobs, coming out of him in bursts and stops like the crackling of frying meat. He brought his hands down on the kid's shoulders. He watched him cry, and felt the vibrations through his fingers.

Looking down, he noticed the kid had come on his pants.

He followed Shepard's eyes down to his pants. "Sorry," he said.

This was his one pair of dress pants. Dry clean only. How was he going to get out these stains: vinegar? soda water? baby shampoo? He pictured himself walking into CVS pharmacy and asking where he could find the cum-remover.

"You sprayed me. Like a goddamn cat."

Farley started laughing, coughing up sounds from the back of his throat. It didn't even sound like laughter except that his face looked happy.

"It's not funny." But Shepard couldn't help but join in. They stood guffawing like a couple of retards, his hands bouncing on top of Farley's shoulders.

Then Farley shifted his weight, from the back of his heels to the balls of his feet—a little movement, hardly perceptible but significant—putting more weight on Shepard's arms which were still holding him a good two feet away. The urge to flee tingled in his calves: out the door and back to his hotel with the cool sheets and satellite TV. The kid's shoulders flinched. More weight shifted onto Shepard. If he bent his elbows the kid would fall into him. Still they looked at the floor. Shepard was tired. His arm throbbed from wielding the belt. His feet ached. His fingers could still feel the soft cords of the kid's throat. He didn't owe him anything. This was a relapse. Relapses don't get better overnight.

The kid slowly raised his head and looked at him; Shepard thought—run. Up the stairs and out the door, back to a hot meal and a hot bath. Call your wife. Talk to your sons. You don't owe this kid anything. But his elbows were bending. He was reaching. Around the shoulders. The hot back. The wet cheek. The bristly neck. Such a thin and brittle body. All the way back—to the place where he held the child in his arms.

❖   ❖   ❖

Notes on Contributors

Thomas M. Atkinson is an author and playwright, and the 2013 Ohio Arts Council/Fine Arts Work Center Writer-in-Residence in Provincetown, Mass. His story, "Grimace in the Burnt Black Hills," received two 2013 Pushcart Prize nomination and won an Ohio Arts Council Individual Excellence award for 2012. "Red, White & Blue" was a finalist for *Tampa Review's* Danahy Fiction Prize. His work has appeared in *The Sun*, *The North American Review*, *The Indiana Review*, *The Moon*, *City Beat* and *Electron Press Magazine*. His short play, *Dancing Turtle*, won this year's 38th Annual Samuel French Off Off Broadway Festival, and will appear in two different anthologies in 2014. He has won numerous honors and awards for both fiction and drama, including four Ohio Arts Council grants. His first novel, *Strobe Life*, is available for Kindle, and he has just completed his second novel, *TIKI MAN*, and *Standing Deadwood*, a collection of short stories.

John Wall Barger's poems have appeared in *The Cincinnati Review*, *The Atlanta Review*, and The Montreal Prize *Global Poetry Anthology*. His second collection, *Hummingbird* (Palimpsest Press, 2012) was a finalist for the 2013 Raymond Souster Award. He lives in Hong Kong and teaches creative writing at the Chinese University of Hong Kong.

Douglas Basford's poetry, translations, and prose can be found in *Poetry, Ambit, Narrative, Subtropics, Diagram, American Poetry Journal, Birmingham Poetry Review, H_NGM_N, Words without Borders, The FSG Book of Twentieth-Century Italian Poetry,* and other venues. He has received scholarships from the Summer Literary Seminars and the Sewanee and Bread Loaf conferences and honors from the National Endowment for the Humanities, the Santa Fe Art Institute, *Southwest Review, The Evansville Review, Smartish Pace*, the New England Poetry Club, and the Dorothy Sargent Rosenberg Memorial Foundation, among others. He teaches and runs the composition program at the University at Buffalo, co-edits the online journal *Unsplendid*, and is prose editor for *The National Poetry Review*.

Angela Belcaster is a writer and poet living in Bellingham, Washington, where she divides her time among six children, performing spoken word, and planting calendulas in solid defiance of the Northwest rain.

James Gordon Bennett, winner of the Danahy Fiction Prize, is the author of two novels, *My Father's Geisha* (Delacorte, 1990) and *The Moon Stops Here* (Doubleday, 1994). His short fiction has appeared widely in journals including *The Colorado Quarterly, The Kansas Quarterly, The Southern Review, The Michigan Quarterly Review, The Antioch Review,* and *The Gettysburg Review*. His stories have been cited in *Best American Short Stories* and have been selected for *Best New Stories from the South* and the Pushcart Prize. Bennett also has written book reviews for *The New York Times Book Review* and published feature articles in *Vogue* and *Glamour*. He is Professor of English at Louisiana State University in Baton Rouge.

Mary Block is a graduate of New York University's Creative Writing Program, where she earned her MFA in poetry. Her work has appeared or is forthcoming in *Conduit, Weave, Saw Palm,* and *Why I Am Not A Painter* (an anthology from Argos Books), among other publications. She was a 2012 finalist for a Ruth Lilly Poetry Fellowship from the Poetry Foundation. She lives in Brooklyn, New York with her husband and their dog. www.maryblock.net

Catherine M. Chastain-Elliott is a contemporary artist whose work is evocative of the American Impressionist style.

She is a graduate of Rhodes College and earned her Ph.D. from Emory University. She is a member of the College Art Association and the Southeastern College Art Conference. She has held two Smithsonian Institution Research Fellowships, one at the Hirschorn Museum and Sculpture Garden and the other at the Archives of American Art.

Bill Christophersen's poems have recently appeared in *Antioch Review, Borderlands, Hanging Loose, Potomac Review, Rattle, Rhino,* and *Sierra Nevada Review*. He lives in New York City and plays traditional and bluegrass fiddle.

Martin Cloutier has been published in *Post Road, Shenandoah, Story Quarterly, Natural Bridge, Upstreet, SmokeLong Quarterly, New English Review, The Bryant Literary Review, The Portland Review, Bombay Gin,* and *The Southeast Review*. He teaches at Brooklyn College.

Sarah Crossland earned her BA in Storytelling (Fiction, Poetry, and Folklore) from the University of Virginia and her MFA in Poetry from the University of Wisconsin at Madison in May 2013. She received the 2013 AWP Intro Journals prize, judged by Ben Grossberg, for the poem published in this issue.

Dana Curtis is the author of two full-length collections of poetry: *The Body's Response to Famine*, winner of the Pavement Saw Press Transcontinental Poetry Prize, and *Camera Stellata* (CW Books). She has also published seven chapbooks: *Book of Disease* (in the magazine, *The Chapbook*), *Antiviolet* (Pudding House Press), *Pyromythology* (Finishing Line Press), *Twilight Dogs* (Pudding House Press), *Incubus/Succubus* (West Town Press), *Dissolve* (Sarasota Poetry Theatre Press), and *Swingset Enthralled* (Talent House Press). Her work has appeared in such publications as *Quarterly West, Indiana Review, Colorado Review,* and *Prairie Schooner*. She has received grants from the Minnesota State Arts Board and the McKnight Foundation. She is the Editor-in-Chief of Elixir Press and lives in Denver, Colorado.

Gilbert DeMeza is an Ybor City native and Professor Emeritus of Art at the University of Tampa. He earned his MFA at the University of Georgia. His work has been shown in numerous exhibitions, including The Southeast Annual, High Museum, Atlanta; Drawing Invitational, Purdue University, and the University of Georgia Art Gallery. He presented a solo exhibition at the HCC Art Gallery, Ybor City, in 2012 entitled "Notes of Interest."

James Doyle's latest book of poetry, *The Long View Just Keeps Treading Water*, was published in 2012 by Accents Publishing.

John Drury is the author of three books of poetry: *The Refugee Camp, Burning the Aspern Papers,* and *The Disappearing Town*. He has also written *The Poetry Dictionary* and *Creating Poetry*. New poems have appeared recently in *Gettysburg Review, Baltimore Review, Ascent,* and *The Journal*. He teaches at the University of Cincinnati.

Martha Grace Duncan is Professor of Law at Emory University, in Atlanta. Her essays and memoirs have appeared in *Gettysburg Review, Columbia Law Review,* and *California Law Review*. Her book, *Romantic Outlaws, Beloved Prisons: The Unconscious Meanings of Crime and Punishment*, was published by NYU Press. Currently, she is working on two projects: a book about her father, entitled *To the Final Cliffs: A Daughter's Journey*, and an essay about the Amanda Knox case, entitled "What Not to Do When Your Roommate is Murdered in Italy."

Santiago Echeverry is a Colombian new media and digital artist with a background in film and television production.

Thanks to a Fulbright grant, he received his Master's degree from the Interactive Telecommunications Program at NYU. He moved to the United States in 2003 to teach interactivity at the University of Maryland, Baltimore County, and then relocated to Florida in the fall of 2005 to teach digital arts and interactive media at the University of Tampa. He started exhibiting internationally in 1992, and his research interests are nonlinear narration, video art, performance art, interactive design, creative code, and web experimentation, with a thematic commitment to gay and lesbian human rights. All his work is available on his personal site www.santi.tv.

Clifford Paul Fetters has poems published or forthcoming in *The Main Street Rag, Cross Currents, The Oxford American, Poetry East, Appalachia, The New York Review of Books, The Seattle Review, The Willow Review, 5AM, William & Mary Review, Ibbetson Street Press, The Wisconsin Review*, and many others. He lives in Miami with his writes-like-a-dream wife, Debra Dean.

Heather Foster lives on a farm in west Tennessee. She teaches English and Humanities at Jackson State Community College. Her poems and stories are featured in *PANK, Anderbo, Monkeybicycle, Graze Magazine, Superstition Review, RHINO, Weave Magazine, South Dakota Review, Word Riot*, and *Mead: The Magazine of Literature and Libations*.

Matthew Gavin Frank is the author of the nonfiction books, *Pot Farm* and *Barolo* (both from the University of Nebraska Press), and *Preparing the Ghost: An Essay Concerning the Giant Squid and the Man Who First Photographed It* (forthcoming from W. W. Norton: Liveright in 2014); the poetry books *The Morrow Plots, Warranty in Zulu*, and *Sagittarius Agitprop*; and the chapbooks *Four Hours to Mpumalanga* and *Aardvark*. Recent work appears in *The New Republic, Field, Epoch, AGNI, The Iowa Review, Crazyhorse, Black Warrior Review, Seneca Review, DIAGRAM, Quarterly West, The Best Food Writing, The Best Travel Writing, Creative Nonfiction, Hotel Amerika, Gastronomica*, and others. He was born and raised in Illinois, and currently teaches Creative Writing in the MFA Program at Northern Michigan University, where he is the Nonfiction Editor of *Passages North*.

Gregory Fraser is the author of three poetry collections: *Strange Pietà* (Texas Tech UP, 2003), *Answering the Ruins* (Northwestern UP, 2009), and *Designed for Flight* (forthcoming from Northwestern in Spring 2014). He is also the coauthor, with Chad Davidson, of the workshop textbook *Writing Poetry: Creative and Critical Approaches* (Palgrave-Macmillan, 2008) and the composition textbook *Analyze Anything: A Guide to Critical Reading and Writing* (Continuum-Bloomsbury, 2012). His poetry has appeared in journals including *The Paris Review, The Southern Review*, and *The Gettysburg Review*. The recipient of a grant from the National Endowment for the Arts, Fraser serves as professor of English at the University of West Georgia.

Kendra Frorup is an international artist with a research focus on the global conversation about connections and identity in art. She has exhibited her sculpture in the United States and in worldwide venues such as the Caribbean, France, Puerto Rico, Martinique, Ghetto Biennale, Haiti, UNESCO in Andorra, and The National Art Gallery of the Bahamas. She grew up in the Bahamas, earned her BFA at the University of Tampa, and completed her MFA at Syracuse University. She and her family now reside in Tampa, where she teaches at the University of Tampa.

Corey George grew up on his grandparents' farm in upstate South Carolina, surrounded by farmers, old pine forests, wildlife, and Southern Democrats. His current work is a study of the rural landscape of the southern U.S. He documents how man and society have shaped and altered the landscape over the past few decades, and continue to alter it in the pursuit of progress. He teaches at the University of Tampa.

Benjamin S. Grossberg won the 2008 Tampa Review Prize for Poetry for his manuscript, *Sweet Core Orchard* (University of Tampa Press, 2009). His first book, *Underwater Lengths in a Single Breath*, won the 2005 Snyder Prize and was published by Ashland Poetry Press in 2007. UT Press will publish his forthcoming book, *Space Traveler*, in 2014. Grossberg's poems have appeared widely in literary journals, including *Paris Review, Southwest Review*, and *North American Review*. He taught for eight years at Antioch College until it closed. He is now an associate professor teaching creative writing and poetry at the University of Hartford.

Lew Harris is Professor of Art and Chair of the Art Department at the University of Tampa. He has exhibited mixed media widely and is the creator of *Electronics Alive*, a biennial digital arts exhibition featuring international artists.

Molly Howes's essays have appeared or will appear in the *Bellingham Review, The New York Times's* "Modern Love" column, *Boston Globe Magazine, Marco Polo Arts Magazine*, and *UU World*. She is a MacDowell Fellow and was invited to the 2013 A Room of Her Own Retreat. Her work was named a finalist for the Annie Dillard Award in Creative Nonfiction and the Writers @ Work 2013 Fellowship, as well as an Honorable Mention in the New Millennium Prize for Nonfiction. She lives in the Boston area and visits the Gulf Coast and her Florida family as often as she can.

Bradford Kammin holds an MFA degree from the University of Michigan, where he taught creative writing and was awarded six Hopwood Awards for his short fiction, nonfiction, and novel. He is the recipient of a residency at the Virginia Center for Creative Arts. His short fiction has appeared or is forthcoming in *The Gettysburg Review* and *Arts & Letters*.

Ina Kaur is a multi-media artist/printmaker who is a native of New Delhi, India. In her studio research she combines various processes including printmaking, drawings, and installations that has been showcased in numerous national and international exhibitions across the US and India, and in countries including Argentina, China, Finland, Hungary, Japan, Korea, the Netherlands, Scotland, South Africa, Spain, Sweden, and Turkey. Her solo exhibitions include shows at Scarabocchio Art Museum in Steven Point, Wisconsin; Overbrook Art Gallery in Muskegon, Michigan; Mehrengarh Museum Trust Gallery in Jodhpur, India; and many others. She earned a Studio Arts BFA from Punjab University, Chandigarh, India, and completed an MFA with honors at Purdue University, Indiana. She has taught at Bowling Green State University and currently is Assistant Professor of Art at The University of Tampa. www.inakaur.com

Jennifer Schomburg Kanke is a doctoral candidate at Florida State University. Her work has appeared or is forthcoming in *Pleiades, Prairie Schooner, Court Green*, and *The Laurel Review*. She currently serves as Poetry Editor for *The Southeast Review*.

Jack King holds his MFA from the University of Georgia. He has exhibited widely in solo, group, and invitational exhibitions including the Montgomery Museum of Art, Evelyn Cobb Gallery, Lakeland Center for Creative Arts., Crealdé School of Art, and Tampa Museum of Art. His work can be found in permanent collections of the Leepa Ratner Museum of Art, Tarpon Springs; the State Art Collection, Atlanta; Walt Disney Companies, Orlando; William R. Hough & Co., St. Petersburg; and others. He is Professor of Art at the University of Tampa and recipient of the Lifetime Achievement Award from Florida Craftsmen, Inc.

J. M. Lennon is an award-winning writer, editor, and photographer whose photographic work appears regularly in national and regional publications and is part of the permanent collections of the University of South Florida's Marshall Center and the University of Tampa's Scarfone/Hartley Gallery.

Frannie Lindsay's fourth volume of poetry, *Our Vanishing*, was selected as the winner of the 2012 Benjamin Saltman Award and is forthcoming in 2014 from Red Hen Press. Her other titles are *Mayweed* (Washington Prize 2010; The Word Works); *Lamb* (Perugia Prize; Perugia Press 2006;) and *Where She Always Was* (May Swenson Award 2004; Utah State University Press). She is widely published and has held fellowships from the Massachusetts Cultural Council and the National Endowment for the Arts. She has also received several Pushcart nominations. She is a classical pianist as well.

Matthew Lippman is the author of three poetry collections, *American Chew*, winner of The Burnside Review Book Prize (Burnside Review Book Press, 2013), *Monkey Bars* (Typecast Publishing, 2010), and *The New Year of Yellow*, winner of the Kathryn A. Morton Poetry Prize (Sarabande Books, 2007). He is the recipient of the 2014 Georgetown Review Magazine Prize.

Priscilla Long grew up on a dairy farm on the Eastern Shore of Maryland. She is a Seattle-based author and teacher of writing. Her work includes science, poetry, creative nonfiction, and fiction. Her most recent book is *The Writer's Portable Mentor: A Guide to Art, Craft, and the Writing Life*. Her work has appeared previously in *Tampa Review* as well as in *Post Road*, *Cincinnati Review*, *The American Scholar*, *The Southern Review*, *Web Conjunctions*, *The Alaska Quarterly*, *Fourth Genre*, *Passages North*, *Bosque*, and elsewhere. Her awards include a National Magazine Award, and she has been a fellow at Hedgebrook, the Millay Colony for the Arts, and Jack Straw Productions. Her MFA is from the University of Washington. She is author of a scholarly history book, *Where the Sun Never Shines: A History of America's Bloody Coal Industry*. She serves as Founding and Consulting Editor for www.historylink.org, the online encyclopedia of Washington state history. For more information please visit www.PriscillaLong.com and PriscillaLong.org.

Tori Malcangio is the winner of 2011 Waasmode Fiction Prize and First Runner-Up for the 2011 Crab Creek Review Fiction Contest. Stories can be found in *Cream City Review*, *ZYZZYVA*, *River Styx*, *Passages North*, *Smokelong Quarterly*, *Pearl Magazine*, *Literary Mama*, *The San Diego Reader*, and *VerbSap*. Her work has also appeared in the anthologies *A Year in Ink* and *The Frozen Moment*. She is an MFA candidate at Bennington College.

Jacqueline Marcus is the author of *Close to the Shore* (Michigan State University Press). Her poems have recently appeared in Hotel Amerika, North American Review, North Dakota Quarterly, Brooklyn Review, and *New Madrid*. She taught philosophy at Cuesta College and is the founder-editor of ForPoetry.com and EnvironmentalPress.com. "Winter Tree" is from her new collection, *Summer Rains*.

Scott Marengo won the 2010 Markham Prize in Poetry, and then set his sights on fiction. He has published stories in *Boston Review* and *Wisconsin Review*, and three of his stories have been finalists in fiction contests at *Third Coast*, *Inkwell*, and *New Letters*.

James Davis May's poems have appeared or are forthcoming in *Five Points*, *The Missouri Review*, *New England Review*, *New Ohio Review*, *The New Republic*, *Pleiades*, *The Southern Review* and elsewhere. He has received fellowships from Inprint and the Krakow Poetry Seminar. In 2013, he won the Collins Award from *Birmingham Poetry Review*. He lives in Young Harris, Georgia.

Peter McNamara's poetry is compiled in four volumes, most recently *Sojourn* and a chapbook, *Orbit's Crossing*, published by St. Andrews University Press. His works as a lyricist/librettist, principally with composer Dean X. Johnson, include *East River Bridge*, an opera for the Brooklyn Bridge Centennial, and *Anthem of Love and Hope*, a choral ode for victims of AIDS.

He has published translations from Garcia Lorca, Neruda, and Castellon; is a founder of the Southern Vermont Poetry Co-op; and has been honored as a Ronald H. Bayes Writer-in-Residence and with the Newcomb Prize, Merilh Medal, and grants from the Florida Council on Arts and Culture.

Peter Meinke is Poet Laureate of St. Petersburg. His most recent books – all illustrated by his wife Jeanne Clark Meinke – are a chapbook, *Lassing Park & Other Poems* (Yellow Jacket Press, 2011), and three books published by the University of Tampa Press, *Lines from Neuchatel* (2009), *The Shape of Poetry: A Practical Guide to Writing & Reading Poems* (2012), and *Truth and Affection: The Poet's Notebook Columns from Creative Loafing*)2013). His work has appeared in *The New Republic*, *The New Yorker*, *The Atlantic*, *Poetry*, and dozens of other journals, and seven of his books are in the prestigious Pitt Poetry Series.

John Messick received the 2013 AWP Intro Journals Award, judged by Rigoberto Gonzalez, for "Discovering Terra Incognito." Its appearance in *Tampa Review* marks his first literary publication. He is a graduate of the creative writing program at the University of Alaska, Fairbanks, and is currently thru-hiking the Appalachian Trail.

Gregg Mosson is the author of two books of poetry, *Questions of Fire* (Plain View, 2009) and *Season of Flowers & Dust* (Goose River, 2007). The poem published here is from his manuscript in progress, "Ripeness." Mosson lives in Maryland and his work has appeared widely. He would like to dedicate this poem's publication to the late, great Adrienne Rich, whose craft, knowledge, and courage forever inspires him.

R. C. Neighbors is a sixth-generation Oklahoman and current Ph.D. candidate at Texas A&M University, where he studies creative writing and the Native South. His work has appeared or is forthcoming in *Barely South Review*, *Red Earth Review*, *Found Poetry Review*, *Parody*, and elsewhere.

Dan O'Brien is a poet and playwright in Los Angeles. His collection *War Reporter*, published in 2013 by Hanging Loose Press (New York) and CB Editions (London), won the Fenton Aldeburgh prize for best first collection. His play about Paul Watson, *The Body of an American*, is a finalist for the inaugural Edward M. Kennedy Prize in Drama, winner of the 2012 Weissberger Award, and premiered at Portland Center Stage.

Brice Particelli is a teacher and freelance writer in New York City. He is working on his first novel, *Nakimoa*, set on Christmas Island.

Doug Ramspeck is the author of five poetry collections. His most recent book, *Original Bodies*, was selected for the Michael Waters Poetry Prize and is forthcoming by Southern Indiana Review Press. Two earlier books also received awards: *Mechanical Fireflies* (Barrow Street Press Prize), and *Black Tupelo Country* (John Ciardi Prize). Individual poems have appeared in journals that include *Kenyon Review*, *Slate*, *Southern Review*, *Georgia Review*, *AGNI*, and *Alaska Quarterly Review*. He directs the Writing Center and teaches creative writing at The Ohio State University at Lima.

Elizabeth Rees's most recent chapbook, *Tilting Gravity*, won the Codhill Press contest in 2009. Her poems have appeared in *Kenyon Review*, *Partisan Review*, *Mid-American Review*. New work is forthcoming in *Agni*, *Atlanta Review*, and *Artful Dodge*.

David Ricchiute lives in Indiana. Fiction and poetry appears or is forthcoming in *NOON*, *The Quarterly*, *North Atlantic Review*, *Interim*, *First Intensity*, *Red Rock Review*, and *Tipton Poetry Journal*, among others.

Gianna Russo is the author of a full-length poetry collection, *Moonflower* (Kitsune Books, 2011), winner of the Florida Book Award Bronze Medal, the Florida Publishers Association Silver

Award, and an Eric Hofer First Horizons Honorable Mention. A Pushcart Prize nominee, she has also had publications in *Tampa Review, Ekphrasis, Crab Orchard Review, Florida Review, Florida Humanities Council Forum, Karamu, The Bloomsbury Review, The Sun, Poet Lore, The MacGuffin,* and *Calyx,* among others. She is also the founding editor of YellowJacket Press (www.yellowjacketpress.org) and Instructor of English and Creative Writing at Saint Leo University.

F. Daniel Rzicznek is the author of two poetry collections, *Divination Machine* (Free Verse Editions/Parlor Press, 2009) and *Neck of the World* (Utah State University Press, 2007), as well as two chapbooks, *Vine River Hermitage* (Cooper Dillon Books, 2011) and *Cloud Tablets* (Kent State University Press, 2006). His individual poems have appeared in *Boston Review, The New Republic, Orion, Mississippi Review, Hotel Amerika,* and *Shenandoah.* He is also co-editor (with Gary L. McDowell) of *The Rose Metal Press Field Guide to Prose Poetry: Contemporary Poets in Discussion and Practice* (Rose Metal Press, 2010). He teaches writing at Bowling Green State University in Bowling Green, Ohio.

Daniel Saalfeld's poems have appeared in many journals, including *The Hopkins Review, The Southeast Review, The Seattle Review, Cimarron Review, Tar River Poetry, The South Carolina Review, Poet Lore,* and *The Pinch.* As a Fulbright Scholar, he lectured on modern and contemporary American poetry and creative writing in Russia. He teaches creative writing at the George Washington and the Johns Hopkins Universities.

Brook J. Sadler is a poet and philosopher. Also: professor, mother, vegetarian, Florida native. Her poems have recently appeared in *GW Review, Ms. Magazine, Cortland Review, Atlanta Review, The Boiler Journal, Mixitini Matrix, Parody Poetry,* and *Connotations Press.*

Sara Schaff graduated from Brown University and received an MFA in fiction from the University of Michigan. Her work has appeared or is forthcoming in *Day One, The Rumpus, The Saint Ann's Review, Fiction Writers Review,* and elsewhere. The recipient of a residency from the Ragdale Foundation, Sara has taught at the University of Michigan and in China, Colombia, and Northern Ireland, where she also studied storytelling. She lives in Ann Arbor, Michigan, with her husband and daughter.

Mark Smith's poetry has appeared recently in *Pleiades, Worcester Review,* and *Gettysburg Review.* He is the recipient of fellowships and grants from the Guggenheim, Rockefeller, Fulbright, and Ingram Merrill Foundations and the NEA. A novelist, he lives in DeLand, Florida.

Matthew J. Spireng's book, *What Focus Is,* was published in 2011 by Word Press. His book *Out of Body* won the 2004 Bluestem Poetry Award and was published in 2006 by Bluestem Press at Emporia State University. His chapbooks are: *Clear Cut,* a signed and numbered limited edition of his poems with photographs by Austin Stracke on which the poems are based; *Young Farmer; Encounters; Inspiration Point,* winner of the 2000 Bright Hill Press Poetry Chapbook Competition; and *Just This.* Since 1990, his poems have appeared in journals including *North American Review, Tar River Poetry, Southern Poetry Review, Louisiana Literature, English Journal,* and *Connecticut Review.*

Judith Skillman's new books are *The Phoenix—New & Selected Poems 2007-2013* (Dream Horse Press) and *Broken Lines—The Art & Craft of Poetry* (Lummox Press). Her poems and collaborative translations have appeared in *Cimarron Review, FIELD, Ezra, Seneca Review, The Iowa Review,* and others. She is the recipient of an award from the Academy of American Poets for *Storm* (Blue Begonia Press). Two of her collections also have been finalists for the Washington State Book Award. Visit www.judithskillman.com

David Starkey served as Santa Barbara's 2009-2010 Poet Laureate and is Director of the Creative Writing Program at Santa Barbara City College. His poetry has appeared in many journals, including *The American Scholar, The Georgia Review* and *The Southern Review,* and in six full-length collections, most recently I*t Must Be Like the World* and *Circus Maximus.*

Chris Valle has had solo exhibitions at galleries including Focus Gallery, Gainesville, Florida; Kresge Gallery, Batesville, Arkansas; and Gallery 414, Fort Worth Texas. His work is held in many private collections, including the Hess Corporation, Houston, Texas; the William J. Clinton Presidential Library, Little Rock, Arkansas; and the Siena Art Institute, Italy. He is Associate Professor of Painting at the University of Tampa.

Gina P. Vozenilek is a freelance writer and the managing editor of *Sport Literate Magazine* (www.sportliterate.org). She earned a Master's in literature at the University of Iowa and is now pursuing her MFA in creative nonfiction at Northwestern. Her writing has appeared in *Literal Latte, Brain, Child, Ars Medica, Notre Dame Magazine,* and elsewhere. "Tri-Level" received a 2012 Intro Journals Award for Creative Nonfiction, selected by Kyoko Mori.

Laura Maylene Walter is the author of the short story collection *Living Arrangements* (BkMk Press, 2011), which won the G. S. Sharat Chandra Prize for Short Fiction, a national gold IPPY, and a *Foreword* Book of the Year Award. Her writing has appeared or is forthcoming in publications ranging from *The Sun* to *Poets & Writers* to *Cat Fancy.* Laura recently left her career as a trade magazine editor to pursue her MFA in fiction at Bowling Green State University, where she serves as an assistant fiction editor of the *Mid-American Review.* She blogs about the writing life at lauramaylenewalter.com

Judith Werner lives in the Bronx, New York, and has had poems published in many literary magazines and several anthologies. Previously an editor and teacher of poetry, she has won the Lenore Marshall Poetry Prize, The Academy of American Poets Prize, a Breadloaf Writer's Conference Fellowship, and Third Prize in the Jesse Bryce Niles Chapbook contest from *Comstock Review.* For *The Lyric,* she has won Best of Issue Prize, Honorable Mentions, the Ronald J. Kemski Prize, and served as judge in another issue. Her poems have been published recently or are forthcoming in *The Aurorean, Blue Unicorn, The Comstock Review,The Deronda Review, The Lyric, The Midwest Quarterly, Plainsongs, Sojourners,* and *Wisconsin Review.*

Dede Wilson is the author of five collections of poetry. Her first book, *Glass,* was published as a finalist for the Persephone Press Award, and her second, *Sea of Small Fears,* won the Main Street Rag Chapbook Competition. *One Nightstand* is a collection of light verse in forms followed by a primer to poetic forms. *Eliza: The New Orleans Years* has been performed as a one-woman show in Mississippi and North Carolina. Her latest collection, *Near Waking,* was issued in 2013 by Finishing Line Press. Dede is also the author of a five-generation memoir, *Fourth Child, Second Daughter,* as well as numerous published short stories. A Louisiana native, she has lived in Charlotte, North Carolina, since 1967.

Jeff Worley published two books last year: *Driving Late to the Party: The Kansas Poems* (Woodley Press), and *A Little Luck,* which won the 2012 X. J. Kennedy Poetry Prize (Texas Review Press). His newest poems can be found in recent or current issues of *Atlanta Review, The Texas Review, The Louisville Review, Boulevard, Poetry East,* and *River Styx.* Jeff lives and works in Lexington, Kentucky, where he does freelance writing and editing, and he also spends time at his Cave Run Lake cabin.

❖   ❖   ❖